Advance Praise For
POLICE CRAFT

"In **Police Craft**, Adam Plantinga provides an unvarnished and eloquent examination of what it's really like to patrol some of the country's toughest streets. It is riveting and refreshing. A must-read for anyone interested in policing." —**Del Quentin Wilber**, author of *A Good Month for Murder* and *Rawhide Down*

"Adam Plantinga's second book is a gift to cops, citizens and crime writers. Adam writes with skill, wisdom, humor, and experience. He's both tough and tender. There's lots for everyone to learn from his behind-the-badge perspective." —**Ellen Kirschman**, PhD, author of *I Love a Cop* and *I Love a Fire Fighter*, and the Dr. Dot Meyerhoff mystery series.

"For anyone who wants to understand law enforcement, Adam Plantinga is an essential resource: a cop who tells the truth about what it's like to police our streets. His eye catches everything and his prose rings with authenticity. **Police Craft** is a terrific read." —**Andrew Klavan**, bestselling author of *Empire of Lies*

"Sgt. Adam Plantinga nailed it again with his second book **Police Craft**, a magnificent inside view of police work from one of San Francisco's finest . . . an outstanding analysis of police work coupled with humility, humor and insight." —**Paul Chignell**, S.F. Police Department Captain (retired)

"You will often hear cops say, 'I could write a book based on everything I have seen and done while on this job!' There is no need to because Adam has done it for us! I encourage cops to read this book. I found it to be therapeutic and a reminder that the thoughts and feelings I wrestle with due to my profession are shared by others. It's also be a great read for anyone in the public because it gives a candid view of law enforcement that many do not see or understand."—**Captain Aimee Obregon**, Milwaukee Police Department

D1565730

POLICE

CRAFT

POLICE

CRAFT

What Cops Know About Crime, Community and Violence

ADAM PLANTINGA

Fresno, California

Police Craft:
What Cops Know About Crime, Community and Violence

Copyright © 2018 by Adam Plantinga. All rights reserved.

Published by Quill Driver Books
An imprint of Linden Publishing
2006 South Mary Street, Fresno, California 93721
(559) 233-6633 / (800) 345-4447
QuillDriverBooks.com

Quill Driver Books and Colophon are trademarks of
Linden Publishing, Inc.

Cover photo by
Rebecca Leimbach of Rebecca Leimbach Photography

ISBN 978-1-61035-331-1

135798642

Printed in the United States of America
on acid-free paper.

Library of Congress Cataloging-in-Publication Data on file.

MIX
Paper from
responsible sources
FSC® C011935

For my parents, Cornelius and Kathleen Plantinga, the two finest people I know.

And for all officers, deputies, and agents who hold the line.

Contents

Introduction

This book is more or less a sequel to my first book, *400 Things Cops Know*, or at the very least, a companion piece. Although I have dropped the bullet point format of *400TCK* in favor of short essays, I have tried to write this work in the same spirit as the original. Why a sequel? Because you, the reader, demanded it. And by "the reader," I am referring predominately to my mother and her loyal coffee circle. I wrote most of the first book while still a police officer. I have now been a sergeant for a number of years, although according to one of my old partners, this promotion was likely due to clerical error. But be that as it may, your perspective on the job changes once you become a supervisor. You are a step removed from the street. You must adopt more of a bird's-eye view. And if you are assigned to an investigative unit, as I was at the time of this writing, you become much more involved in casework, evidence, and interrogations. This book is reflective of those changes.

After *400 Things Cops Know* came out, the response I received was gratifying. The other day I got an email from a cop in Australia. He's a constable in New South Wales attached to the Redfern command. He said the book had been helpful and aided him in avoiding injury. This made my week. But I also heard from officers and citizens alike who said the book was fine and all, but you left out the part about this. Or you should have talked more about that. A number of cops, noting that I wrote in *400TCK* that police commandeer cars only in the movies, regaled me with accounts of vehicles they had commandeered. (With one or two exceptions, I found these accounts, even being kind, less than justifiable.) But point being, on other matters, I have listened to you. As such, this second volume contains things I left out of the first one and then some. It is made up of some material I had waiting in the wings, but a good deal of it comes from other cops, who are subject matter experts in everything from firearms to explosives. I have credited those officers' contributions in these pages, unless it was a really interesting passage, in which case I pretended it was my idea from the start and then began an aggressive campaign to discredit the source. Like the first book, this second assembly is largely a collection of other people's wisdom on the craft of police work. I am merely the fellow who put it together. This has been a reoccurring theme throughout my police career; when smart cops do and say smart things, I take good notes. And that is what makes books like this possible.

I wrote the first book, and am writing this second one, in part to give the reader an insider's look into urban police work. Most folks' contact with the police may stem from a traffic ticket or reporting an auto break-in. But I don't think most people know what cops do all day. Or what the job looks like. Or what it feels like. This book is about those kinds of things. And in presenting police work the way it actually is, I hope that the reader will understand and recognize the contributions of the men and women in law enforcement. Because it's a noble calling, if done right. It isn't always done right. I know this because I watch the news and read the papers. I know this because I don't always get it right. But I'm not doing anyone a favor by serving up a sanitized view of how the job works. Life isn't always tidy. And law enforcement is one of the untidiest professions around.

So, the reader might wonder, is this second book going to be another bead on a string of never-ending sequels? Like the Godzilla movies? Will there be a *Jungle Made of Concrete: 400 World-Weary Musings from an Administrative Lieutenant*? Nah. This is it. Police work is a rich, complex field and could likely sustain such a series. But that will have to be written by someone else, for my pledge is two and done. So I can still exit the room with some dignity.

The reader may notice I have included gentle jabs at firefighters in these pages, much like in the first book. I don't have anything against firefighters—in fact, they are some of the toughest, most courageous people I know. I write this the day after I dropped two cases of Gatorade off at my local firehouse as a thank-you after they battled back an intense grass fire that came uncomfortably close to my family's home. I also point out the flaws in my own profession far more than those of our fire counterparts. No, the jokes are here because cops and firefighters have a natural rivalry and because firefighters are big boys and girls and they can take it. And, truth be told, the jokes are also here because, after the first book, people have come to expect them.

As in *400 Things Cops Know*, I make generalizations in this book, but they come from seventeen years of police experience at two different metropolitan agencies as well as from other officers about how things work at their own agencies. I also make suggestions and recommendations for a way forward on such thorny issues as police–community relations. But I'm not the last word on any of these matters. If someone has a better way to go, let's hear it. And I'm not just talking about listening to other police officers. Some of the most discerning voices in the area of urban violence and law enforcement come from folks who have never driven a radio car or put handcuffs on a suspect. Like David Kennedy, Jill Leovy, and Geoffrey Canada. The stakes are far too high not to have all hands on deck.

So who is this book for? It's for people who want to better understand police officers and perhaps for police officers who want to better understand people. It's for crime writers wanting to get the details right. For readers who wish to know how they can help keep themselves safer in dangerous situations. And it's for everyone who had kind words for the first book—thank you, by the way. I'm glad you're joining me for this second go-around.

1

Getting the Job

Why are we doing so much running? Aren't we all going to be in cars?
—Christian Slater as a police recruit, *Kuffs*

Before they'll let you enter the academy's doors, police applicants must run a gauntlet of tests. First up, the written portion, that gauges everything from reading comprehension to short-term memory and includes a personality inventory that analyzes how well you work with others. If you are looking to be hired by a big-city police department, you will likely take the written exam along with thousands of other hopefuls. Traditionally, a handful of convicted felons will apply, perhaps under the mistaken assumption that the department has relaxed their standards and they'll understand that although I pistol-whipped a guy in 2008, hey, 2008 was a trying year for everyone what with the downturn in the economy and all.

After the written exam is a physical agility test where you have to demonstrate the strength and dexterity needed to do the job: climbing over a 6-foot wall, dragging a weighted dummy to safety, using a Nautilus machine to simulate handcuffing a resisting suspect, and pulling the trigger of a replica handgun ten times with each hand in rapid succession in a set amount of time. I have been told by members of the academy staff that a disproportionately high number of female candidates fail the trigger pull portion of the test—something to do with basic physiology and having smaller hands than the male applicants.

Somewhere in the process will be an oral interview, where you enter a room and are questioned by a panel of police and/or civilians about various aspects of the job. You don't need any formal law enforcement training to pass this section, but common sense sure helps. I myself have served on a number of these panels because I am deeply committed to ensuring the quality of future law enforcement officers and also because a tasty hot lunch is often provided. You can learn volumes about a candidate by how hard he or she knocks on the door before entering for their interview. If it's a meek, almost subservient rap, no good. If you hear a commanding Boom Boom, now we're talking. As a street cop, you'll regularly be going hands on with yoked-out parolees who don't have your best interests at heart. Meek and subservient isn't gonna cut it. As one of my coworkers diplomatically put it, "Sound off like you got a pair."

For the psych exam, which is typically a standardized test like the Minnesota Multiphasic Personality Inventory, the department is looking for signs of stability. For anger issues. For indicators that the candidate generally enjoys a positive outlook on life. For susceptibility to stress and booze. A cynic might point out that the brooding and heavy drinking can come later, once you have some time in on the street, but the department just doesn't want you to start out like that. The two questions I remember best from my psych exam for the Milwaukee Police Department were whether I enjoyed handling the personal articles of others (gloves, socks, etc.) and did evil spirits at times possess me. I felt pretty confident answering no to both. I wasn't really sure what the sock question was getting at, but I've never been overly interested in my own socks, much less the socks of others.

Most departments these days also submit candidates to a polygraph test. The examiner, who in my case with the San Francisco Police Department was a dour woman on a mission to remove all joy from the universe who didn't believe me when I admitted I was a boring square who'd never smoked marijuana, will question you on everything from substance use to driving history to the worst thing you've ever done. Then they'll ask if you've researched ways to beat the polygraph, like the ol' nail in the shoe trick where examinees seek to artificially increase their heart rate during the control questions by skewering themselves with something sharp so the test results won't show any significant increase in heart rate once the tough questions come along. There's growing research that the polygraph has limited effectiveness for preemployment screening, but it sure felt effective to me when I was hooked up to all those sensors and graphs. I would have dimed out my own kinfolk if pressed. *There's no point in trying to hide it. They already know.*

Throughout the police application process, you will be the subject of an extensive background check. Hope you kept good records and had amicable breakups, because the background investigation covers every place you've ever lived, including interviews with all of your exes, and every job you've worked along with the name and contact info of your direct supervisor there. Leave something out, even inadvertently, and you will be bounced out of the process for failure to disclose. A speeding ticket (or around four in my case) won't submarine you, but recent hard drug use will. Even bad credit can be grounds for disqualification. Because police departments are looking for responsible people who play by the rules.

A few applicants, who look great on paper, will confess to crimes at some stage in hiring to either their background investigator or the polygraph examiner. Sometimes crimes from long ago. Sometimes serious crimes, like sexual assault. The end result is that they will be eliminated as a candidate, and the department they are applying to is going to contact the jurisdiction where their crime occurred and ask some hard questions about both the statute of limitations and extradition.

Rounding out the testing process is the medical screening and the drug test, where you provide urine and a lock of your hair to be checked for narcotics. A few candidates, fearing the results of such scrutiny, will research such products as the Whizzinator. Google it if you must.

If you clear all those hurdles, and the department still has open slots, you're in. I still remember the uniformed Milwaukee officer who came to my apartment and had me sign for my acceptance letter to join up. He seemed tired and distracted.

"Good luck," he said with a prescient sigh.

Typically when you start a new job, your coworkers seem happy to see you and welcome you aboard. The first day might feature roundtable icebreakers. Cookies. Punch.

But on Day One of the police academy, no one is happy to see you and you will encounter no refreshments. You file into a classroom and you sit down. To dead silence. There are no exchanges of "What did you used to do before this?" or "Hey, is this going to be fun or what?" because your recruit training staff will have entered the room by now and it is clear they will brook no chatter or nonsense. The initial impression they leave is of fear, awe, and the promise of pain. My primary Milwaukee academy instructor was Officer Darryl Ponder, a massive, glowering man who looked like he could snap recruits over his knee like kindling and spoke in a deep, grave voice that seemed to originate from some wellspring of hard-earned authenticity. PO Ponder didn't waste much time going over the class rules. There were only three.

"Show up," he said. "Put up. And shut up."

The academy staff will make it clear they are your instructors, not your pals. Like kids from the '50s, recruits are to be seen and not heard. If you have a question, you raise your hand, and if called on, you stand, identify yourself, and say sir or ma'am before proceeding with the question. Recruits don't ask many questions. Except the ones who do. You'll see their kind everywhere from high school to law school, shooting their hand up at every available opportunity, desperate to make a favorable impression. My brother Nate calls them gunners. But such student enthusiasm is handled a bit differently at the police academy level.

"You're annoying," an instructor said matter-of-factly to a gunner in one of my academy classes, after which her cascade of questions slowed to a drip. But perhaps Officer Ponder put it best. "Some of you," he intoned, "raise your hands and then I don't call on you. If I don't call on you, it's not because I don't see you. It's because I don't want to call on you. It's because I don't care what you have to say."

But not all of Ponder's sayings were meant to diminish us. "Let's get through this," he said once. "So when it's over, we'll be proud of what we've done here."

Every police academy runs a bit differently. Some are more like the military where the recruits shave their heads, stay in barracks overnight, and do an inordinate amount of marching. Others approach more of a collegiate atmosphere. Some are seven months long and some are significantly shorter, although gone are the days when you'd spend a few weeks in a classroom and then be handed a gun and badge and told, "Okay kid, go get 'em."

But one unifier among these various academies is the police recruit's uniform, which looks just like a real police uniform. Except shittier. They are typically made of canvas and resemble the coveralls you might throw on to do asbestos work. That's the point. It's a uniform sure enough, but a uniform that indicates you're nothing but a recruit. You haven't earned the right to wear something that actually looks good. You haven't amounted to much yet. No one is the least bit impressed by you. As the academy staff will dutifully point out, they harbor strong suspicions that you are, in fact, a turd.

Another unifier among academies is the rigors of morning inspection, during which recruits stand at attention while the academy staff walks down the line making sure uniforms are lint-free, belt buckles are shined, shoes are gleaming. Many shoes are found not to be sufficiently gleaming.

If one recruit falters in inspection, the whole class pays for it. This is to promote a sense of togetherness and teamwork. Payment often comes in the form of the front leaning rest, which is a vehicle for introducing the police recruit to a combination of stress and pain. It involves getting into a push-up position with elbows bent and chin a few inches from the floor and then holding that position until your muscles quiver and your sweat pools on the floor in front of your nose. You will be astonished by the volume of sweat you have in you. Can all of that perspiration really be yours? Or is some of it sweat transfer from the recruit next to you? There will be groaning from the class as the seconds tick by. You will be told to shut the hell up. There will be more groaning and you will be told to shut up more. A few recruits will cheat by arching their backs or briefly taking a knee. These shortcuts will be quickly addressed by the staff in a withering diatribe and will serve only to lengthen the duration of the front leaning rest. The academy staff will think quite highly of your physical stamina because the front leaning rest will stretch on and on until recruits collapse under their own weight and splay out on the floor.

But no matter how hard you think you have it, veteran cops relish talking about how much tougher the academy was when they went through. An old-timer will reminiscence proudly about the concussion he suffered in a hand-to-hand combat scenario and then grouse about how recruits now, a bunch of pansies, get to wear protective helmets and mouth guards in the mat room. My old partner Steve Pinchard graduated from the Milwaukee academy in 1991.

"They put us in cages," Steve insists. "They fed us beans."

Early on in the academy, you will be shown a series of survival videos, many of them taken directly from police dash or body cams, where officers are badly hurt or killed on the job. In these videos, cops are stomped on repeatedly until their bones snap. Officers are splashed with acid. Deputies are shot in the face at close range, leaving them grossly disfigured. The theme might be survival—many of these officers fight back and win, even under tremendous pain and duress—but there is also a Can You Hack This? philosophy at work in showing the footage to new hires. (After this video onslaught, some recruits will quit and return to their old job at Applebee's or Home Depot, where acid exposure and face shootings are less commonplace.) Then someone from Payroll will inform the class that if you are killed in the line of duty, your chosen designee will receive a base payment in compensation, not including life insurance settlements. In Milwaukee, in 2001, that figure was $250,000. That seemed high to me at the time, but maybe because I was single and childless, my main possession a ratty futon. But the $250,000 figure inspired quite a few "I am worth far more dead than alive" quips among my classmates.

The training staff goes hard at you, especially in those first six to eight weeks. Then they lighten up a tad. A few of them may even smile or crack a joke. But if they sense complacency among the recruits or anything that even remotely resembles cockiness, it's back to shouting. Throwing things. The front leaning rest. Workouts that don't stop even when recruits are wilting on rubbery legs and upchucking in the hallway. It's not unusual to see an ambulance show up to the academy and cart away a recruit for dehydration or a bone fracture.

More recruits will quit during this stretch. Usually around 20 percent of an academy class doesn't make it to graduation. The staff won't make any rousing speeches urging anyone to stay. As one instructor told my class, "Don't like the way things are going here? Then leave. We don't want you."

Physical fitness stands front and center in the training room, for police work is a stressful, physically demanding career that requires officers to get in shape and stay that way.

"If you do not eat healthy foods, exercise, and take care of yourself, I have one word for you. Stupid. Because you are going to die," Officer Ponder said during a course on nutrition. I dutifully scribbled this in the corner of my notebook: "Eat well or die, stupid."

The academy will force you to become acclimated to pain and fatigue, your constant companions through months of training. You will be forced to sprint until you have nothing left and then be told to keep on sprinting. You will undergo Defense and Arrest Tactics (DAAT) Training where you will be put through a punishing workout after which you are so exhausted you can barely raise your arms. And then and only then do you battle with an instructor clad in a heavily padded suit. And not the diminutive instructor either. No, the other guy. The one with MMA or Olympic judo experience and no discernible neck. The guy they keep in back.

The recruit staff is trying to accomplish a couple of things with these rigors. The first is to prepare you, hopefully, for a lifetime of fitness. The second is to measure how much quit you have in you. This is vital to know because your life, your partner's life, and the life of the civilians you have signed on to protect could all depend on how deep you can reach into the reservoir. Staying in shape and being used to pushing against your physical limits could mean the difference between having to shoot some thug who is going for your gun and being able to spear that same suspect into the ground like he's a tool you're using to dig a trench. The academy staff knows there will come a time when it's just the two of you in a dead-end alley, the criminal and you, and backup isn't there yet or maybe you've just lost your radio in the fight. And he doesn't want to go back to jail. In order not to go back to jail, he has to go through you. And when the fight is on, you will think I cannot hold this man off for another minute. Not one more minute. And then you do. Because you must.

During DAAT, you practice punches, elbow strikes, wall stuns, and firearm retention. You will drill on handcuffing to the point where you can literally cuff someone with your eyes closed. DAAT takes its toll on some recruits, who miss workouts with maladies ranging from banged-up limbs to "stomachaches." While the rest of the class presses on, they are sequestered on the sidelines like lepers, the instructors openly deriding their tolerance for pain, sending the clear message that police recruits are too new to be hurt.

One of the key phrases in DAAT is "Stop resisting." It's what you're supposed to say to suspects who fight with you. Even if it doesn't make them stop, the instructors tell you, it sounds good. Maybe a neighbor will hear it and when the news interviews him, he'll say, "Well, the guy didn't do what the officers told him too. He kept resisting."

But DAAT isn't all about fighting. It's about knowing how to talk to people so you can try to avoid a fight. This approach is often called something like tactical communications or verbal judo, the latter pioneered by the late, great Dr. George Thompson, a former street cop turned teacher and author. In verbal judo, you learn how to de-escalate people with the right choice of words. They're called peace phrases. So you lead off with something like this:

"I understand that, sir, but . . ."

"For your safety and mine, I'm going to . . ."

"Can you work with us here?"

"Is there anything I can say to get you to comply with my lawful order?"

"You seem like a reasonable person . . ." (I once said this to a man whose hair was strewn with ramen noodles, who proudly wore his Department of Corrections inmate ID around his neck like a lucky charm inside his own apartment, and who smelled strongly of piss. Maybe a peace phrase doesn't have to be true to be effective.)

Some of these peace phrases sounded straight-up hokey, but it was a calm script to fall back on if things got heated with citizens. And it was all about treating people with due respect and earning their cooperation, thus accomplishing one of the primary goals of law enforcement—gaining voluntary compliance.

The acronyms fly thick and fast in the academy. The staff from the Vice Control Division teaches you what signs to look for in a drug addict (crystal meth tends to dry out the mouth so users lick their lips a lot) and the street value of an eight ball of cocaine. You'll take the Emergency Vehicle Operation Course (EVOC), where they tell you that if you have to drive quickly through an accident scene to something more pressing and want to avoid pinballing off other cars, aim right for the smoke. Because the smoke isn't where the accident is. It's where the accident used to be. EVOC is great training but isn't nearly as exciting as you had hoped, probably because the city doesn't have the budget to keep replacing squad cars that enthusiastic recruits total on the track. Special Weapons and Tactics (SWAT) shows you how to clear rooms for suspects and how to handle hostage takers and active shooters. They'll guide you in the use of simunition guns, similar to paintball guns, to hone your skills in Shoot/Don't Shoot scenarios. You realize how difficult it is to tell a wallet from a handgun under stress in low light. Recruits shoot role players in these scenarios who shouldn't be shot and don't shoot people who should be. Things are not always as they seem. I remember one video-based training scenario where a fellow recruit and I entered a tavern on a subject with a gun call and approached a winsome blonde who greeted us warmly just before she took out a revolver from her purse and shot us both repeatedly before we had even cleared our holsters.

"She had us at hello," my partner said glumly.

In the academy, you will get diversity training. Plenty of it. Courses on Hispanic Issues, Native American Issues, Gay and Lesbian Issues. In the History of Women in Policing class, you'll learn that women used to be marginalized. No one thought they could handle the job. Male officers wrote the female officers' names over the urinal and taped tampons to their lockers. Their acceptance into law enforcement has been gradual and grudging. An LGBT group came in to talk to my Milwaukee class about tolerance. One of them, a 200-pound male-to-female transgender woman was visibly nervous and I admired her pluck; police recruits probably weren't the easiest crowd for such material. She fielded quite a few questions, such as which restroom did she use. One of my Milwaukee classmates told the LGBT guests that he was glad they came.

"I thought gay people lived in, like, caves," he offered.

And that, folks, is why we have diversity training.

As you push on in the police academy, your coursework became weightier. Someone from the Special Victims Unit will talk to you about speaking frankly with the victims of sexual assault. "You people have to get used to saying penis and vagina," one instructor told my class. He then had us repeat the words in a rhythmic monotone. You will learn about shaken baby syndrome and sudden infant death syndrome (SIDS). You will learn that your city's average response time for a med rig is under four minutes, which you are incredibly grateful for as you fumble around with dressings, splints, and bandages in your trauma class.

During handgun training, you will be taught that the first order of business when confronted with a weapons malfunction is Tap, Tilt, Rack, where you tap the magazine in hard, tilt the weapon at an angle to free any obstruction, and rack the slide to chamber a round. You will become familiar with the failure drill, which is shooting two rounds to the upper body and one to the head in case a suspect is wearing body armor. You will know the importance of having a clear field of fire when you make the decision to shoot—the mantra for this is Target, Backstop, and Beyond, because you are accountable for every round you deliver downrange.

In addition to handguns, you are trained on the shotgun, often the Remington 12-gauge. It is a devastating weapon, especially up close. But the instructors teach you to check the barrel of the shotgun before going into the field, because twigs, leaves, and sometimes even chewing gum can end up in there. Basically, some cops use it as a trash receptacle. This sounds absurd to you as a new cop. But, as an instructor once explained to me, "There are some sloppy bastards on this job."

The police academy will teach you the hard skills essential to the job. Shooting, fighting, emergency driving, first aid. But one of the softer skills, report writing, is the one you'll use the most. For every hour of police work, there is, on average, two hours of reports to write. And, as the staff will tell you, if you don't document it, it didn't happen. You will be introduced to your state's motor vehicle accident report, a form with so many different pages and Scantron-esque bubbles that at first it appears to be some kind of cruel joke. You will be given memorandum books where you are to record your daily academy schedule and, beyond the academy, all pertinent information about assignments you took on the street. When one fills, you are to get another, and many departments require that you retain them for the duration of your career in case the information is ever needed for an investigation or court. The typical officer goes through one memo book every month or so, the academy staff tells you. One a month for twenty-five years. Three hundred memo books. You picture yourself after retirement surrounded by these books, piles of them spilling over each other as you tell visitors about your august years and the crimes you once tried to solve.

Another skill you must master as a police officer is attention to detail. The academy teaches you to drink in the whole room when you enter on an assignment. The instructors will do things like leave a handgun out in plain view while recruits talk with a suspect role player in a training scenario; the recruit is often oblivious to the instrument of death just a few feet away. That's why the academy staff will come down on you hard if there's lint on your shirt collar or you botch a radio code. Attention to detail is everything. On the street, you want to be constantly taking mental snapshots. That's why you'll see an experienced officer drive at patrol speed. Not too fast, not too slow, but just the right clip to keep a watch out for everything from road hazards to recessed doorways where criminals like to linger. That same officer will often make a sharp U-turn when he hears a radio broadcast of a street robbery. But not in the direction of the crime scene. In the opposite direction. Because even though he was driving and joking with his partner, and simultaneously listening to two police radios and Rock 103.1, he had his head on a swivel and remembers seeing someone matching the suspect description three minutes ago walking westbound on the north side of the street carrying the same property taken in the robbery.

Especially these days, police academies also place a heavy emphasis on ethics training. It doesn't get too philosophical; no invocations of Nietzsche or Aquinas. It's a lot of classroom lecture and scenario-based coursework, but it boils down to this: If it isn't right, don't do it. If it isn't true, don't say it.

There's also a lot of capping on the firefighters in the academy. The academy staff might describe being a firefighter thusly: you'll work an average of seven minutes a day and get paid the same as cops and everyone will love you and you get to sleep on duty and make brisket in a well-stocked kitchen and grow a powerful mustache and watch *Backdraft* over and over while trying to figure out which of the brooding yet heroic McCaffrey brothers most resonates with you.

But if you want to do some real work, the police instructor will continue, stay in this room. Because, as the bumper sticker posted outside several police stations says God Made Police So Firefighters Would Have Heroes.

All of this is okay, you see, because you know that the instructors at the fire academy are capping on you even harder.

On the morning of September 11, 2001, my Milwaukee academy class was put on hold when the instructor rolled in a television and we watched the towers burn. The MPD was on high alert, as was every police department across the nation. Our education had taken a backseat to a state of wartime readiness. I wanted to take action, to bring someone to justice, but I felt small and ineffectual in my canvass recruit uniform, my duty belt empty of handcuffs and weapons, just a boy playing dress-up. I wrote in my memorandum book, "9:30 a.m. Class suspended due to terrorist attack." That night, I stayed up and watched the news until it felt like there was sand behind my eyes. Learned that it was a day when ordinary people at work in the Towers in New York City had to decide whether to leap to their deaths or be burned alive.

The next morning, one of the sergeants brought up the horrific events of the previous day. "This," he said, "is what you signed on for."

The class was quiet after that.

Our workouts were punishing, almost frenzied that week. Everything had changed, and we would need to be in the best shape of our lives.

Because this could happen again.

And there would be stairs to climb.

Toward the end of the academy, you bid good-bye to your recruit clothes as you're fitted for your regular uniforms. You have a gun, cuffs, a ballistic vest, and a star or shield. You haven't taken a single assignment or arrested anyone, but you almost feel like a real cop. It seems like the academy has stretched on forever, but it takes eighteen months to get a hairstylist license in some states, so you aren't coming out too badly in comparison.

I gave a speech at my Milwaukee academy commencement. It was a lot of highbrow stuff I probably hadn't earned the right to say yet. Afterward, at the reception, I was asked several times what my goals were on the job. I pondered something profound about serving the common good and protecting the weak and the innocent. But then I thought of something more immediate—my primary goal was to avoid accidentally shooting myself in the leg.

You don't think about it much at the time while in the academy's halls because you are too wrapped up in your own myopic recruit world, but the police instructors' task, that of molding unformed civilians into functional cops, is nothing short of herculean. And there's ongoing pressure on the academy staff to push classes through, as each recruit represents a sizable investment by the city in terms of time and money. That's perhaps why a smattering of new officers will make it to graduation even though they appear to have no earthly business walking around with a loaded firearm or making split-second decisions. But such cops tend not to last on the street. They quit, are fired, or find some roundabout way to escape patrol duties; one day, poof, they're transferred to Records or Crime Analysis or the Midday Metro Aquatic Investigative Task Force, which looks exclusively into crimes that occur in fresh water between the hours of noon and three.

After you've left the academy, walking under the sign that says Enter to Learn, Depart to Serve, you are assigned to a field training officer (FTO). And he is the law enforcement deity who rules your universe. The rising of the sun. The rhythm of the tides. The earth's gravitational pull. These are just some of the things he controls.

You get in the patrol car. Your FTO will probably drive, at least that first day. Until he sees what kind of hand he's been dealt.

You are raring to go.

You are likely in terrific physical shape.

You have large swathes of the criminal and traffic code committed to memory.

Other than that, you don't know anything about street-level police work. Not one doggone thing.

So you roll out of the parking lot toward your first call, something rising in your gut that mixes elation and self-doubt, pride and apprehension.

It begins.

2

Violence

The nation that will insist on drawing a broad line of demarcation between the fighting man and the thinking man is liable to find its fighting done by fools and its thinking done by cowards.
—Thucydides

A question for the reader: when's the last time you got in a fight? For some, it might harken back to grade school, when Robby McPherson stepped up to you, words were exchanged, and you went at it before the playground monitor pulled you apart. Perhaps that's why, when some adults fight, you see a lot of the old fourth-grade moves come out. Pushing. Hair pulling. Biting. Slapping. This is because the combatants likely have no training or technique, no memory bank to draw from other than grammar school scuffles, and they don't quite know what to do with the adrenaline rush that accompanies physical conflict. You can't just turn that adrenaline off, like a water spigot, because it represents the equivalent of pharmaceutical grade chemicals rushing through your system.

When it comes to fighting, such arrested development isn't just limited to civilians. I once observed a cop involved in a winter melee get so jacked up that he washed a suspect's face out with snow. Not sure where that one falls on the official police use of force continuum. Maybe one step above Wet Willy and one below Noogie.

In a fight, instinct tells you to back away from the man swinging his fists or a weapon at you. If you're quicker and faster than your opponent and intend to run away, go for it. Live to fight another day, when the odds are better. But if you are committed to a fight, and as a cop, you are committed to them all, you may want to resist that urge and instead move in and tie the suspect up like a boxer. This guy needs the right amount of distance to land blows, and if you take away the distance, you take away the blows. And while you're up close and personal, you run through your response options. Maybe it's a baton day, maybe it's a gun day. But this guy throwing haymakers or swinging a wrench? You're going to make sure it isn't his day.

The prospect of fighting is why female officers with long hair keep it tied up. You leave nothing for the bad guy to grab onto. No feathery Heather Locklear tresses from *T.J. Hooker*. It's the same reason you wear a clip-on tie. Prevents the bad guy from strangling you with it. The other nice thing about clip-ons is that they're so cheap and shoddy-looking that you don't feel bad when you spill condiments on them.

One way to dispel violence as a cop is to give off the appearance of being readily able to dispense violence. Do you look like you'd be comfortable going a few rounds? Or is your shirt untucked and your stomach suggestive of a diet made up primarily of assorted rich cheeses? Physical presence counts for a lot. Some crooks will take a pass on brawling with you only because they're not sure they can beat you. That's one of the reasons you cringe when you see some of your academy classmates who let themselves go not long after graduation, as if they've embarked on some kind of misguided quest to get into the worst shape possible. When they were in training, they were lean, fit, and hungry. Fast-forward a couple of years and they've got a beer gut and they're smoking a half pack a day. There's a box of bear claws on the break room table and they're good for three of them. One of my former coworkers became so overweight that he couldn't reach down to tie his own shoes. His wife would tie them in the morning, but if they became undone during the course of his shift, they stayed that way. He'd walk down the hallway of the district station, laces flapping. It was hard to watch. Another officer I know got so heavy, he wouldn't walk up the stairs to the locker room. His locker was the trunk of his car.

Some police departments, like the SFPD, incentivize staying healthy, awarding officers bonus off-time if they score well on a biannual fitness test. But I don't know of any department that penalizes cops for getting doughy; Personnel has enough trouble recruiting and retaining officers that they can't afford to drop one for a failed PT test. Street cops worth their salt stay fit because they take pride in themselves and the job. You don't want to be the guy whose shift resents you because you wheeze before the fight even starts and are too pudgy to climb over a fence in pursuit of an armed suspect. Your fellow pudgy cops will be sympathetic to your plight, but everyone else will think you're a slug because they understand that when you put on the uniform, you lose the right to be out of shape.

There's a photo up in some police stations that speaks to this issue. The picture is of a line of heavily muscled, shirtless cons standing in the prison yard. Underneath is the caption They Worked Out Today. Did You?

One of the essential philosophies to understand in police work is Ask/Tell/Order/Make. Those four words are the rungs of the ladder you climb when giving direction to the public. You first Ask them to do something, like step to the sidewalk or take their hands out of their pockets, etc. If that doesn't work, you Tell them, with a little more steel in your voice. If you still aren't getting results, you Order and then transition to Make if need be. If you're in Make territory, someone is getting handcuffed. What you want to avoid is getting stuck in a ridiculous "Stop or I'll Order You to Stop Again" loop, which is fine for mall security but makes you, as a lawman, look like an incompetent boob. You may also skip ahead a few steps when the situation calls for it. If a suspect soccer-kicks you full-on in the groin, you don't just politely Ask him to cease and then wait an appreciable time and raise your voice just a tad and Tell him the same thing. No, in that situation, you may commence with the hostilities of Make, really at any time you'd like.

If the fight is on, you quickly learn there's no perfect calculus for the police use of force. There never will be. Sometimes you'll go too hard at suspects. Sometimes too soft. But the bottom line is, you have to be able to flip a switch and go from civility to savagery. You must out-violence a violent suspect to take him into custody. No half-measures. A man is strangling you. You can't reach your sidearm. You are a half tick away from passing out. But there is the suspect's nose, right in front of you. So bite it. Maybe that will take some of the starch out of him. *But they didn't teach me that in the academy.* No, but they also didn't teach you to be murdered in a filthy apartment by a berserker drug addict. So bite his nose, bite the whole thing off if need be, and when that's done, look for something else to bite off. Because you need to understand this is on him, not you. He threw this party. All you did was show up.

Some officers, especially newer ones, don't have this violence switch. They are too good-natured for the job. They simply don't have the Make of Ask/Tell/Order/Make anywhere inside them. Physical stature doesn't always have much to do with it—you'll see cops the size of a vending machine turn tentative and ineffectual at the start of a fight whereas an officer half their size will roll her sleeves up and jump right into the fray. The nonfighters, the one who don't possess that extra gear, are frequently identified and either shunned or dismissed from the department because they're going to get themselves or someone else hurt. The job isn't for everyone.

If you punch someone in the face, you run a high risk of injuring your hand up to and including breaking it. That's because, while the human nose has some give to it, pretty much everywhere else on the head is hard as shale. You'll know plenty of cops who have shattered phalanges and metacarpals from striking people who are resisting arrest. During the summer of 2013 when I was working Street Crimes, my partner and I were taking someone into custody every day and not all of them were wholly agreeable to the arrest process. I punched so many violent felons in the face that summer that I was placed in the Early Intervention System, which is designed to track problem officers but more often than not, simply reveals proactive cops who make quality arrests and aren't big on retreating. I was so punch-happy that summer that even now, years later, when I hit the heavy bag in my garage, the knuckles on my right hand start to protest and burn after only a few minutes.

Now, I could justify every blow, but to onlookers, all those face strikes may have looked like police heavy-handedness. They may have viewed me the same way my wife does when I am doing something questionable like eating a greasy meat platter without utensils while hunched over the sink. At which point I tell her, "I do not expect you to understand or approve of what is happening here."

One school of thought holds that you aren't a real street cop until you've been socked in the face yourself by a suspect. I think there's something to that. Because when you get out of the academy, you often harbor the notion that people are going to do what you say solely because you're a uniformed legal enforcer. After all, you sport police patches and a shiny cap and you're infused with lawful arrest powers granted to you by your state's legal code. But then you run into the guy who doesn't think much of you or your dress blues and he doesn't give two squirts of cold piss about legal authority. You take the handcuffs out and approach him. Pop! Facepunch. And the fight is on. This type of altercation can only serve to make you a better officer. It's a gift to you, the gift you never knew you needed. It helps remind you to keep your guard up because violence can jump off at any time. And you gotta watch the suspects' hands. Watch 'em with the attention of a Beverly Hills manicurist. Because it's the hands, and what's in them, that will hurt you.

After a donnybrook with a suspect, sometimes you'll give the guy grudging respect. He fought hard. He went all out for a cause, even if it was the wrong one. And once in a while, he'll give it right back to you. "That was a real good takedown," a heroin dealer told me earnestly after I flipped him on his back in a hotel lobby after he fled from my partner and me. "Never seen anything like that before." I was so proud I went home and told my wife. A career doper paid me a compliment today on my scuffling ability! Hey, you're a cop. The compliments are few and far between. You'll take it, no matter the source.

Although some suspects will fight you, many are nothing but tough talk. They want to sound hard in front of their buddies, or they're drunk, or they're just fundamentally silly. And as long as they're not threatening you and they are going with the program, there's no need to get grabby with them because of what they say. That's where some officers get in trouble. They lose their cool because the criminal has committed the offense of Contempt of Cop, which they believe may not go unpunished. But best to let it be. If a suspect calls you a bitch-ass punk, you simply accept the constructive feedback without any payback, because this is America, the cradle of free speech, and a crook can say pretty much whatever he'd like to you as long as he follows your commands.

If your suspect doesn't follow your commands, things probably aren't going to break his way. I once chased a drug dealer on foot down Mission Street who was tossing his crack cocaine as he fled. Knowing that drug dealers in general are dangerous and carry weapons and knowing that this particular corner where this particular dealer was selling has been the site of several recent drug-related shootings, I told him to stop, but he didn't so I caught up to him and threw him onto the hood of a parked Honda Accord. He bounced off and landed on the street, separating his shoulder. He claimed police brutality, but it was hard to feel bad for him. It wasn't just his thirty-five prior felony arrests. It was because he called the play that day. If he had stopped when I told him to, none of this would have happened. Often when the police have to hurt people, it's because you're reacting to their poor decision-making. It's also because you know you cannot wait too long for the threat to materialize. If you give the bad guy that kind of head start, you're headed to the hospital or you're already dead. Raymond Chandler understood this when he wrote, in *The Big Sleep*:

"Perhaps it would have been nice to allow him another shot or two, just like a gentleman of the old school. But his gun was still up and I couldn't wait any longer."

As an urban police officer, you will patrol streets that are neither orderly nor safe. It is not a gentleman's game.

Skin is easy to break. It's about four millimeters thick. And because of their heavy concentration of capillaries and veins, scalps bleed a lot, so much so that even a small gash will appear life-threatening to the layman's eye. A concerned citizen will call 911 and report there's a man bleeding on the sidewalk, come quickly because this guy is really gushing, maybe he's dying. And you show up and all this fellow really needs is a Wet-Nap and a butterfly bandage.

But while a scalp injury could be a big nothing, one of the factors you must key in on when responding to a street fight is the possibility that one of the participants has sustained traumatic brain injury (TBI). Only in cowboy movies can people withstand staggering numbers of cranial blows without ill effects. For the rest of us, it's delicate wiring up there and a hard knock to the head, be it from a blow or a fall, can concuss a person's brain against his skull like a wave breaking over a water piling. The symptoms of TBI include slurred speech, disorientation, headaches, and blurry vision. Victims might repeat the same question or insist on going to sleep. (In the past, conventional wisdom advised keeping TBI victims awake because going to sleep could increase the risk of a coma. Most medical professionals now believe this risk is overblown, especially if the victim is on the way to a hospital where they can be monitored.) It can get a little confusing out there because many street fights are alcohol related, so you have to figure out if the person you're looking at has TBI or is just some party boy feeling the effects of seven consecutive wine coolers. And those with TBI are rarely in the best position to judge their own fitness. "I'm fine," your victim insists, waving you off and then taking one step forward and sagging into the wall like his legs don't have bones in them. You always call an ambulance for these folks and ensure they get in it, even if they loudly declare they won't go because that eighth wine cooler beckons. Let the medical experts give them the once-over at the hospital, and if they want to leave against medical advice, that's on them. Legally they can refuse treatment, but they can't refuse transport.

Beyond TBI, another hallmark of street violence is that people who have been stabbed often don't realize it right away. They feel the impact of the blow but think they've only been punched. They may actually continue to fight and even chase the suspect for a time. Then they look down and see blood flowing out of holes in them. Internal injuries aside, the mere sight of gushing blood is as alarming as it gets. But you can safely lose sixteen ounces of the red stuff before you're officially in trouble. Sixteen ounces is quite a bit. That's a standard bottle of water. It's how much they routinely take at the blood bank.

As an investigator, you will watch many surveillance videos that capture the intense, split-second violence of shootings. Even without audio or a direct view of the gunman, it's clear what's happening on screen because folks will be going about their business and then people's heads will whip around in the direction of the shots and they'll start running. Some of these bystanders, particularly those who seem a bit past their prime, run in choppy, ungainly strides, as if they aren't accustomed to moving at a pace quicker than a stroll. As if all their parts aren't connected right. But they get out of the way as quickly as they can, because that's the human body's wet-wired response to danger. For most people, that is. Others, often the down-and-out types who hang out on a hard corner, will continue to trudge along in the same direction they were going. Gunshots? Ain't nothing they haven't heard before.

Some take it even a step further. In the annals of municipal legends is scribed the confirmed tale of a San Francisco crack dealer who was conducting a dope deal in the projects when a gunman began shooting in his direction. The dealer had just passed off a corner cut to the buyer, who ducked for cover. The dealer didn't budge, because he hadn't yet been paid. "Where the fuck my money at," he demanded as bullets pinged off the walls around him. Admirable pluck, to be sure, but all of these folks would do well to remember the words of '40s Dallas gangster Benny Binion. "Courage is a fine thing," he is credited as saying, "but when the shooting starts, get down on the floor."

One of the police responses to such gunplay in the neighborhood is to go high-profile. This means taking a number of slow rolls in your squad car down the streets with light bars blazing and spotlights on. It's a show of force. You are trying to be seen. And the message you wish to impart is this: We're here, okay? See us? All right, good. Now, stop shooting people, assholes.

As a police officer, you are taught that in a deadly force situation, you fire until the threat is stopped, which often means the suspect is literally down on the ground, incapacitated or dead. (And when the scene is safe, you immediately try to save his life with first aid and CPR. Not a lot of other jobs like that.) Many citizens wonder, after a publicized police shooting incident, why the officers had to fire so many rounds. Firearms experts will tell you that the difference between four shots and a dozen shots isn't as significant as you might think. First off, most officers have no idea how many shots they fired in the heat of the moment. Intense situations create all sorts of physiological effects. Time slows. Your hearing and sight are affected. You sometimes don't remember crucial parts of the incident until much later when you have the time and space to decompress. Second, you typically don't have time in a gunfight to turn and ask your partner how many rounds he's firing so you can respond accordingly.

But anyone who thinks there should be a cap on police bullets fired would do well to study the '86 Miami shoot-out between two bank robbers and eight FBI agents in which approximately 145 rounds were exchanged. The two suspects, despite being outnumbered four to one, went down hard. How hard? One of them, Michael Platt, was shot twelve times, including a 9-mm bullet that entered his right rib cage and stopped an inch from his heart. He kept fighting for four more minutes, eventually killing two of the agents, Jerry Dove and Benjamin Grogan. The other suspect, William Matix, was shot six times, the primary hit being a .38 round to the brain. He went unconscious for over a minute, woke, and rejoined Platt in the gunfight, which injured five other agents.

Both Matix and Platt had military training but wore no body armor. They were found to be drug-free during autopsy, sustained only by a powerful will to live and a desire to destroy what was in front of them.

A placard honoring Agents Dove and Grogan can be found in Miami at the corner of SW 82nd Avenue and SW 122nd Street where the gunfight played out. As for the suspects? Platt is buried in Jonesboro, Arkansas. Matix was laid to rest at the Mound Hill Cemetery in Eaton, Ohio. I found this information on findagrave.com. When I scrolled down Platt's page, I read this: "The Virtual Flowers feature has been turned off for this memorial because it was being continually misused."

Sounds about right to me.

3

Addiction

First you take a drink, then the drink takes a drink, then the drink takes you.
—F. Scott Fitzgerald

Gambling, which novelist André Malraux called "suicide without death," works on the basis of intermittent reinforcement; you win just often enough to think you can do it on a regular basis. That's how gambling sinks its hooks into you. It's like when Charles Barkley used to shoot three-pointers—he hit just enough of them to think he could sink them every time.

Some gamblers are so desperate to end their cycle of addiction that they will sign a sworn statement in the casino office banning themselves from that casino and agreeing to be arrested for trespassing if they return. And then they often do return and you arrest them, although they've essentially arrested themselves. That oath they swore not to come back—that was a lie. Just another entry on the list of deceits addicts tell themselves. Theologian Lewis Smedes speaks to this when he observes in his book *A Pretty Good Person*: "Nobody ever says, 'I think I will lie to myself today.' This is the double treachery of self-deception: First we deceive ourselves, and then we convince ourselves that we are not deceiving ourselves."

If you're wondering if your office NCAA tournament pool is illegal, it was up until May of 2018, when the Supreme Court struck down the 1992 federal law called the Professional and Amateur Sports Protection Act, which outlawed betting on nearly every sporting event outside the confines of Las Vegas. How about your poker night with the fellas? Depends on the state. About half of them outlaw private poker games where money changes hands, the violation typically being a misdemeanor. But the more important question is, do the police or anyone really care about this type of gambling? No, not especially. Not when your local circuit court judge is in on the pool and just sagely picked Lehigh to go to the Sweet Sixteen. Not when the district attorney is among the guests at Texas Hold 'Em night. But if you have transformed your basement into a mini-casino with a roulette wheel and craps table with cash payouts and you aren't being particularly discreet about it, it's conceivable that the law will come knocking. What will happen next sort of depends.

Years ago, my partner and I were going door to door dropping off crime prevention flyers in the Ingleside district of San Francisco when I walked into a community center and saw a sea of people playing an organized card game with a video screen and an emcee. It was clearly for money and did not give off even a whiff of a charity event. Lo, a large-scale illegal gambling operation right in front of me. But it didn't look like there was a single person in the room under sixty and I got the sense that not a lot of English would be spoken. I started to imagine how many cops, how many translators, how many vans it would take to properly shut this operation down and book all the evidence. Whatever that number was, it was more than we had.

My official police response? I said, "Uh . . ."

My partner did me one better. He said, "Uh, yeah." And we both slowly backed out and shut the door softly, leaving a lone crime prevention brochure in our wake. If the community made a complaint about this geriatric gambling den, we would revisit it.

Otherwise, some doors are perhaps best kept closed.

Good people work in addiction and recovery and they know far more about this topic than I ever will. Many of them are addicts themselves who have found their way back. What I have learned from them is that addicts cannot fix themselves. It's like cancer patients trying to perform their own surgery. But the waiting list for drug treatment tends to be prolonged, unless you have comprehensive insurance and/or the money to go to the programs they advertise on television that look like high-end spas with infinity pools and attentive masseuses. If you are underinsured or you don't happen to have six thousand a month in discretionary income to spend on in-patient care, be prepared to wait for a city- or state-funded program where a six-month backup on treatment is not uncommon. For hard-core addicts, six months might as well be a century. That's another half a year to be out on the streets committing crimes to support their habit, risking contracting hepatitis C and HIV, and generally walking through the rubble of their own lives.

Addiction is everywhere. If you don't think you know an addict, give it time and one will be revealed. Addiction ruins jobs and implodes marriages. You'd think, with all the societal debris caused by addiction that cops see on a daily basis, that they'd be able to sidestep these pitfalls themselves, but not so. Ask anyone from a department's Behavioral Health Program and they'll tell you a growing number of police officers are finding themselves addicted to pain killers. These pills are often prescribed for a duty-related injury, but the officer battles to wean himself off them long after the prescription has run out. And cops and booze are so inextricably linked that if you're an officer who doesn't drink, some of your coworkers just won't trust you. You will have friends on the job who are chronic drunks, a condition often handled with breezy nonchalance:

Cop 1: "I didn't know vodka and cranberry juice could make you shake like that."

Cop 2: "At least I get vitamins from the juice."

Some of your colleagues disguise their affliction well and you have no idea they're struggling until you hear they've been sent to the farm (police speak for a drug program). Others don't even bother to hide it. They come into work classing up the joint in a T-shirt that says Tequila Police, unshaven, hair unkempt, already swigging Pepto-Bismol. You gotta drive the squad car that day because they're still hung over. In the macho Don't Need Help subculture of law enforcement, recovery and the language of recovery are often treated as a cheap joke; one cop will sarcastically ask his addict partner, "Hey, you practicing good self-care?"

None of this, of course, is the way it should be. To act as a counter-weight, many police departments staff their employee assistance programs not with civilians but with police officers who are also experts in chemical dependency and understand the stress and depression that can accompany the job. They are well versed in both calling out Tequila Police and his ilk on their bullshit and helping them find a way forward.

Even if you can sidestep the booze and pills, quite a few cops smoke. More so, I think, than the general public. One of my police academy instructors in San Francisco used to give our class a 10-minute break as soon as he showed up to teach so he could pop outside and have a cigarette; I didn't think we had quite earned a break yet, but hey. I have a vivid memory of another cop knowingly pushing through an alarmed door in police headquarters so he could have a smoke, bravely weathering the blaring siren for the sweet promise of nicotine. A few decades ago, it wasn't uncommon to see a cop in the station weight room smoking a cigarette while doing the bench press.

The heavy smoking is due in part to the high number of ex-military on the force. Soldiers are known smokers ("You get bored," one ex-Marine told me). There's also something about the job that at times suggests, even demands, a cigarette. After my first FTO, Gilbert Gwinn, and I engaged in a fierce battle with a drunk domestic violence (DV) suspect armed with a knife and wrestled him into custody, Gwinn lit up a smoke on the suspect's front porch. Then he turned to me, a nonsmoker, and asked, "Does this kind of thing make you not want to be a police officer?" My first thought was no, but it really makes me want one of those cigarettes.

When you park your car, run an errand, and return to find your rear passenger window broken and your valuables gone, odds are the culprit was a drug addict. The man who just shoved that eighty-year-old woman down and ripped away her purse, causing her to shatter her hip? Likely an addict. They can't hold down regular jobs so they take other people's things through guile or force in order to sell and finance their habit. You can lament the vice grip of addiction while still acknowledging the boatload of crimes drug addicts commit on a regular basis.

Not all of these addicts seem to understand the scope of their problem; you'll ask a guy if he smokes crack and he'll tell you, in all earnestness, "I smoke socially," as if he's talking about benignly puffing on the occasional Pall Mall outside a bar with friends. Or you'll find yourself in conversations with people like James, a meth user who was peering into car windows in an area known for auto break-ins. As my partner ran a wanted check, I asked James what he did with himself. Did he work? Did he go to school?

"I go to school," he said. "But I think it's canceled tomorrow. Do you know if it is?"

"I'm not sure," I replied. "What school do you go to?"

"I'm homeschooled," he explained with no trace of irony, nicely illustrating the mush heavy drug use makes of the human mind.

But the brain of the drug offender does kick into high gear when it comes to picking out creative hiding spots for their dope so the police can't find it. Like fake hollowed-out cigarettes. Liquid heroin disguised as eye drops in a Visine bottle. A can of soda with a secret screw-off top. But when you are talking about drug dealers, the go-to hiding spot is their vagina and/or anus. This area of the dealer's body is known as the Vault. And if you have a dealer in custody and suspect such a storage method, there is a quick test to help confirm it. You smell the hand. Because if the dealer's hand has been in the Vault, it will carry the corresponding strong body odor, as personal hygiene is not the hallmark of many street drug pushers. Smelling the hand is not, as you might guess, the most enviable part of the job. Usually you'll have a couple of cops doing Rochambeau to determine who the hapless sniffer will be.

If you get a positive hit on the hand, or have other probable cause to go on, you'll likely do a strip search for narcotics. You'll put an officer in the backseat of the squad car to watch the suspect, as some dealers like to take this opportunity to cram their contraband more deeply into the Vault. Once at the station, female officers will search female suspects, male officers will search males, and no cop who is of an opposite gender of the suspect is allowed in the room when the search occurs. If you have a transgender suspect, they get to pick the gender of the searching officer. Once in a while, a drug suspect will be in the midst of gender reassignment surgery and have the intimate parts of both genders. They may ask for a male officer for one portion of their body and a female officer for the other. And that's no problem. As police, we are flexible and will accommodate this request. So you glove up and get to work. After the males disrobe, you instruct them to lift their penis and scrotum. Women are to raise their breasts. Both genders are to bend over, spread their buttocks, and cough hard. If a suspect is carrying some extra pounds, they must lift up their folds of fat. One of my coworkers, Lt. Angela Wilhelm, worked a number of years in the Tenderloin, a neighborhood in San Francisco infamous for street-level drug dealing. She told me of finding a softball-size mass of dope in the creases of one woman's stomach. In another woman's blubber, she unearthed some lottery tickets. Sometimes there's drugs socked away in a suspect's hair too, so you tell them to vigorously ruffle it as you step back to avoid the dandruff and critters.

If you see suspected narcotics and any portion of the package is wedged in a bodily crevice, the suspect has to remove it. You yourself may not, because that's considered a body cavity search that only trained medical personnel are allowed to perform. Body cavity searches require a warrant. Some doctors, at least in San Francisco, have refused to do them even when presented with the lawful warrant signed by a judge ordering them to, the reason being they don't want to compromise the trust of the doctor/patient relationship, especially for something they don't consider a medical emergency. This conflict can touch off a So Do I Gotta Arrest This Doctor for Obstruction of Justice carnival, which benefits absolutely no one except the local newspaper, which finds such a debate riveting.

So you unleash your full arsenal of rhetoric and persuasion on the dealer. Perhaps bluffing is involved, even wheedling. You try to convince them to take the path of least resistance. And if all else fails, you advise them to go ahead and march right into county jail with a sack of crack cocaine deeply lodged in their assholes. Bringing contraband into a correctional facility is a high-end felony and you are totally going to tell the jailer on them.

Methamphetamine was started in the 1900s by a Japanese chemist. It comes in ice-like shards and can be purchased on the cheap, with one hit going for around five bucks. You can snort, smoke, or inject it, although smoking is the most common. Its users include factory workers, suburban mothers, and bankers. Meth addicts claim the drug makes them feel wide awake, sexy, and smart. They'll also tell you it is the most addictive substance known to mankind. That it makes crack cocaine seem like caffeine. That you can stay up for days without food or sleep, your brain shot through with dopamine. But when the high wears off, it's replaced by depression and hopelessness. Heavy meth users can look forward to bouts of paranoia and hallucinations. Liver damage. Skin sores. After a few years, a meth addict will look like something that shuffled off the set of a George Romero film. Meth mouth, the dental horror show found among many methamphetamine addicts, is caused by the wearing away of tooth enamel because of the corrosive chemicals found in crystal, the constant teeth grinding spurred on by the drug, a general disinterest in tooth brushing, and a pronounced craving for sweets that is one of the drug's many side effects. You'll hear of meth addicts who drink forty bottles of cola a day, which is a lot to log on the MyFitnessPal app.

The active ingredient in meth hails from the pseudoephedrine found in cold pills. That's why drugstores had to move the nonprescription cold pills behind the counter, because meth addicts were stealing them all. A meth cook will extract the "pseudo" from the cold pills in a lab setting and mix it with a host of other chemicals like anhydrous ammonia and iodine. Every pound of meth generates about five pounds of toxic waste, making meth labs a work environment OSHA would frown upon. OSHA also would not approve of the volatile chemicals, open flames, and a lack of adherence to safety protocols, all of which cause meth labs to blow up fairly regularly. So, as a street cop, if you enter what looks like a meth lab, you touch nothing, slowly back out, and call for a hazmat team. And when some meth cook starts a fire, melts off his skin, and runs up a few hundred thousand in medical bills at the hospital burn unit, guess who pays for that? You and me, for all of it, because the cooks don't have anything remotely close to health insurance.

So if you want to put a dent in the trade of meth and other street drugs, how do you do it? Here are the most common police tactics:

1. Patrol. Drug use is so prevalent that you'll run into it while in full uniform. You round the corner and there they are, doing a hand-to-hand— sure, their lookouts were supposed to whistle to warn of your approach, but sometimes it's hard to find good help in the turnover-prone field of narcotics sales. Bicycles, by the way, are great for picking off drug dealers. You can roll in and stop on a dime. And they can't outrun you, although it's enjoyable to see them try.

2. Spotting. You find an elevated position, usually an apartment or office building with an unobstructed view, and watch the dealers with binoculars. You can use binos for about fifteen minutes before your eyes start to tire, but if you're surveying a hot corner, you'll see a deal long before that. Junkies have a distinctive walk on the way to get their fix. They move briskly, looking straight ahead, often with their money already clutched in their fist, like a kid heading to the ice cream counter for a root beer float. And you often see an extreme case of tunnel vision accompany the junkie walk. This was brought home to me one day when my partner and I were in plainclothes with our police stars clearly visible around our necks putting the kibosh on a local crack dealer in front of a liquor store. An older fellow attempted to buy a hit of crack from the dealer right in front of us. We simply didn't register with him, two white guys with conservative haircuts who looked exactly like what we were—street cops. The dealer said nothing, perhaps uncertain as to what social decorum dictated under such circumstances. The buyer seemed embarrassed when I wordlessly pointed to my police credentials. "I'm awful sorry," he said and shuffled off, no doubt in search of the dealer on the next block.

The first of the month is a fine time for spotting operations because folks have just cashed their government subsistence checks and are flush with cash to buy their poison of choice. When you see through your binos that the sale is made, you radio in to have an officer pick off the buyer out of sight of the seller. If the buyer still has the dope on them, you have a few more officers grab the seller. Sometimes there's a hook involved (someone who ushers the buyer over to the seller). You grab them too as party to the crime.

If the case goes to court, the defense attorney will ask you exactly where you were when you observed his client. You may elect not to answer this question under your jurisdiction's applicable evidence code, citing a need to protect the property owner from retaliation from the dealers who may not look favorably on anyone allowing the police to use their building as a perch. Depending on how much leeway the judge gives the defense, this often touches off a cat-and-mouse exchange where you will be asked how far vertically and horizontally you were from the dealer when you made your spotting observations. I was in court on one such case where the defense attorney invoked the Pythagorean theorem in an attempt to calculate the precise distance between the officer and his client. Somewhere, a high school geometry teacher raised her fist in the air.

3. Buy busts. You send an undercover cop in to buy dope from the dealer and then an arrest team makes the bust. Buy busts are often as simple as walking over to the corner where the dealer posts up and asking him for a rock or "some of that hard" or whatever the going slang is. But sometimes a cop will get the phone number of a dealer and set up the sale over the phone via text. Best alias for the cop to use? J, as in "What up, its J." If you write "it's J" with the apostrophe, you may give yourself away; this is not the best forum to be a stickler for punctuation. So why J? Because J could be anyone—Jeff, Jerome, Julia, Johann. If the dealer gets suspicious and wonders if you really are one of the Js they know and tries to call you, you fake a bad connection or claim you're up in the club and can't hear. You tell them to stick to texting. And you set up the deal over the phone and when they show, they're yours. You'd think something as simple and crude as the J technique wouldn't work, but it surely does.

4. Buy/walk. An undercover buys narcotics from the dealer, but nobody is arrested, not yet. Both the cop and the dealer "walk" from the sale. The suspect is arrested later, once you have identified their coconspirators, stash house, and supplier, or, ideally, the supplier's supplier. These are long game investigations that take patience, skill, vision, and, if you really want to make the case, some serious surveillance. You're usually in a car during surveillance and rarely get to hang out in the apartment across the

street like where Estevez, Dreyfuss, and Estevez's mustache lay in wait in the film *Stakeout*. Surveillance kind of sucks. The food is brown bag. You can't smoke or listen to music because it draws attention. You whizz in a bottle. You endure long stretches where absolutely nothing happens. Some of the dullest waking spans of your life. In surveillance, there's a mental place you need to get to, where you keep your eyes on the target but shut your system down and just let things filter in. But you will come to know galactic boredom. The most interesting thing in the car is the putrid stench blooming out from your partner's pants because he forgot to take his lactose pills. It gets to the point where you will miss the squirrel that scampered by twenty minutes ago. You'll construct a short narrative about his life. He seems lonely. You'll call him Quincy. What he's all about? Why isn't Quincy with the other squirrels? Do they not get along?

Higher-ups in police admin aren't always fans of the long-game investigation because they want to see dope and guns on the table right now, not six months from now. Six months from now, your lieutenant may have been transferred to the Midday Metro Aquatic Investigative Task Force because his narcotics team hasn't produced.

Some members of the public hold that drug enforcement is elitist and unfairly targets the poor. The cops go after only the street-level drug offenders and leave the cocaine addicts on Wall Street alone, they argue. They're right. We're street cops and, accordingly, deal with street crime and its accompanying violence. If the bankers and executives were doing hand-to-hands on the corner, we'd be grabbing them too. But they deal in offices and restrooms, which we do not patrol. I suppose I could go into some high-end business and ask the receptionist if I could look around to see if any suits were snorting lines off the boardroom table, but until the employees of Judson, Norquist, and Henkel start gunning each other down over drug feuds as the corner boys do, I don't see that happening. You deal with the crimes in front of you.

Cops understand the arguments for legalizing drugs. They're made by some pretty sharp people, and there's even a police group that advocates legalization called Law Enforcement Action Partnership (LEAP). Those in this camp argue that the drug war cannot be won. That it's a public health issue, not a criminal issue. They note that the government is spending an obscene amount of money to wage this war. All the while, drug use, if anything, is rising. You can't even keep drugs out of prison, they say, so how do you hope to keep them off the street? Isn't it better to have drug use controlled, regulated, and taxed as it would be if legal? This would also help stem the street violence associated with the illegal drug market.

Compelling arguments to be sure. And if they legalized drugs, would law-abiding adults suddenly throw caution to the wind and start shooting up heroin? Probably not, because they know how destructive that would be. But what about teenagers? Adolescents? My daughters? I don't know. Maybe that's unknowable. Some countries have tried this approach. In 2001, Portugal decriminalized even hard drugs and politicians there tout that there's been no dramatic rise in drug use and that drug overdoses are significantly down. But while marijuana is now legally available in San Francisco at a number of convenient dispensaries, criminals still sell it on the street. Some of these dealers are benign. Others have guns and will use them to maintain their turf.

Regardless, as a working street cop, odds are you won't buy into the drug legalization philosophy. Odds are you'll still hold fast to the belief that you and a hundred guys who think like you could reclaim those drug corners. Maybe it's akin to the same delusion that some NBA scout will see you shooting around at the Y and think, let's sign this guy to a 10-day contract and see what he can do for us at off-guard.

So is there a way to win the drug war? Robert Mitchum said it best in *Out of the Past*: "There's a way to lose more slowly."

It's easy, I suppose, to take potshots at addicts. They make soft, inviting targets. You can claim they're weak and lack discipline and fortitude. That they are trapped in a prison entirely of their own making. But you change your tune when an addict surfaces among your close friends or family. Because now when you talk about addiction's hold, you are no longer talking about a stranger, no longer talking about the Other, but rather, someone you care about. Someone you'll fight for. Someone you love. That's when you realize most addicts are in the same boat as the rest of us, trying to make it, to be better than they are, to stay afloat, but in the end, when the siren's call beckons, they cast away reason, turn their back on prayers and promises to stay clean, and embrace their drug warmly, like an old friend.

The whole business of addiction reminds you of the sermon about the man who decides not to build his house on a rock.

He builds it on the sand.

And it washes away in the storm.

4

Policing the Community

Maybe this is what it feels like for civilians when they see cops doing some of the dirty work. A lot of times they don't understand what's happening. They see something they don't like and it upsets them—because they don't have the full story, aren't personally facing the problem, and don't know how much worse the alternative could be.
—Jim Butcher, *Proven Guilty*

Now and again, a member of the community will call the police on the police. You'll respond to a dispatched assignment and the citizen won't like the way the conversation is going so he'll get on his cell and ask for different cops. Dispatch will ask you if everything is all right, because another 911 call for your location has just been received by the telecommunicator. You tell Dispatch all is well. And you let the caller know that you sense his anger and frustration and you will renew your pledge to help him in the best way you can, but he had best get off the line unless he wants to be cited for 911 abuse.

Some callers won't be satisfied with the police services you're providing and will request an officer of a specific race. "I want a black cop," they might insist. Now if a female assault victim wants a female officer, you accommodate her because it can help make her more comfortable and forthcoming. If it's a translation issue, you find an officer who speaks the language. But other than that? You don't do such special requests. Because it's a police department, not a restaurant. You can't tailor your order. You may not demand an athletic, bi-curious Tongan officer with just a tinge of rakish insouciance. As the old saying goes, which I sometimes use with my five-year-old, you get what you get and you don't throw a fit.

If the aggrieved caller wishes to file a complaint against you, they'll demand your name and badge number, which you are required to provide. If the person requesting your information is drunk or high, some officers have been known to take a few liberties with this policy. You'd like my name, my good man? You bet. It's Officer Nasium. Officer Jim Nasium.

One type of fellow who frequently asks for your name and badge number is a member of the community who holds a special place in the hearts of law enforcement. He is a white male, typically heterosexual, between sixteen and thirty years old. He is well-off, or at least his family is. He favors pressed khakis and designer golf shirts worn with the collar popped. His hair is artfully tousled. He is not battle tested, unless you count Twitter wars. A bad day for him is when his tennis racket comes unstrung. He probably drives a Fiat and he tends to get huffy if you pull him over, because stop signs aren't for him, they're for other people. He tends to lack perspective but ooze entitlement.

This storied individual is known in police parlance as a Chad. Because that's usually his name, or something like it. It could be Lance. Trent. Damian. Blake.

Still confused about this terminology? I'll use it in a sentence.

Cop 1: "What's your victim like on the 9th Street robbery?"

Cop 2: "He ain't much. Some Chad from Marin County."

Not every rich kid is a Chad and, moreover, there's nothing wrong with Chads per se. Their heavy reliance on styling gel and valet parking stimulates the economy. But when they leave their high-end laptop on the coffee shop table and go to the bathroom and are shocked when it's stolen, you have to let them know that, sorry, we can't call in the gunships and ground-penetrating radar. If you have tracking on that thing, we'll do our best to run it down. We'll check for video surveillance and put your serial number in the system, but other than that, you're going to have to chalk it up to a loss.

If they don't like the way things are going, Chads are known to invoke the lame standby "Do you know who my parents are?" The automatic cop response is "Excuse me, can anyone locate this young man's parents? He does not know who they are." Which is kind of lame in its own rite. But you play stupid games, you win stupid prizes.

Even worse is the "Do you know who I am?" question, which is still alive and kicking among the upper crust. Everyone from Reese Witherspoon to Alec Baldwin has trotted it out when stopped by the police. I'm not aware of it ever working. ("Dammit man, you can't arrest him! He played Agent

Nick Kudrow in *Mercury Rising*!") However, there is one circumstance under which "Do you know who I am?" can potentially reap dividends. I'm talking about diplomats. It doesn't quite go like in the movies where they can murder away with impunity. But if a diplomat commits an act he claims is performed in the exercise of his consular function, you can't arrest him except in the case of a serious felony that endangers public safety. And if you pull over some ambassador and have reason to believe that she is blitzed out of her mind after a consular visit to the local brew pub, San Francisco Police Department General Order 5.13 essentially states that in lieu of a drunk driving arrest, you are to escort her back to where she's staying and write a report that will later be reviewed by the FBI and the State Department. The bottom line is if you stop anyone who flashes fancy international credentials, you need permission to take police action and will end up setting off a string of phone calls that will run from your Special Investigations Division up to at least a deputy chief, which might mean calling them in the middle of the night, which I am told they do not care for.

In addition to celebrities and diplomats, another class of people vying for special protection these days seems to be United States college students. Quite a few viral videos of late show some college kid being arrested by law enforcement. There's a violent struggle during which a young man is taken down and handcuffed and comes up bloodied. At some point, tomorrow's leader proclaims, "But I go to State!" Yep, the public seems to think, there the police go, assuming everyone is a hoodlum and brutalizing all in their path. Look at that educated young man with the scraped-up face—de facto proof of police terrorism.

But what the police see is someone they have just cause to detain or arrest trying to pull away from them. Someone showing the beginnings of fight or flight. This is against the law. It's called Resisting/Obstructing an Officer. If you don't think the police are justified in stopping you, have your friends videotape the whole thing and file a complaint afterward. But if you resist the police, you are probably going to the ground. Hard. This is what police training dictates. A member of the public isn't just allowed to ignore your lawful directives without consequence. Otherwise you'd just have a bunch of police out there shrugging and saying things like: "I tried to arrest him, but he pulled away and I was like, rats, there goes another one!"

When the kid cries out "But I go to State!" you search your brain for any blanket immunity from prosecution one receives upon enrolling in college, even a well-thought-of institution. And you don't come up with anything. You aren't high-fiving your partner because his face got scraped up. You are not in the pain game if you can help it. Moreover, suspect injuries, however slight, are just more paperwork for you and likely a hospital run.

Here's some good news for all young undergraduates. There is a simple yet elegant solution to avoiding this fate and it is this: refrain from resisting arrest, especially whilst standing on hard pavement. Pavement hurts. And it is unreasonable to expect the officer to say to his partner, "Hal, we got a violent young adult on our hands. Let's try to maneuver him over to that soft, dewy field I saw three blocks from here."

Regardless, when the fight is over, you clean the university student up and guide him through the arrest process. Maybe he gets a few stitches. Perhaps he spends a weekend in jail. He is left with a painful lesson about submitting to just authority. See. You do learn stuff in college after all.

Professor Stephen L. Carter, in his magnificent book *Civility*, holds that we can be civil without being familiar and cautions against the danger of saying the first thing that comes into your head. "Words are magic," he writes. "We conjure with them. We send messages, we paint images." Saying Please and Thank You to the public is simple but goes a long way. It can also be all too rare. Some officers mistake civility for weakness. And we aren't always careful with our words. When the community says "Fuck You," it's tempting to respond in kind. But as the old aphorism goes, never wrestle with a pig, because you both get dirty but the pig likes it. So you gotta take the high road. Because when you police neighborhoods where the citizens' reaction to you ranges from mistrust to hate, the wrong word at the wrong time can be the spark in a mine full of coal dust. When you talk down to or outright goad a member of the public, be it a career felon or just some regular Joe you happen to find annoying, the damage is twofold. First, you have sunk to a level not befitting someone who is supposed to be a trained de-escalator and problem solver. Second, you have made the road tougher for both yourself and the next cop who works with that person. When you approach citizens and ask for their cooperation and you don't get it, maybe it's because you look quite a bit like the last cop they dealt with—same uniform, same gun belt—and that cop gave them the strong impression that he found their problems amusing. And then he called them "fucksticks." The citizens saw inscribed on the side of that police car the words Integrity, Dedication, and Professionalism, but they weren't shown even one of those things. As a result, when the police need help from the community, they'll be stonewalled. That's why one of key rules of law enforcement is this: Don't Be a Dick.

The Don't Be a Dick rule is also why you'll find yourself performing various tasks that aren't technically part of your job at all. Like helping a kid fix a flat tire on his bicycle. Or assisting an elderly woman with a blown fuse in her darkened home. Or taking phone calls at the station from senior citizens who are having problems with their credit or want to complain about the state of the world and public morals. This is why all across America desk sergeants are on the phone with citizens attentively sort-of listening to a litany of complaints that they can't do anything about. "Okay, Mrs. Hargreaves," the desk sergeant says. "I don't quite understand those rollerbladers either. Thank you for keeping me informed. I'll talk to you again next week." My old Milwaukee partner Rolf Mueller (remember his name because I'll be talking about him again) used to sweep up the broken glass caused by vandals, especially if the homeowner looked at all elderly or ailing. He'd politely ask for a broom and dustpan and then go to work, emphasizing the second word in the title Public Servant. No, you're not a bike tech or an electrician or a member of a cleanup crew. It's not written anywhere in your mission statement. But it is your mission to connect with the community. To build goodwill and a sense of trust. So in a sense it's precisely your job. There are, of course, limits to this. "Go get me a beer," an especially soused weekend reveler once demanded of me during a disturbance call. The beer remained ungotten.

Civility and good community relations call for giving the backseat of the patrol car a once-over before you give a citizen a courtesy ride home or take them to a crime scene to look at a suspect. You respond to a lot of assignments in the city, which cuts into opportunities for vehicle maintenance and beautification. This means that although you put a lot of gamey characters in the backseat, you also wash out those back seats infrequently. You want to avoid a "Hey! I think I just sat in piss!" moment with your citizen passenger.

Community relations also means looking professional but still approachable. So take the aviator shades off once in a while and limit the number of tough guy upward head nods to no more than three per shift. And if you put on latex gloves to search someone because you are wary of hep C and staph infections, the suspect you are searching will sometimes protest: "What, you think I got AIDS or something?"

The proper diplomatic response is "No. I'm trying to protect you from *my* germs."

Community organizers concerned about police-society relations say officers should live in the kinds of black and brown neighborhoods they police. I understand why they say this and I believe it comes from a well-meaning place. And some cities have programs where cops can live in public housing for free or at a greatly reduced rate. The federal government has a HUD initiative called Good Neighbor Next Door that allows for teachers, firefighters, and police officers to receive a 50 percent discount on a home price on eligible properties in certain low-income zip codes provided they live there for a certain number of years.

It wasn't part of any program, but I tried living in such a neighborhood for a few years when I was a Milwaukee cop. I was single at the time with no kids. I figured if anyone was to do it, it might as well be me. To call my experience a nightmare might be melodramatic, but not by much. I went in with honorable intentions. I thought I could add stability to the block. Maybe troubleshoot a few neighborhood problems. Generally be a force for good.

I was shockingly naïve.

The highlights of my stay included waking up to a gun-related homicide down the street, being surrounded by an angry crowd when I tried to break up a street fight off duty, and going to the laundry mat and coming face to face with a violent drunk I had arrested the week prior. The whole block knew who I was. I wasn't trying to hide it, but it didn't matter, because the toothless drug addict next door told everyone; I might as well have worn a blinking neon sign that said Cop. I became embroiled in a running conflict with the crack house across the street, which culminated in one of its occupants throwing the extension to a socket wrench at my head while I sat on my front porch. It whizzed past my left ear. I began creeping out my backdoor and crossing over the rear neighbor's vegetable garden so the crack house wouldn't know when I was home—it didn't help, someone broke into my place presumably looking for my gun, which they didn't find because, ironically enough, I always had it with me due to the wretched neighborhood. One night while off duty, I was flagged down by a man who said his sister was getting beaten up by her boyfriend inside their house—I responded alone even though I had no radio or backup—a foolish decision that I wouldn't have made if I had been on duty, but somehow felt compelled to do off duty because, well, I was the cop on the block. A series of armed robberies close by had me walking to and from my car with my hand on my unholstered gun hidden in my front sweatshirt pocket, ready for close encounters. It was an extended period of danger both real and imagined, stress, hypervigilance, and unrest. I would spend all shift at work dealing with violence and strife and come home to more of the same. I looked over my shoulder a lot. I felt constantly under siege. Made it a bit hard to unwind.

I did, however, enjoy paying $375 a month for a three-bedroom apartment. As a guy living alone with low overhead, I didn't have a lot of stuff so I used one of the bedrooms just to store my single raincoat. A raincoat storage room. I bet not even the Koch brothers have that. At night I would open my window and listen to people argue about unpaid bills, infidelity, drug abuse, and loneliness. It was the kind of neighborhood where the police had to fight the feeling to just let crime go, to battle the attitude that these people, in the end, deserved each other and the fate they had accepted or been dealt perhaps long ago.

Not all of my neighbors made me wary. Among them was Andre, the cheerful Frenchman next door, who shook my hand so enthusiastically when he found out I was a cop that I wasn't sure if I'd get that hand back. He'd regularly invite me over for coffee and tell me how the neighborhood used to be better, some twenty years ago, before the dealers moved in. And I wasn't in the same lot as those who lived around me. I wasn't trapped there. I could have afforded to live elsewhere. And eventually I did. I have a family now, and our home is near a serene cul-de-sac far from the city I police. It's an oasis away from work. There's no chaos and little drama. People clean up after their dogs. They jog. They wave cheery hellos to each other. They take pride in their properties. In many ways, it's the exact opposite of work. That's why I like it. I feel my family is safe here. I want my family to be safe.

So this is just one man's account of living in a rough neighborhood. Maybe another cop could pull it off. Maybe they wouldn't have abandoned Andre as I did. But if so, they are forged of stronger stuff than me. As police officers, we are willing to put ourselves in harm's way for an eight- or ten-hour shift, but when we're off, we'd prefer to live in peace. There has to be some separation between the worlds of work and home. Otherwise, it's liable to drive a fellow just past crazy.

The dissenting voice in society. Nothing could be more American. Protestors aren't always right, and sometimes they fail to meaningfully advance the discussion and just yell a lot. But civil disobedience has created profound, lasting change in everything from women's suffrage to civil rights, and if you think you've been marginalized, you're gonna want to make some noise. However, if you are taking to the streets and clogging up traffic in support of a cause, especially if your demo is spontaneous and without a permit, allow me to present a modest proposal. It is this—have a point and a plan. A point is a clearly defined goal—get City Hall to change a policy, support a gay marriage amendment, rail against soybean tariffs. A plan is something like, we will march for thirty minutes, be peaceful, and stay off the freeways. Because if you have no point and no plan, you are just protesting for protesting sake. People are less likely to be drawn to your cause when you annoy the crap out of them by blocking intersections and spray-painting their property. You've just given them more reasons not to listen to you. And you are burning up a tremendous amount of finite police resources to swing traffic and prevent violence from breaking out among your ranks. Bet you'd be steamed if you got robbed at knifepoint and there were no available police cars to send to you because all units were tied up dealing with the gridlock, vandalism, and melees generated by the Occupy Anarchy Everything Sucks Demo.

Now, if you are a protestor who hates the police and everything about them, perhaps this argument won't sway you much. But you know the kinds of people stuck in your manufactured gridlock who you may want to consider?

—Parents, especially single mothers, who are paying a dollar for every minute they are late to pick up their child from day care.

—People who are trying to get to a job interview on time.

—The sick, injured, and dying whom ambulances are rushing to the ER.

—Folks who really have to use the bathroom.

When you're standing on line at an angry protest equipped with your long baton, your professional game face, and your riot helmet (which will start to smart after a while, like your head is wedged deeply in a metal waste basket), the protestors on the other side of the line—many of whom may not care about any particular cause but are just using a social controversy as a convenient hook to hang violence and looting on—will have quite a bit to say to you. Not much of it is a tribute. It's a lot of this: "Fuck you, pig, you're all wife-beaters, oink oink, bad cop—no donut, sucking at the public trough, faggot-ass cops, hope you all die." They say these things both to express their heartfelt disdain for you and in hopes of eliciting a negative reaction from you. And you are not to respond. There's absolutely no upside to it. It's not the time or place for a civic-minded dialogue (you shouldn't even point out to the protestor with a cardboard sign that there are two *l*'s in Orwell), and under those circumstances, even your most benign utterance can only serve to inflame a crowd that is already inflamed. You are there to keep the peace and facilitate their constitutional right to assemble and repeatedly call you vile names. That there is the police nurturing democracy.

But even given the whole sticks and stones philosophy, sometimes their rants can get to you. Some punk is in your face calling you worthless and commanding you to suck his dick and you're thinking, hey, I helped catch a trio of armed robbers the other night and this week I solved an attempted murder case. What, pray tell, have been some of your own recent accomplishments, assface? And getting to level 38 of World of Warcraft doesn't count. Let's compare achievements and see who is found wanting. It's a bit childish, but you do it anyway. And you can't get in trouble, because it's all in your head. Your thoughts, although exceedingly unprofessional, are still your own.

One thought you may wish to share with the protest community is that being disenfranchised isn't a license to do whatever you want. You can understand the rage that stems from a divisive police incident and still hold people accountable for the crimes they commit during protests. But sometimes the chaos unfolding all around you reaches such a critical mass that your righteous indignation flames out and is replaced by something more coldly analytical. You'll see a rioter coming out of a store with something that doesn't make any sense, like three left shoes. Hey man, don't you want to go back in there and get a right? If you must loot, do so properly.

Police-citizen community meetings are where the rubber meets the road, especially if the mood is especially testy between law enforcement and the public. Some supervisors will look frantically for a subordinate to send in their place.

"Kuchac, I need you to go to the public safety forum at the Santos projects tonight."

"But lieutenant, I went to the last one . . ."

At such meetings, cops addressing a skeptical if not outright angry crowd will emphasize their roots, i.e., "I grew up four blocks from here."

Some familiar words words and phrases get trotted out. "Stakeholder." "Gatekeeper." "We're working with our community partners." "We're working with the mayor's office."

If done right, community meetings can be an invaluable way of bridging the gap between the police and the public. A prevailing police weakness is our inability to seriously consider a point of view other than our own. The public might be wrong on some issues, or have unrealistic expectations of the police. But we have to listen to them. What was it that Atticus Finch said about really understanding someone? How you have to climb in their skin and walk around for a while? A lot of cops aren't willing to do that with people. And a lot of people aren't willing to do that with cops.

But if things go south, what you get is a free-for-all where everybody shouts, no one can understand anyone, and nothing gets done. The ugly irony is that protestors who (rightly) demand police accountability and transparency will attend these meetings and make it a point to drown out the cops with chants, name-calling, and boos so the police aren't afforded an opportunity to demonstrate either accountability or transparency. The representative from the department usually tries to hang in there as long as he can. But there comes a time when there's really no point in trying to make a lone voice heard in a cacophony. So he'll leave.

"Yeah, fucking run away," someone from the crowd will say.

Then the protestors will go to their websites and brag about how they shut the system down. Way to go guys, cutting that meeting short so everybody loses. Do you see how you're working against yourselves? For your next trick, why don't you go scatter antilittering pamphlets all over the town square.

One of the recurring themes at community meetings is the complaint about the over-militarization of law enforcement. And it's true that the police don't have to respond to every whiff of unrest with armored vehicles and long guns with scopes, because it can make us look less like public servants and more like shock troops. But this anti-militarization movement has its limits. Like when citizens say, "Why do those cops have helmets and shields? That just incites the crowd." Don't know about that. Most crowds seem to have a way of inciting themselves on their own just fine. You like your shield and helmet because it can stop a brick or bottle from knocking you unconscious. You hate being unconscious, especially in the midst of an angry mob. How about this tentative social compact—stop throwing dangerous shit at our heads and we'll lose the helmets.

As a cop, you are out there to serve everybody equally with dignity and professionalism. From the stumblebums to the Chads to the male hipster with a Faux Hawk, gauged ears, and iridescent green shoes whose name is Thistle. You don't have to necessarily understand them all, mind you. Just serve them.

But serving them requires getting out of your patrol car. Your relationship with folks must be more than being their arresting officer. Police departments organize toy drives, deliver food to elderly shut-ins, and referee youth sports leagues not just because it is right to do so but because it lets the police have positive contact with the citizens we serve. The societal problem does not exist that the police can buckle down and arrest our way out of. These issues are too complex, too entrenched. A guy I know on the Milwaukee Police Department used to aggressively pursue street hoodlums, and once he nabbed them, he would just as aggressively try to help them find meaningful work.

"Get a job with UPS, man," he'd say. "They got clean uniforms. They teach you how to lift boxes right."

I don't know how successful he was with this approach, how many jobs were obtained, and how many were held down for any length of time. But regardless of the statistics, he understood that the police aren't just in the crime-fighting business. We are also in the business of housing anytime we take someone to a shelter or refer them to Homeward Bound, which can provide a bus ticket for a stranded traveler to go home. We are in the education business when we go to schools to read to students. We are in the mental health business when we approach someone in crisis, assure them that they aren't in trouble and we're there to help, and transport them to an assessment center where they can be stabilized.

There are cops, especially old-timers, who resent these additional duties and bristle at being labeled anything that sounds even remotely like "social worker." But if you're serious about leaving your patrol sector just a bit better than you found it, you better get used to it.

Even when you do all you can to bridge the gap with the community, you'll still occasionally return to your patrol car after completing an assignment and find one of your vehicle windows punched out or your door awash in graffiti, like "SFPD sux dix." You're irritated at the vandals. What a bunch of dix. But you know what never gets vandalized? That's right, fire trucks. They remain immaculate, even gleaming, thanks to the frequent hose-downs by the fellas at the station house. And if they did ever suffer graffiti, it would probably be something tasteful, even honorific like: "Metro Fire: could they *be* any more courageous?"

In terms of bridging the gap, on my last day as a police officer before I was promoted to sergeant, my partner and I were on the unit block of 6th Street and I encountered a man I'll call Mike. Mike was a man in his late fifties, a constant on the corner, usually drunk, although not so drunk that he couldn't warn the drug dealers we were coming. He would occasionally threaten to kill me, although it was hard to tell because he always mumbled. I told Mike I was leaving to become a sergeant. He mumbled something. Then I took out a pack of Newport Lites that I save for suicidal jumpers and reluctant witnesses. I gave him one and had one myself. We sat at the corner and smoked.

"Hey," I said. "You remember all those times you threatened to kill me? What was that all about?"

Mike just smiled his mysterious smile and kept smoking as we continued to broker an uneasy peace. For just a moment, the gap felt bridged.

But although Mike doesn't quite crack my top ten list of favorite community members of all time, one of the slots on that list definitely goes to Ms. Vickie Williams-Tillman, a fifty-six-year-old woman from Baton Rouge. In the spring of 2017, she was listening to gospel music in the car on her way to Sam's Club when she saw a man repeatedly striking a Baton Rouge police officer in the head with the officer's baton. Williams-Tillman called the police and then jumped on the attacker's back, helping fend him off until other officers arrived. She hurt her wrist in the process.

"I could see in his eyes he needed help," she told a reporter. "You don't have time to think about it . . . I did what God needed me to do."

Thank you, ma'am. I will be sending Ms. Williams-Tillman a copy of this book. Plus a gift card to Sam's Club.

5

Street Crime

Everything decent is held together by a covenant. An agreement not to go batshit. You broke the covenant.
—William Hurt, *Changing Lanes*

The numbers are in and street crime is up, the experts say. Or it's down. Or it's the same as it ever was. A spike or dip is a statistical fluke, they surmise. Or perhaps it's a long-term trend. And criminologists can't seem to agree on *why* these stats fluctuate so. Downturn in the economy where desperate people are committing crimes just to get by? Maybe. A flood of offenders let back on the street on early release because of prison over-crowding? Possibly. But these hard numbers don't mean much to you as a street cop or investigator. Even if CNN features some bow-tied law prof claiming violent crime has plummeted, you are still constantly responding to calls where people are being shot, stabbed, and beaten. Where the covenant William Hurt talked about is being broken but good. In all my years in the field, there's never been a significant period when I've thought to myself, boy, there isn't much crime these days; in fact, I don't really have anything to do. Crime always seems to be up in our world.

Banks have gotten wise and tightened up their security of late, but for a long stretch, one of the most popular street crimes out there was ATM Shoulder Surfing. This involved some petty crook either standing to the side of the victim and pretending to conduct their own transaction at the adjoining ATM or taking up a position behind the victim all in the hopes of watching the vic enter their PIN. Then the suspect would see if the victim neglected to properly sign out of their account when they left or the suspect would actually pressure the victim to complete the transaction ("Hurry up man, I gotta catch the bus!") in hopes that they'd be rattled into leaving before they signed out the right way. Then the suspect would move in and enter the PIN and raid the account up to the daily max, which is often a cool grand. I have watched surveillance videos at ATMs and have seen suspects' eyes constantly flickering over to the screen of the hapless victim next to them, taking such an interest in that person's banking activities, it's as if the two of them just opened a joint account.

There's a persistent belief out there that if you are being forced to withdraw your money against your will at an ATM, you can enter your PIN backward and the machine will still dispense money but will also alert the police. This isn't the case. Some states have tried to introduce such legislation, but it died in committee. Such a tactic could potentially be useful, but odds are, the victim's uncertain fumbling on the keypad would alert the suspect that something was amiss and make him more prone to violence.

When someone is the victim of a crime, you want to get the relevant information from them as soon as possible so you can put a suspect description out to your fellow officers. If the victim doesn't speak English, you show them your language reference card, which lets the victim point to the language they speak. You then call for a translator because hand gestures will get you only so far. When the translator shows, you think, finally, we can make some sense of all this. But given the different dialects and idioms out there and given that some recent immigrants to this nation have, at most, an elementary-school education and are sometimes drunk, the translator doesn't always do much better than you.

"What's he saying?" you ask.

"No idea."

"Aren't you a Cantonese translator?"

"Shit, I don't think this guy even speaks Cantonese."

As an investigator, your antennas need to be up when you're working a street crime and a victim or witness doesn't recall enough ("I was just walking and I got shot. Didn't see nothing."), or recalls a bit too much. If a suspect description reads like a fashion catalogue, they're likely filling in the mental blanks in a misguided effort to be helpful, or are flat-out lying to you. Once they start giving detailed descriptions of, say, all three suspects' shoes ("The second assailant wore cross-trainers, officer, aqua and burnt sienna in color, the soles of which bore a crescent pattern."), you know something's up. I couldn't even give that good of a description of my daughter's clothing and not only am I a trained observer but I dressed her this morning.

A trained observer who is serious about stopping street crime must be in tune with the fashions, styles, and accessories of the day. Because you will look at an endless assortment of suspect clothing, hairstyles, and accoutrements in surveillance footage and crime scene stills. And since criminals don't regularly change their clothes or general look between offenses, either because they're homeless or because they just like to stick with an outfit that works for them, you can often match the clothing/appearance in a Crime Alert with the clothing/appearance of the suspect when you arrest him. So you have to be able to differentiate between Sean John and Rocawear. Is that teal ball cap from the San Jose Sharks or the Jacksonville Jaguars? Are those the new Jordans? The Carmelo M11s? Look, that guy has a little rattail at the back of his head in the video and so does this fellow. There's the glimmer of a hoop earring. A light spray of freckles. A hook-shaped scar, a Roman nose, a lantern jaw, oversized ears, a crimson birthmark, an oval face. Particularly thin or especially bushy eyebrows. It's the little things that add up to make your case. So you drink it all in. You're a haberdasher, jeweler, tailor, cosmetologist, cobbler. You're a man for all seasons.

Just because you can arrest someone for a street crime doesn't mean you have to, or even that you should. If an aging transient tries to sell a limp-looking bag of weed to an undercover, he'll likely get a pass on that soft felony as the working cop looks for bigger fish. I was presented with a case not long ago where an intoxicated man was walking down the street on a Friday night and kicked a trash can apparently just to demonstrate his zest for living. The can rolled into a parked car. The car owner came out and claimed the trash can had caused $1,500 in damages to his vehicle. Some newer cop heard the $1,500 figure, panicked maybe, and booked the guy on a felony vandalism charge. But that's not a crime. There's no criminal intent. That's called Drunk Guy Being Silly, and if you booked every such person, buses wouldn't run and food wouldn't be served and garments wouldn't be sold because half the city wouldn't have shown up to work that day on account of being incarcerated.

But if the offense you're dealing with is serious and malicious, you gotta go out there and get the offender. Because street criminals do not present themselves to you, subservient, putting their hands out to be cuffed because they're experiencing deep moral pangs for the wrongs they've committed.

That's one of the key differences between the police department and the fire department. Firefighters lounge on plush recliners awaiting their next call as they sip kale smoothies feathered with just a wisp of almond. As a street cop, you don't wait for things to happen. You make them happen. So you love it when staffing levels allow the shift lieutenant to send a bunch of cops out to do street sweeps in high-crime zones, which means finding a lawful reason to stop people and run them for warrants. Some days all you find is some geezer with a couple of unpaid traffic citations. Maybe that's good news. Perhaps all crime has been vanquished. But most of the time, if you have the right eye for the street and dispatch is leaving you alone, you can make a quality pinch of a career criminal.

But after your commendable arrest, there is one single factor that can bring you and your investigation to a shuddering halt. And it isn't the victim's convoluted narrative, or a reluctant witness, or a tricky crime scene.

No, it's something else altogether.

It's a copy machine or printer that doesn't work.

Copiers and printers are as essential to your investigation as a ventilator is to a terminal patient. For you aren't going home until the blizzard of paperwork you must complete is properly printed and documented and collated and accounted for. An arrest means nothing without the appropriate reports for the district attorney to review. So you hit Print. And the printer, purchased at the lowest bidder, says "Calibrating." You come back twenty minutes later and the display still says "Calibrating." This is going to be one calibrated print product—no sheet of paper will ever be as holistic and finely balanced and pristine as this particular sheaf. Or you try to print and some error code pops up with a number to call for service Monday through Friday from 8 a.m. until 5 p.m. Too bad it's two in the morning on a Saturday. Sucks to be you.

So you educate yourself on such things. You learn to keep the copy machine at least six inches from the wall so it doesn't overheat. You figure out how to change the toner cartridge. But that won't stop the copier from the semi-regular jam in seven different places (how can one machine even have so many crevices?) or the fax from spitting out faint yet crumpled copies streaked with vertical lines. I have seen officers break policy by taking their guns out of their holsters and pointing them at malfunctioning office equipment with intent to do it harm. Have I been one of these officers? Let me wait until the investigatory statute of limitations passes before I answer that question.

If there's a rash of, say, fast-food robberies in a certain part of town, sometimes the higher-ups will order officers to stand a fixed post at those locations. But that begs an important question. Do you want to catch the suspects or do you want to stop them? If you put a marked patrol car in front of every fast-food restaurant, you'll stop them. But you won't catch them.

Commercial robberies after hours are often inside jobs. An employee will tell their criminal pals the best time to hit the store, will leave the back-door open, and then feign shock and surprise as the suspects rush in with guns drawn. One clue that points to the inside man? When every store employee gets pistol whipped except the one guy.

Street robbers set up their crime by asking the victim a simple question. Got a cigarette? Got a dollar? Got the time? They're trying to feel you out, to see if you're wary of this question (harder target) or if you seem friendly and complacent (softer target) and fish in your pocket for a smoke or take out your wallet to peel off a dollar, or pull up your sleeve to reveal your watch. Then they can see if you have a timepiece worth stealing. And how fat your billfold is. And if you actually have a pack of smokes. Because there are animals out there who will stomp your face in for a single cigarette. Silly world, isn't it.

Robbers, especially the younger ones, like to mass up on a victim. At some level, many know that individually, they aren't much. But they can get things done if they work together, just because of their sheer numbers. Like harvester ants. You get a pack of hooligans acting in concert and it can be nearly impossible for a victim or witness to identify who was who and who did what and who ran where during a street rip that may have taken only a few seconds to unfold. We're talking about trying to differentiate between, say, a half dozen juveniles of the same race, roughly the same age, and all wearing dark clothing with the hoods up.

"He might have been one of them," a victim will tell you doubtfully when viewing such a suspect who has been detained for the crime.

Another commonality among street robbers is to tell the victim to "break yourself" or "break your pockets." This is urban slang for "I am robbing you so give me all of your belongings." Someone unfamiliar with this phraseology might hesitate, wondering what exactly is transpiring here, but the gun shoved in the face or the blow delivered to the abdomen usually gives them a situational key as to what this person wants.

Some robbers don't have to say anything at all due to the fact that many people walk around oblivious to their surroundings, a condition worsened by being absorbed in their smart phones. They make inviting targets and they never see what's coming. When the suspect wordlessly punches them in the face and steals their stuff, these victims are unable to provide any description at all to the police. Not race, not even gender. Was their assailant even human? They're not sure—it could have been a large carrion bird that flew away clutching their new iPhone in its talons.

Wondering what happens to that stolen cell phone once it enters the criminal underworld? Thieves will try to untether the phone from its carrier, which some guy on the corner will do for as little as fifteen bucks. Or they'll factory-wipe it for resale. I'm told some crooks have the know-how to electronically scrub out the old serial number and replace it with a new one.

Once a phone is wiped, it can be sold on Craigslist or a similar site for a few hundred bucks. Some of them get shipped overseas. Kill switches on stolen cell phones are the new trend, but my guess is the phone thieves have already figured out a way around that. These people are criminals by trade. They don't go to regular job-type jobs or attend Daisy Scout meetings. They have all day to sit around and think about this stuff.

Police departments share information with other law enforcement agencies, often in the form of emailed Crime Alerts. It's sorely needed, because plenty of criminals' crime waves aren't stopped by the invisible boundaries that separate jurisdictions. But it can be overwhelming to try to keep up with what's happening in your own metropolis, much less in the cities across the bay. And while larger departments tend to issue crime alerts solely for felonies, a smaller jurisdiction will take the time to put out an informational bulletin with multiple photographs alerting everyone across fifty-eight counties that the stolen moose head from Garvey's Lodge has been recovered, in more or less its original condition, but the suspect(s) are still outstanding.

Investigating a street crime often involves showing the victim a photo array that consists of your suspect's picture plus five filler photos of people of the same race and gender and similar age and appearance. If your suspect has a distinctive facial tattoo, you have to use a marker to conceal it and then make the same color mark on everyone else's face so your lineup isn't unnecessarily suggestive, unless, of course, you can find five fillers who also happen to have Fuck the World inked on their forehead. If your suspect has blue hair, everybody in your photo spread is getting doctored hair. You try to color within the lines, just like in grade school. If your suspect is crossing his eyes in his booking photo, well, then I don't know what to tell you. I suppose you could blacken in everybody's eyes and your lineup would resemble one of those movies where aliens inhabit human bodies. Some of this stuff you just make up as you go.

The problem with photo arrays is that witnesses aren't always reliable. Sometimes they were drunk or high or didn't actually see anything at all but just heard about it and decided to make the story their own. Even wholly sober, well-meaning people struggle to accurately describe what occurred. One of my favorite examples of this is the classroom simulation where a professor is lecturing to a group of students and then a man comes in, takes the professor's briefcase, and runs out. It's all a setup. But when the students have to write down a description of the man, the variations are astounding. Ever observe something noteworthy with a group of friends and then talk about it later and discover you differ on key details? People's mental lenses all function differently. Which is why you can have a victim describe the suspect as 6'5" wearing a red shirt and then say there he goes, Officer, and point to some 5'11" guy wearing a black shirt. So you review surveillance video and realize it really was the 5'11" guy wearing the black shirt who committed the crime. So where did 6'5" and red come from? Descriptions can get muddled, especially when a victim is in an intense situation. Memory degrades under stress.

Because of this general muddle, I have had a host of crime victims confidently pick out filler photos in a photo array. "That's him!" they insist as they select some utterly random fellow's picture out of the six. "I'll never forget that face." It's possible, I suppose, that a filler photo could actually be the correct suspect. I don't know what the odds of that would be, but not even the most adventurous bookie would take them. Occasionally, just out of curiosity, I'll run up the filler suspects they identify. Usually they were in jail during the time frame of the crime. One guy had actually been dead for six months—pretty sure he didn't do it.

I do believe, however, that most victims of crimes are telling the truth when they make a police report. The incident happened the way they said it did, or at least to the best of their memory. They don't have any ulterior motive. They were legitimately wronged and you do everything you can for them.

But there are exceptions to every rule. You get your fair share of sketchy victims too. I remember one named Rico, who had some teeth knocked out in a fight. He fit into the sketchy victim category because he knew his assailant, the attack concerned a $1,000 debt, and Rico was a drunk and argumentative felon. Rico questioned why we didn't fucking believe him. If we weren't going to help him, he'd settle this himself. He didn't want to wait for the detective. Fuck this. Fuck us.

"Normal, law-abiding people do not get their teeth knocked out by friends over monetary debts," I told Rico. "For instance, it's never happened to me."

Rico was precisely the kind of victim investigating officers loathe, a known criminal telling a tale less than credible. But you can't quite tell him to take a hike, because, knucklehead or not, he had been the victim of a violent felony and as long as he remained at least semi-cooperative, you have a professional and ethical obligation to fully investigate his complaint and check for the suspect. You do this even knowing that it was the kind of case unlikely to be charged by the DA even if an arrest was made, for Rico would be a train wreck on the witness stand and probably wouldn't show up in court at all if he had something better going, like, Margarita Mondays.

So you spend a wealth of time, energy, and resources on a case going nowhere.

You deal with these types of victims by picking their stories apart, asking them legitimate, credibility-testing questions ("Tell me again why you were in an alley at 2 a.m. wearing no pants with a girl you know only as Peaches?") that sometimes make them so frustrated that they curse and storm away. That's fine by you because, as the saying goes, no victim, no crime. You are required to investigate felony complaints, but if the sketchy victim walks away from you, you aren't required to jog at their side, notepad in hand, and beg them to reconsider.

When I think about questionable victims, I recall the day when a description came over the police radio of a car taken in an armed robbery. It was a Chevy Monte Carlo with 20-inch custom rims. Etched on the side of the Chevy, the dispatcher told us, was "20s, Bitch." My partner and I burst out laughing. No one deserves to be carjacked, but some you don't feel as bad for as others.

Auto burglars are out there in every town in America plying their trade. The other day I saw a sign on a car in the SF Mission District that read "Please don't break my windows. No valuables left in car. Thanks!" But breaking a car window is a bit harder than you think. A chip of porcelain from spark plugs, otherwise known as a "ninja rock," works best, and some car burglars will keep that chip tied to a string for easy retention. The bold thief will break the target window, reach in, grab what they can, and go, all in a matter of seconds. Others stretch the crime out. They'll break the glass and then walk away and see if anyone notices. If the cops arrest them at that point, it's just for misdemeanor vandalism, not felony auto burglary. But if the coast is clear, they'll move in and load up and if they're caught then, they'll claim, hey, I didn't break into that car! The window was already like that. I've heard there's been a rash of broken windows around here . . .

Even though an auto burglar will break into your car solely for the six cents he sees in your center console, because that's six cents he didn't have before, oh what a haul he might encounter when he digs a little deeper. I constantly review police reports where thousands of dollars of luggage are taken. High-end jewelry. Expensive cameras. Laptops. Passports. Firearms. All items left by people who thought a rolled-up window or locked trunk was some kind of magical barrier against theft.

If the thief decides to take not only what's in your car but the car itself, here are some of the ways he'll do it.

1. Get a shaved-down key and turn it in the ignition just like the real key. This works best on older Hondas and Toyotas.

2. Peel the steering column and disable the steering lock with a screwdriver.

3. Glove up and cut the power wires, which are usually red, underneath the steering column. Strip the ends and touch them together briefly. Then separate them and tie them off. This turns on the juice to the car. Repeat this process with the starter wires, which are usually brown. This will start the engine. (If you don't tie off the wires, they can deliver a nasty shock.)

Now you may ask yourself, why is this cop giving people tips on how to commit vehicular felonies? What if a criminal reads this? Well for one, I've found that most street criminals aren't big readers. But more importantly, I'm not giving away any trade secrets here. Most criminals know this information already, and if they don't, it is readily available online. And I'm not talking about some obscure encrypted site on the Dark Web. Nope, it's on YouTube.

You will have at least one street criminal nemesis on the job. I have several, but the one I'm going to talk about is Devin (not his real name), a prolific burglar and sometime crack dealer. He is my nemesis not because he's the worst of the lot, although he's no saint. No, he's my nemesis because he keeps getting away from me. My first encounter with Devin came one fine spring day when I was rolling around in an unmarked car with a few coworkers and I saw him at a bus stop. I recognized him from a wanted flyer. "Hey, is that Devin?" I asked and got out of the car. Devin answered my question by sprinting away. He disappeared around the corner and I ran after him. Poof, he was gone, leaving me trying to catch my breath as I checked around on the ground to make sure I hadn't coughed up my own spleen.

My second go-around with Devin was in the lobby of an apartment building maybe six months later. My partner and I had just cleared a weapons call so my shotgun was slung over my shoulder. I saw a guy standing by the front desk. "Hey, is that Devin?" It had been awhile and I knew him mostly by seeing the back of his head and the soles of his tennis shoes. I called my partner over and took hold of Devin. But when he calmly said he was someone else, I paused for just a tick when I took the cuffs out, a pure rookie mistake. He capitalized on my hesitation and once again bolted. I still had my hands on him, but it didn't matter. He dragged me across the lobby. All 250 pounds of me, 235 with duty belt and long gun. He pulled me along with a surge of horsepower that belied his unassuming frame. The strap of the shotgun got tangled up between us and I tripped over it and him and went sailing into the lobby wall, hitting it full bore, the impact putting my blocky midwestern head right through the drywall. When the cobwebs cleared, I heard my partner outside on the radio giving chase. Again, it didn't matter as Devin once more vanished into the night. I was left with three things: handcuffs with no hands in then, a piercing headache, and a lengthy incident report I had to write explaining the property damage I had caused with my own face. 0 for 2. Outwitted, outclassed, outplayed.

I took a photo of the face crater in the wall, documented proof of my futility, and for a time looked at it whenever I felt myself getting cocky. I found comfort in the words of writer M. H. Anderson, who said, "If at first you don't succeed, you're running about average."

Sometime later, sharp-eyed cops in the Tenderloin district of San Francisco arrested Devin for selling crack. I believe it's for the best that someone else besides me got him. Given my track record, my encore probably would have been chasing Devin into a waste treatment plant and stumbling into a vat of raw sewage. Then this conversation would follow among my coworkers:

"Where's Plantinga?"

"Oh, you didn't hear? He went after Devin a third time, tripped, and drowned in human waste."

"Huh. How 'bout that. So can I have his desk?"

One of your favorite types of street criminals is the fugitive who will spray-paint his face while on the run. He must think it will provide sufficient camouflage so he can blend in with his surroundings. Or if the police stop him, he can say, "Officer, you seem to be looking for a light-skinned individual but here I am, clearly dark-skinned. My flesh is just runny. I have a condition."

Some of these face-painters are, as you might suspect, really drunk.

Another police favorite is the fleeing suspect who will actually call 911 and demand the police stop chasing his car. As if he's being quite put out by the whole experience. The nerve of those cops. This is *ruining* his evening.

But best of all is the gun hoarder. Given the ability of modern ballistics to link a firearm to a crime scene, information that is common knowledge to anyone who has ever watched even half an episode of *Law & Order*, you'd think it'd be a no-brainer that if a criminal commits a violent crime with a gun, they'd ditch it as soon as possible. Drop it in a river, or disassemble the pieces and scatter them around town. Not so. A fair number of street criminals operate on a narrow profit margin. They aren't exactly knocking over the Bellagio so their take tends to be small, which means they can't afford to get rid of their gun and pick up a new one. And if the violent crime they committed was against a gang rival, they're going to need that gun to defend themselves against likely retaliation. So the gun stays in circulation. And by "circulation," I mean it stays tucked in their pants, or stored at their house, because there isn't anywhere else they can put it where it won't be stolen, with there being no honor among thieves and all. So you write the search warrant, hit the house, and there the gun is in the top dresser drawer. And when you tie the gun back to the crime in question, you know that you have been successful because your suspect is poor, dumb, and desperate. These three salient qualities have helped police officers put away a staggering number of violent felons.

One of the long-standing interactions law enforcement enjoys with street criminals is the name game. In this contest, crooks try to sell you on an alias because they have warrants under their actual name. The consequence for unlawfully lying to the police about your name is a low-level misdemeanor, so some crooks figure it's worth it. But they are inclined to take just one stab at it. They'll verbally serve up a name and date of birth ("I'm sorry, I left my ID at home, officer") and you run it. You quickly figure it's bogus info when nothing comes back in the system for this ghost man, or if there is a match, the height and weight are way off. You are also aided by the fact that these days, nearly every squad car is equipped with a computer program that can display mug shots or photographs of state IDs. When you call them out, 95 percent of the time, they'll give you their real name. The remaining 5 percent will apologize for lying and then try to pass off a second fake name, as if maybe you won't try to verify this one, because you got that nice apology just a minute ago. And when this second name turns out to be a nonstarter, 99 percent of the 5 percent will know the gig is up and cough up their birth name or just clam up, at which point you take them to the station to verify their ID through fingerprints.

Once in a great while, you'll have some undaunted felon shoot for three different names. The hallowed trifecta. After the first two swings and misses, they'll often say something like "Okay, you guys just make me really nervous. My real name is _____. I swear I'm telling you the truth." Maybe they're thinking, If I can pull this one off, I will become a legend of the streets.

One of my favorite name game stories was the fellow who tried two different monikers with some SF cops, the second of which was Roger Hawkins (name changed to shield his reputation). When the second name didn't match, the cops pressed him on his real identity.

"I'm going to stick with Roger Hawkins," he said. At some level you must admire a man who is willing to go down with the ship.

Kidnappings are rare and often domestic violence related. Stranger kidnappings are rarer still. Why? Because they are among the most labor intensive of crimes. First, the kidnappers have the challenge of removing the victim from their home or a public place without getting caught. Then they have to transport them from Point A to Point B. The victim has to be watched, possibly fed, and kept quiet in a remote location where no one will notice. It takes patience, manpower, and planning and there are too many opportunities for things to go all sorts of wrong. Your average criminal doesn't want to mess with that. Give them a grab 'n' go street rip any day.

What's more, enough kidnappings are hoaxes that you must be constantly on guard for them. Victims claim they were taken by force, but their story starts to unravel. Maybe they are surprisingly clean for someone who was allegedly abandoned in the woods for days. Or they report they were tightly bound by their captors, but there are no corresponding ligature marks on their wrists. Or they are found safe and immediately retain an attorney, not a typical move for a true victim.

So why would someone make a false claim of abduction? It could be drug or prostitution related. Or sometimes it's a college student with a misguided need for attention (see the Audrey Seiler case in Madison, Wisconsin). Or a boyfriend/girlfriend team hoping to squeeze a parent for ransom money (see the Hackensack, New Jersey, case from May of 2014). Or it could be just some dopey kid who stayed out too late and now fears the wrath of his parents for busting curfew. The reasons are often spectacularly inane.

These hoaxes poison the well for legitimate kidnapping victims, and local, state, and federal resources invested in working a kidnapping can reach upward of a hundred grand. As such, some of these alleged victims are criminally charged for obstruction or filing a false police report. The victim says she faked her own kidnapping because she needs time away. Need time away? The police can arrange that . . .

But one need look no further than the 2015 Denise Huskins kidnapping in Vallejo, California, to realize that some abduction accounts, however questionable they initially appear, turn out to be wholly true. The Huskins case featured, among other things:

1. A boyfriend witness with an incredible tale of drugging and blind-folding.

2. A several-hour delay in reporting.

3. An unlikely ransom amount ($8,500)

4. The victim being dropped off at an illogical spot (her family's home some 400 miles away).

5. The victim initially agreeing to meet with police but then not showing and hiring an attorney.

These are all red flags, classic signs of a ruse, and the Vallejo Police Department, after working the case round the clock with some forty detectives, said as much publicly. And what spun this case even more into the realm of the fantastic was when the alleged *suspect* contacted the media to defend the victim and report that the victim's account of her kidnapping was accurate. But after a similar offense occurred in a neighboring jurisdiction, an arrest was made of one Matthew Muller, a disbarred attorney and former Marine who claimed to be bipolar. He confessed to the crime and has been indicted on kidnapping charges with the possibility of life in prison.

I don't possess any inside knowledge on the Huskins case, and I seek neither to vilify nor to exonerate the Vallejo investigating officers. From what I have gathered, my guess is I'd have arrived at the exact same conclusion they did, namely, that this was one giant make-'em-up. It's a conclusion steeped in hard-earned experience. A conclusion that was entirely understandable and entirely false. And it leaves victims like Denise Huskins with that awful fear, the stuff nightmares are made of.

Something horrible happened to me. The worst thing that has ever happened to me in my entire life. I'm trying to tell people.

And no one believes me.

Street crime pisses you off, especially if the victim is an innocent. And generally speaking, anger doesn't help you much as a cop. All it tends to do is get you in trouble. But sometimes a little justified anger is just what this town needs. Because anger spurs on effort. So you hit the block one more time in search of the suspect and that's when you find him. You listen to jail call after jail call and finally catch him slipping with an offhand but incriminating statement. You write a warrant for his house, his phone, his car. You call the shopkeeper who might have video of the crime, but he doesn't call you back so you keep calling and calling and you stop by his store and stay on him like a telemarketer from hell until you get your hands on that crystal-clear surveillance shot of the suspect punching a senior citizen in the teeth and yanking her rent money away as she collapses to the ground like a puppet with cut strings.

And if you can't get the suspect for the crime you know he committed but can't quite prove, you figure something else out. Like a parole search that turns up the drugs he's packaged for sale inside the storage unit he rents. Or a traffic stop that reveals his 9mm underneath the driver's seat. Follow those train tracks long enough, eventually you see the train. And if he tries to make a deal to trade up for bigger fish, you let him know he's the only fish you want. He's your special project. You're gonna bird-dog him.

Today is Johnny Felon day. And tomorrow will be too and the day after until you send him to state prison where he is meant to be.

You do these things because you're a cop and it's the very essence of your job. And you do them because your operating philosophy hails from the Latin *reliqua autem impius non est.*

No rest for the wicked.

6

Special Operations

The Tactical Enforcement Unit, otherwise known as SWAT, has a language all their own. They talk about disturbance resolution models and they diagram wedge formations for crowd control. Threat matrixes. Fatal funnels. Deterrent zones. And they're constantly discussing the high ground and where it is and how to get there and how long you want to remain once you arrive.

Just as impressive as their linguistic arsenal is their arsenal of weapons and gear. Like explosive breeches and hinge-melting torches to get through doors. Pole cameras to survey tight quarters, like attics. Shotguns that shoot .40 beanbags as a less lethal alternative to bullets. Armored rescue vehicles with extension ladders and a door built into the undercarriage so you can enter a hot scene, position the rig right over the victim, and pull him in. The LRAD (long range acoustic device) that targets a suspect with a beam of sound so piercingly irritating that it tends to make people just give up or try to find a dumpster to hide in to avoid the noise. Plus thigh holsters for handguns, all hail the thigh holster, which instantly transforms a SWAT cop from whatever he was previously into a bona fide badass. And then there's the almighty flash bang grenade.

Most people's experience with flash bang grenades comes from the video game *Call of Duty*. Police tactical teams use the real deal. I spoke with Sgt. Tim O'Conner, a longtime member of SFPD's Specialist Team, who gave me the rundown. First used by British SAS troops in the late '70s, flash bangs are designed to temporarily disrupt an enemy's senses. They accomplish this by producing a blinding flash of light and an intensely loud "bang" of around 175 decibels, which causes temporary loss of hearing. The flash activates the photoreceptor cells in the targets' eyes. This makes vision impossible for approximately five seconds until the eye can recalibrate, followed by a lingering afterimage that inhibits the target's ability to aim a weapon with any precision. The audible blast not only momentarily deafens but also scrambles the fluid in the target's ears, causing sustained loss of balance and general screwed-upedness.

Flash bangs are ideal for when a team is about to make a dynamic entry into a building, or has eyes on an armed suspect who needs to be incapacitated to be safely taken into custody. But sometimes you pull the pin on the flash bang and prior to throwing it, circumstances change dramatically such that now you shouldn't throw it. Maybe a small child enters the room, or the suspect surrenders. And there you are with the active flash bang in hand. And you gotta do something with it. Trying to put the pin back into a live flash bang is ill-advised and this isn't a hot potato—you can't just toss it to a teammate. No, you have to absorb it, the proverbial falling on the grenade.

This, Sgt. O'Conner informed me, is affectionately referred to as "eating the bang."

SFPD tactical teams drill on flash bangs every six months, with an orange traffic cone playing the part of the suspect. They give verbal commands, which of course the suspect does not obey because he's an orange cone. Then they pull the pin, toss the bang, and duck out of the way. After that begins the nonducking portion of training where someone has to eat the bang, all part of a rich police tradition of experiential learning. That selected someone cringes because he knows what's coming. Then he deploys the flash bang right next to himself, voluntarily entering the sound and light party from Hell.

This is all part of the SWAT philosophy of train, train, and train some more. Your average street officer qualifies at the range twice a year. SWAT gets on-duty range time twice a month. Some officers practice handgun reloads every night for an hour in front of their television or get to the point where they can field-strip their weapon with their eyes closed. They run on treadmills wearing ballistic vests and backpacks. And if you've ever wondered just who on earth works out with those gigantic tires you see at some gyms—rest assured, it's the SWAT guys.

Whenever possible, SWAT maintains a good working relationship with the media. Because what you don't want at a high-intensity scene is some news station giving your location and setup away by filming it live and letting the suspects holed up inside the house watch the whole thing unfold on TV or their phones. "Hey look, there's the entry team approaching the front door. Let's greet them with gunfire." Media channels by and large respect this. They'll take footage of cops standing by their cars away from the action and they'll film the aftermath, but nothing that would give away position or tactics.

When the scene is safe and the crowds have gone home, SWAT supervisors will hold a tactical debrief with the officers involved where they'll talk about what went well and what went shitty. SWAT debriefs can be especially brutal, because the team holds itself to high standards and there's not much room to screw up. So if someone made a mistake, a sergeant or team leader will tell them they fucked up, how the situation had to be unfucked, and how to avoid future such fuckups.

These debriefs are often conducted with the understanding that rank is not an issue, which means that if a police officer thinks a sergeant is the one who blew it, he'll say as much. "I speak my mind to the bosses," I once heard a tac cop say. "I just add 'sir' at the end."

The SWAT team has all sorts of tips for the common patrolman. They talk to you about having the proper combat mind-set. They tell you never surrender ground you already own. They're the experts, and you'd be fools not to pay attention to them. But a handful of the suggestions seem a bit much. Like the SWAT advice that you shouldn't wear white T-shirts under your uniform because if you're in a low-light situation, that's exactly where the bad guy is going to aim—at that illuminated patch of white underneath your neck. But what about the older cops with white hair. Wouldn't that present a convenient target as well? Should they dye it? And how about those lucky ducks with pearly white teeth? Must they brown them with coffee stains? How far do we want to take this?

One knock on SWAT you'll hear from patrol cops is that they're stand-offish and aloof and they all wear Oakley sunglasses. If you're not one of them, line officers will grumble, SWAT won't give you the time of day. This perception may be tied to the tight bonds forged on SWAT teams. You're talking about a group of officers of similar age, interests, and abilities on an elite unit who spend so many hours training together and so many hours hanging out off duty that after a while they start to look and act the same.

SWAT cops have to know and trust each other; when they're taking down the dope house, the guy in front hooks left because he knows, without anyone saying anything, that the guy behind him has got the right side covered. They're working operators taught to think on their feet. And yes, they do all wear Oakley sunglasses, but that's only because there's one guy on the unit who has a hookup so he gets all of the guys the same sweet deal. There's an insularity that comes from such a work setting and that's okay. You don't want a SWAT team to stop and make time for idle pleasantries and chitchat with their patrol support at a critical scene, because there's a man with an assault rifle in that building and if the team doesn't get this one right, some people are going to get shot and some people are going to die. No, you want them to be terse and focused and say some technical shit to each other you don't fully understand as you stand aside to let them pass into the darkest valley.

At a critical incident where a suspect is presenting an imminent, deadly threat, a special operations supervisor will, on occasions both rare and extreme, give the officers on scene what's known as a green light. This means the go-ahead to shoot the suspect on sight. A green light is only given when negotiations have failed, lives are at stake, and the suspect has crossed a line that cannot be uncrossed. The only time I'm aware of this order being given by the San Francisco Police Department was on May 9, 2012, when a homicide suspect named Dennis Hughes, wanted for the murder of his sixty-six-year-old mother, shot at officers responding to his apartment at 861 Post Street. The units backed off and held the perimeter as Hughes remained inside, firing shots through walls and floors before he set fire to his own apartment, endangering everyone in his multi-unit complex as well as neighboring buildings. There was no talking with Hughes. He had decided his own fate and was trying to see how many people he could take with him. So the incident commander gave the green light and when Hughes passed by a window, an SFPD sniper ended the standoff with a single bullet.

That night is still painted in my mind. Streets were cordoned off and clogged with cops and firefighters, residents were being evacuated, and pedestrians were running away as they looked back over their shoulder like they do in disaster movies. There were three different police command posts, a media throng, and a sense in the air that anything could happen next. I remember going door to door evacuating tenants from an adjoining building and hearing shots ring out from an open stairwell and hitting the deck. I remember listening to the crackle of radio traffic, each update more impossible than the next ("Now he's setting his apartment on fire?"). I recall being ordered to hold fast at the building's front door to accompany Hughes to the hospital and waiting there for some time because he never came out. The whole night was surreal, intense, cinematic. And I remember thinking that when the world ends, it might look a little something like this.

The police command van was in place for the Hughes case. The van is a staple for any large, complicated scene, be it a criminal investigation or, more frequently, a large-scale festival where lots of coordination is needed. The command van is fairly sweet. It has a wall of television monitors and radio banks and tables with space to spread out maps and charts. It bristles with antennas. Seats come at a premium. Usually it's just the brass in there, plus the one guy on the department who knows how to operate all the equipment. If you are a lowly patrolman, you may get a quick glimpse inside of how the other half lives, but then the door shuts and you're like a passenger in coach straining to see what's happening in first class. If you are on, say, POTUS detail and are assigned to guard a street corner outside the president's hotel for ten straight hours, you will yearn for the command van and the soft comforts it promises. Stood on your feet for hours on end recently? Around hour five, your lower back already feels like it's been trampled by bison.

The command van is air conditioned. It has its own bathroom. There's a couch you can fully stretch out on, and when someone with a bunch of insignias on their collar does it, I think it's technically referred to as Forward Observation from a Fixed Post, but if you ask me, it looks suspiciously like lounging. There is a refrigerator that I have heard is stuffed with platters of cold cuts and flavorful beverages. "You look tired, Commander. Would you care for a Snapple? Come recline over here so you can Observe from a Fixed Post." And that's just the police command van. I can only imagine what the fire department command van looks like. Probably memory foam mattresses and oysters on the half shell.

The media will report on high-profile incidents of what seem to be overzealous actions by police while serving search or arrest warrants. A SWAT unit stormed in, shot the family dog, terrified the children, or maybe used extreme force against a resident under questionable circumstances. And once in a great while, they do these things and it's the wrong damn house. If you're at all appreciative of the Bill of Rights, you may be deeply troubled by this.

It's a given that the police have every right to make hard entry into a felonious residence because many of these homes present imminent danger. The vast majority of search and arrest warrants are served without a hitch, and officers I have worked with have time and time again shown heroic restraint in dealing with violent suspects during high-risk raids. But you may not ram down the door of the incorrect house any more than an air traffic controller may guide two 747s down the same runway at the same time. So you gotta do your homework. You are obligated to gather intel and conduct surveillance so you get it right. In the past, when doing the briefing for a search warrant, I have printed out large photographs of a duplex and written in large block letters THIS ONE on the door of the target location and NOT THIS ONE on the nontarget just as some paranoid patients will write on their limbs prior to undergoing surgery so the doctor doesn't carve up the right appendage when it's supposed to be the left. Because sometimes the upper unit holds the Newton Boys while downstairs is an assembly of Mennonites in a prayer circle. The Mennonites should remain undisturbed by you.

Some SWAT units will insist that one of their officers physically touch the front door of the target location during the recon prior to executing a search warrant. This can cut down on mistakes and confusion when you actually hit the house. Is it a metal door with a wooden frame? A wooden door with a metal frame? Any sign of the door being reinforced? Is the walkway strewn with children's toys? The front yard dotted with gopher holes? (You don't want your lead guy stepping in one and going down with a torn ACL.) The answers to those questions will dictate everything from which breeching tool you'll use to how many officers will make up the approach team.

Any discussion of special operations must include canines, a staple of the police department. Police dogs bring a lot to the table, not the least of which is their legendary sense of smell. Just how good is it? I asked Sgt. Davin Cole, a cheerful, loquacious fifteen-year canine handler, who told me you could put a grain of salt in a 10-gallon bucket of water and a dog would detect it. When Cole does presentations for schoolkids, he illustrates a dog's sense of smell as follows: Ever been home and smelled your mom making cookies in the kitchen? Smells good, doesn't it? Now how about if you go outside? Can you still smell them? Maybe, maybe not. How about if you go next door to a friend's house? Not likely. But a trained police dog can pick up on that odor from two blocks away and, what's more, can break down the smell *by ingredient*—eggs, flour, sugar. Human beings have only a few square inches of membranes in their nose to detect scent. In contrast, dogs are working with a few feet of membranes because a canine's nose is like a honeycomb—the membranes just keep wrapping around themselves and trapping the scent for analysis. The longer the dog's nose, the better it smells. And one of the reasons bloodhounds are such legendary trackers is that they use their large ears close to the ground to, in effect, scoop up scents as they go.

Trained police dogs can locate certain accelerants used in fires. Cadaver dogs pick up on the chemical plume given off by decaying human remains. Cole told me that after a rash of sexual assaults in Amsterdam parks, dogs were specially trained to detect semen to help locate crime scenes when a woman was raped but couldn't say exactly where in the park the assault took place. Dogs can be trained to sniff out electronics like thumb drives and microcards, which aided in the prosecution of former Subway pitchman Jared Fogle for possession of child pornography. Sheriff's deputies use prison dogs to find the silicon in contraband cell phones.

But the main function of police dogs is to go after bad guys. K-9s are specially trained to pursue, bite, and hold (although some departments train their dogs to bark and hold). Bite-and-hold canines will not release the suspect until commanded to do so by their handlers.

Handlers give fair warning before any chomping goes on. They make a loud announcement to the suspect or to the area where they believe the suspect is hiding. The warning advises that a dog is going to be released and the suspect could get bit. If the suspect doesn't give himself up, then he has only himself to blame when the 100-pound missile launches his way. The warnings can compel a suspect to surrender because criminals fear dogs. They can't outrun them. Can't bargain with them. Can't reason with them. Dogs don't believe their excuses, tricks, or lies. The canines are trained to do two things and two things only, which is to find them and stop them. So sometimes even when a police dog isn't available, cops will get creative and try to fool the suspect into thinking otherwise. A veteran Chicago cop named Joe Wagner told me that when he was hunting for a suspect, he used to get a bullhorn and announce that a police dog was being released. He'd even make barking sounds so suspects would think a dog was hot on their tail and give up. I listened to Joe's bark imitation. It wasn't half bad. And it worked, he told me. Nobody wants to get bit.

Police dogs aren't trained to bite only a certain area of the body, because you never know which part of the suspect will be exposed, but they frequently go for forearms or legs. In bite training, handlers protect themselves with full bite suits, mixing up the colors so the dog doesn't get too used to going after only a certain shade. If they want to gear down a bit, they might use only an arm sleeve, which they hide under civilian clothes to simulate how suspects are dressed on the street. Cole has a friend on the LA County Sheriff's Department who would don a thin leather gauntlet covered with layers of newspaper to simulate human skin. The problem with this approach is when the dog clamps down on the newspaper, it hurts like a mother. Officers in the Netherlands favor pigskin from the butcher shop to wrap around the trainer's arm because it's the closest to human flesh. But using the sleeve alone isn't sufficient because that teaches dogs to go only for arms and leaves them confused about what to latch on to if, for instance, a suspect's arm is folded under his body and inaccessible.

During training, the dogs go hard. Cole once suffered a concussion when his canine hit him full bore and flipped him over, padded bite suit and all. He described this almost fondly, like he might recount an incident when he got a little banged-up playing a fun game with one of his children.

Cole has had suspects, especially those hopped up on drugs, actively fight his dog. Punch his dog. Try to strangle his dog. Cole would jump in and tackle the guy while the dog was still biting him, risking, with all those flailing arms and legs, a bite himself.

The dog's natural bite is the front canines, which is what they use on their prey in the wild. The rear teeth are just for chewing. Handlers teach the dogs to go in deep on the bite because it isn't about damage, it's about pain compliance and holding the bad guy in one place; you don't want the dog treating the suspect's limbs like corn on the cob. In order to teach a proper hold, trainers put the dog in a harness tethered to a 20-foot bungee cord. If the dog lets go of the bite, it is propelled backward on the bungee, which isn't fun at all. But most dog training is heavily concentrated on both play and rewards and it is nonstop, which is why police dogs don't make good house pets. The owners don't have the commensurate energy to keep up.

K-9s are typically German shepherds or Belgian Malinois. (Rottweilers, Cole told me, get fatigued too fast.) Shepherds aren't as common as they once were because they have a problem with their hips wearing out, hence the more recent move to the Malinois. A police dog costs about ten grand. Most hail from Germany or the Netherlands. Cole's last dog, Zigi, was a Malinois, and he had to learn some Dutch to give Zigi commands. Cole described Zigi as a Jack Russell terrier in a shepherd's body and described

Malinois in general as strong alpha dogs with an abundance of energy and phenomenal recovery time. They can go eleven or twelve years on the force as working canines.

SFPD's police dogs are all dual purpose. They first and foremost serve as patrol dogs, which means they look for suspects. Their secondary function is either narcotics or explosives detection. You don't want dogs trained for both narcotics and bombs in order to avoid, among other things, the confusion of whether the dog is indicating he just found a pound of cocaine or a pound of TNT. This distinction would be important in the field.

Dogs alerts come in different forms. Some sit and stare at the source, be it narcotics or explosives. Others scratch, although you'd want to avoid that indicator for bombs for all the obvious reasons. The hit is a generic one and not drug specific, so a dog won't have one tell for cocaine and another for heroin. Same deal with explosives—the indicator for Semtex is the same as C4.

One type of canine SFPD doesn't currently have on the roster is a tracking dog; they have trouble in an open urban environment due to the population density. If a suspect flees into the housing projects where he lives, his scent is going to be spread around from his previous time there, and even if the dog can narrow down the location where he fled, it can be an uphill battle to get a search warrant solely off a canine track to a house. But if a good tracker has something to get a scent off, like abandoned clothing, and is operating in a more rural environment, the handler will put them on a 40-foot lead and make a go of it. Some tracking dogs are better on old tracks and some need fresh ones. Because of how the dog is trained, if they find someone at the end of the track, they are going to bite, so if the dog gets onto the wrong trail, the homeless guy who happens to be sleeping in the bushes along the way could be in for an unpleasant surprise.

But while canines don't always get it right, Cole pointed out, they still make far fewer mistakes than people do. They do well in finite, enclosed spaces; they are going to find that late-night burglar tucked away in an upper corner of the three-story warehouse. They are going to hone in on him like his pockets are stuffed with pork chops.

On the SFPD, only the K-9 handler or the officer in charge of the unit may say whether a dog will be deployed. It's their call, because they know the dog's capabilities. This policy prevents some green lieutenant from sending a dog into a house where, for instance, there's a gunman who has already shot at cops. All this will accomplish is to sacrifice a valuable asset, the dog, for no gain. But sometimes it goes the other way where a supervisor doesn't think to use a dog when it would be the very thing to do. Cole told me of a time when a suicidal boyfriend reportedly barricaded himself in an upscale house after physically assaulting his girlfriend. A member of the police command staff drove up, demanded SWAT respond, and tasked them with pumping the house full of tear gas. Twenty-one volleys of tear gas to be exact. When SWAT was done, they had broken every window and every door. One gas canister sent a chandelier crashing down on a dining room table. There was so much tear gas shot into that home that it left a powder residue thick enough to show footprints. The whole house became a hazmat scene. All the carpeting had to be replaced. And after all that, turns out the guy wasn't even in there.

"I was just going to open the door with a key and send the dog in," Cole said, but he was overruled by the higher-ups. The projected cost of Cole's plan? Zero dollars. The homeowner's claim submitted to the city? A cool quarter million. Our bad, taxpayers.

Police dogs are practically one of the fellas. They often wear ballistic vests. They have their own badge or star number. They go home with their handler because they're pack dogs and their handler is part of their pack. If they are killed in the line of duty, they receive a stately funeral. Mess with a police dog and it's a felony. And don't expect understanding treatment from the dog's handler, because the bond between cop and canine is family strong. In fact, if you're the suspect in an incident that hurt or killed a police dog, you should probably just catch the first bus out of town.

Handling things that might blow up also falls under the umbrella of special operations. As a patrol cop, you will occasionally be called to someone's house because they were cleaning out the attic and found some of grand-dad's stuff from the war or a few items from weird Cousin Kenny's duffel bag. The homeowner isn't sure what it is or if it's dangerous. So you have to be able to do some on-the-fly explosives recognition before you just start picking stuff up and holding it close to your face. Blasting caps look like long silver whistles with a wire sticking out. C4 resembles pliable Ivory soap. Anything remotely explosives related that's moist or exuding crystals can be deadly. And explosives can age well, which means World War II ordnance could still be good to go.

Most suspicious package calls are baseless; a transient left a bag of his stuff in a doorway and someone passes by and calls it in as a potential device. The temptation as first responder is to walk up and open it yourself and get this over with, because the last time anything exploded in your district was when Tolliver from midnights ate too many chimichangas and lit up the station bathroom all shift. But if you like your arms attached to your torso, you don't want to take too many chances. Bombs don't always look like bombs, especially not to your untrained eye. So you gotta show bombs some respect. Because it only takes that one time when you casually stroll up to the abandoned package and open it without any protective equipment and the resulting explosion turns you into pink mist. The names that should be on your mind are Ted Kaczynski, the Tsarnaev brothers, and Eric Rudolph. You need to call the experts, the bomb techs, who use X-rays to examine suspicious packages, have liquid nitrogen to freeze destructive devices, and still employ Geiger counters to detect radiation.

But at times, even the experts step wrongly and pay the price. In 2008, a suspicious device was left outside a bank in Woodburn, Oregon. Senior Trooper William Hakim, a Navy vet, eleven-year cop, and bomb tech, brought it inside the bank because he thought it was a hoax. When he examined it more closely, it detonated, killing Hakim and Captain Tom Tennant and seriously wounding Chief Scott Russell and a bank employee, whose name has not been released. Hakim was a bomb tech in the Navy, who had real-world experience dealing with actual explosives. He was in the major leagues of bomb cops. It is not speaking ill of the dead to say you can learn from the Woodburn tragedy. No one gets it right all the time. Not the first responders and not the experts. But when it comes to explosives, there is no margin for error.

To get a better handle on explosives, I sat down with an SFPD sergeant who spent a number of years on the department's bomb squad. He preferred to remain anonymous, citing a desire to "reduce his Net presence." The first question I asked him was if he had ever encountered a bomb with a digital countdown timer like you see in movies. He had not. He described the devices he had encountered in his career as fairly crude. He was too polite to inform me my lead-off question was fairly stupid. It also probably helped that I was buying him lunch.

An exploding bomb is shrapnel plus concussive force. The shrapnel shreds your flesh, but the blast overpressure liquefies your organs. You may see a police bomb tech in a bulky bomb suit walking slowly toward a potential explosive and think, hey, that guy will be fine, look at that ginormous suit. Nothing is going to get through that—guy looks like one of the Transformers. But while a police bomb suit protects against shrapnel, it offers only a limited defense against the concussive effects of a high-end explosive. If the bomb goes off, your organs are still on their own.

The sergeant thought it was hard for the general public to understand how fast explosives move. Bombs are different from bullets and different from fires, he explained. A bullet from an M16 travels at roughly 2,800 feet per second. The slowest of the high-end explosives travels at 17,000 feet per second. He invoked the scene from *Lethal Weapon 2* where Murtaugh is sitting on an explosive-rigged toilet and Riggs pulls him into a nearby bathtub and pulls a bomb blanket over them. Both men survive the blast and live to crack-wise some more. But, the sergeant pointed out, a bomb circuit closes at the speed of light so Murtaugh "would be instantly incinerated as soon as his butt cheeks left the toilet." The debunking of this scene made me somewhat forlorn, as this is an awesome cinematic escape that I wanted to be possible.

The sergeant observed that it's common for patrol officers to peer around the corner at a suspicious device from, say, a block away. But given the velocity of explosives, if it does detonate, you won't have time to duck your head back behind cover. Your head will be gone, and you won't even have time to miss it because the whole thing will be over before you see the device go off. I nodded, knowingly, while thinking back to the multiple times I've been that guy peering around the corner at the weird package. Patrol's tendency to underestimate devices is why, on the SFPD, the bomb tech has complete control over the scene. He's the expert and cannot be vetoed. He can tell a deputy chief what to do, and if the deputy chief doesn't like it and insists on doing things his way, the tech will shrug, pack up his gear, and leave.

One of the biggest misconceptions of bomb work is that it's really exciting. It's more of a methodical and technical slog. "Once you get past the skin," the sergeant said, "they're all exactly the same." He talked about the paranoia bomb work brings with it. "Once you become a bomb tech, everything looks like a bomb." He eyed the ketchup container on our table. "I know how to make that into a bomb," he said matter-of-factly. Made me glad he's one of the good guys.

If you have a hostage situation or a person threatening suicide, you get on the horn for a special operations negotiator. They have the requisite training and the snazzy pins on their uniforms to prove it. You don't send just anyone up there to talk to the troubled soul, certainly not the patrol lifer on his third marriage and struggling with both the bottle and diabetes; he might be thinking of jumping himself.

You want to use lateral thinking when dealing with jumpers. In October of 2015, SFPD negotiators used the suspect's beloved cat to help coax a distraught car thief down from an upper-story window, ending a three-hour standoff on Harrison Street. My old Southern Station coworkers Jordan Oryall and Ronnie McGoldrick once responded to a rooftop on 6th Street where a despondent young woman was threatening to make the leap. Both natural-born schmoozers, the two cops chatted with her for a time, found out her favorite song (Bobby Brown's "My Prerogative"), and then played it on a cell phone. I am told one or both officers may have even accompanied the music with a few dance moves, the Running Man chief among them. She laughed and stepped away from the brink and the officers were able to transport her to a mental health center. You do what works. I once tried convincing a naked, suicidal, and grease-covered man to get off the top of a crane with the promise of a pack of cigarettes and two donuts. He was unimpressed with my offerings, claiming he didn't smoke, but my negotiator coworker smooth-talked him down by playing a song from the Cranberries. And he still got the donuts. Well, one of them, anyway. A cop ate the other one. You probably saw that coming.

Negotiators avoid lying to the person they're negotiating with and never make promises they can't keep. If you lose the person's trust, the negotiation is effectively over. One seasoned cop I spoke with said he had gone his last thirty negotiations without lying, save for one. Curious, I asked him about the one. He told me he was in an extended conversation with a barricaded suspect who was on the brink of suicide. The suspect said he would emerge only if the negotiator promised to attend a Trump rally with him. In a move born of desperation, the negotiator agreed and the suspect promptly walked right out.

The negotiator ended up taking a pass on the rally, perhaps concluding that nothing was worth that.

7

Collisions

Know the difference between knives, bullets, and brick walls. If you show up in the ER with a stab wound to the heart and no vitals, your survival rate is 40%. With a gunshot wound to the heart and no vitals, 4%. If you have blunt trauma from smashing into something like a brick wall, your odds are less than 1%. Blunt trauma is the worst, because there's no one fixable thing. It's a whole body of hurt.
—Ben Sherwood, *The Survivors Club*

When you're investigating a traffic collision, you're looking to see if the car is in or out of gear. You're checking the radio volume, because if it's cranked up, it may have made it difficult for the driver to hear an approaching siren or car horn. You're surveying the car's interior for cosmetics, in case the driver was distracted from the road while she was applying lipstick. You're seeing if anything is obstructing the brakes, like food wrappers or a wadded-up shirt or any one of the other hundred things people leave strewn about their car that can interfere with its operation.

Newer cars are equipped with black boxes called SDMs that are about the size of a videocassette and located under the front seat. They provide a wealth of information to traffic investigators in a collision. The SDM can tell you if the air bag was deployed and when the driver hit the brakes. It records engine speed, the position of the gas pedal, and whether a driver was wearing his seat belt. These newfangled cars have other features too like warning signals to help you when you're backing up. I didn't have any fancy gadgets or an SDM on my first car, which was a 1985 Olds Delta 88, a wide hunk of metal that just barely fit in the lane. As a new driver, I relied on my father to inform me when I was about to hit things.

If the collision you're responding to is at an intersection shared by another department that turns out to be just on their side of the street, a responding officer from the department with jurisdiction will say, "We thought about moving the cars ten feet over so it would be yours." Something like this is always said. It is never not said.

Many horrific collisions are caused by felons fleeing the police, collisions that can injure the pursuing officers, other motorists, and pedestrians. The suspect might be injured as well, although, as if to give a lesson in the resiliency of the human body, many crooks hit by cars while on foot will pop right back up and keep running, buoyed by a wash of adrenaline. Spike strips can work in slowing the suspect vehicle down if you are in the right place to deploy them at precisely the right time, but roadblocks tend to be both dangerous and impractical. There has to be a better way. What if all cars were equipped with a remote kill switch that only the police could tap into, so you could make the suspect vehicle glide to a graceful stop? Or a button you could press that would reroute the suspect vehicle to the nearest police station? I feel like Microsoft should be working on this stuff instead of Windows 48.

In a high-speed collision, the hood can fold, flip up, and shatter the windshield as the back wheels rise from the ground. Though the force of impact has slowed the car, the passengers haven't slowed at all, bound by the unblinking laws of physics. Heads strike glass, feet come out of shoes, the brake pedal can shear off, and the seats sometimes tear free and rush forward.

Cops understand high-speed collisions because you get what it's like to drive at high speeds. It's odd—when you're doing 130 on the freeway chasing a robbery vehicle, it doesn't actually seem that fast because there aren't any buildings or traffic lights around that act as a frame of reference to gauge your velocity. 130 feels more like 70. Except when the suspect vehicle swerves onto an exit ramp and you try to make that same ramp too. Then, Judas Priest, does it feel like 130 again.

The homeless and the down-and-out are frequently victims of collisions. They cross the street against the light into heavy traffic because they're drunk or largely indifferent to the 5,000 pounds of metal racing toward them. Or they use the curb as a pillow and stick their feet straight out into the roadway until an SUV splinters their legs. Some transients fall asleep in a stranger's driveway, unbeknownst to the homeowner, who backs over their head on her way to work in the morning. It is an ignominious end for the victim and a traumatic encounter for the driver.

Other hazards in collisions? Vehicle airbags contain a toxic gas called sodium azide. According to a recent bulletin from OSHA, this gas is completely consumed in the deployment of the bag and doesn't represent a threat to the occupants. OSHA's no slouch, but if you are in an accident and the airbags deploy, I'd still open my car windows if I were you.

Sometimes cars will collide with buildings, like straight through the glass doors of a hospital. Then the fire department will be called to check the integrity of the building and see if it needs to be shored up. That's a good assignment for firefighters. It's refreshing to see them out there doing an actual job-type job instead of spending hour upon hour in the firehouse developing their lats in the gym or thinking of a whimsical name for the new house Dalmatian.

At times you'll be called to a traffic collision that's a low-speed affair with little damage to either car. However, one of the parties is claiming assorted pains or is completely passed out for no apparent reason. Maybe their injuries are legit—you're no surgeon, and even a minor traffic impact can cause serious dysfunction inside the human body. But if it looks like you have a thespian on your hands pretending to be unconscious in order to gun for a big insurance payout, and you get to the hospital and the doctor can't find anything wrong with the guy either, once in a while you'll be tempted to do the hand drop test. You lift one of this actor's hands away from his body, position it over his face, and let go. If his hand thwacks his own face, he may actually be passed out. If he stops his own hand, he's likely not. But the true test is if the doctors elect to intubate. You can't very well play possum while someone is vigorously stuffing a tube down your throat. This causes the possum to awake.

On rainy days, officers scramble to keep up with the traffic accidents the wet weather brings and neighborhood kids do backflips onto the sodden mattresses in their front yards. If a hot call comes out during a deluge, you gotta dial it back a notch when responding, a lesson learned on the streets of Milwaukee when I was sent to a robbery in progress and I floored it. When I made the left-hand turn onto S. 35th from W. Greenfield, I hydroplaned into a fast counterclockwise spin, coming to rest about two feet from a parked car, having rotated just over 360 degrees, like a Tinseltown stuntman. Better lucky than good.

If I had wrecked that squad car during the hydroplane, I would have had to fully answer for it because in our current progressive departments, police vehicle accidents are, for the most part, handled thoroughly and professionally. If the cop is at fault, the report will say as much. But in the olden days, things were . . . different. Some sector cop would approach a weathered desk sergeant and report that he cracked up his patrol car taking a turn too fast because he was rushing to make it to the station bathroom on time. The sergeant's reply? "Listen, dummy, my report's gonna say you were going to an emergency call with your lights and siren on, okay? Also, I drink Chivas Regal." At some point during the shift, a bottle of the latter would mysteriously appear on the sergeant's desk. Those were the days of yore, and they were highly questionable but often entertaining.

Accidentally run over some broken glass from a traffic collision? Got yourself a flat tire? A lot of new cars don't even come with spares anymore, part of automakers' goal to make cars lighter to increase fuel efficiency. My mechanic, an insightful fellow named Ravi, recently told me some contemporary models have underbellies made of a wimpy carbon polymer that will crinkle like foil if you try to hoist it with the jack that comes with the car. You have to take those vehicles straight to the dealership, robbing a generation of the rite of passage of changing a car tire on their own.

Modern cars also collapse like accordions when rear-ended. Folks will grumble about how they don't make 'em like they used to. But this is all by design. The backs of cars are now outfitted with what's called a crumple zone, which more evenly distributes the impact of a collision. If something is to be crumpled, you want it to be the car, not the driver.

Everything from a minor collision to tailgating to being cut off can lead to road rage, which is the launching pad for all manner of mayhem. Road rage transforms the meek into the seething, the calm into the sputtering. The gates are flung open and anything goes. The wronged driver will follow the offender to his house and fight him in his driveway in front of his children. Fish a tire iron out of the trunk and shatter his windows. Beat him to death with a motorcycle helmet.

When road rage starts simmering, we all need to suck in a contemplative breath (I'm talking about myself here too—I'm far from immune). We have to let some of these things be. It is rarely a good idea to confront another motorist with an angry lecture that we think at some level may be a teachable moment but is actually just us screaming like a loon. Call 911 for flagrant offenders, but keep a safe distance. Indeed, the best outlook on road rage comes from comedian Dobie Maxwell, who said, "Driving a crappy car changes your entire mind-set. If someone cuts me off on the freeway I can't flip them off, because I may need that guy to jump-start me in a few minutes."

Hit-and-run collisions showcase how vital paint chips and glass are as evidence, because of their distinctive chemical compositions. Both can potentially tell you the make and model of the striking vehicle. Tire tracks will give you the size of the vehicle and the load and the make of the tire. Experts can usually say that this particular tire track was made by this particular tire on this particular car.

Once you find hit-and-run vehicles and the corresponding drivers, you'll hear all sorts of excuses. They may claim they weren't driving at all. They lent the car to a friend. Which friend? Oh, hard to say. They lend their vehicle out so frequently. Could have been any number of people. Playing along, you ask for the names and phone numbers of these beneficiaries of their largesse and they suddenly get all vague and elusive, as if you asked for the contact information for the Society of Druids.

Another common move for hit-and-run suspects is to claim their vehicle was stolen and the thief must have been the one who caused the accident. Maybe. According to recent FBI statistics, a car is stolen in the United States every forty-four seconds and people driving stolen autos rarely stop and check on the welfare of people or vehicles they've just struck. But a telltale indicator of deception is when the reporting party stumbles over simple details like when they last drove their car and whether it was taken with keys. Every so often you find yourself asking what their stolen car is doing sitting right there in their driveway.

If the offending motorist is accused of hitting a pedestrian, the excuse of "I thought I hit a deer" is commonplace, despite the fact that the concrete slums where this particular accident occurred haven't seen a deer since people hunted them with spears. Or they'll say they might have hit some road debris. Or an especially nasty pothole. These excuses might fly with an elderly driver or someone operating a big rig. But nearly everyone else is lying and doing so with stunning audacity. There are documented accounts of hit-and-run drivers who flee an accident scene, go home, and park in their garage, all the while with the victim wedged in their windshield. Makes it harder to claim they didn't notice. Or maybe they'll claim, hey, I recently bought the car and it just came like that. With a human being on the hood.

Wondering why your car insurance rates are so high? Insurance companies have to jack up your bill to recoup their losses from insurance fraud. Such fraud includes organized rings of hustlers who stage phony auto accidents in order to collect benefits.

The classic hoax goes down in a parking lot. One pedestrian will pretend to be hit by a car backing out of a spot. He'll slap the car dramatically and collapse to the ground with a series of medical woes. Someone else who pretends not to know the first person but is really an accomplice will serve as a convenient witness. This scheme often targets the elderly, who are more vulnerable to being swindled.

But other false accident claims are more spur-of-the-moment. Take, for instance, a collision involving a municipal bus. Knowing the city has deep pockets, passersby have been known to actually climb inside the damaged bus through a window so they can claim to be injured passengers and fish for a settlement.

Auto accidents are the place where tragedies live. I remember a car crushing a eleven-year-old boy who darted into traffic while playing tag with his friends. He was on a stretcher with a neck brace, his face a mask of blood, staring at the ambulance ceiling, eyes shot through with panic, as if the familiar, safe world he had known moments ago had spun away. Or the two-car fatal where one of the victims was a college student in a vehicle with a bumper sticker that said Dare to Dream. Or the intoxicated driver who crashed through the backyard of an apartment complex, killing a woman and her infant daughter and critically injuring two other children. He just had two beers, the driver later claimed. Just two beers.

But sometimes you're not quite sure if you're looking at a tragedy. I recall responding to a fatal traffic accident where a T-bone crash left one driver dead with a shattered neck. It was five o'clock in the afternoon and maybe he was just getting off work. But I looked closer and saw the dope packaged for sale scattered around the passenger compartment of his car. Noted the electronic monitoring bracelet on his leg I later learned was due to his parole for armed robbery. Took in the tattoos: MOB (short for Money Over Bitches) and the cocaine eight ball inked on his forearm. He just got off work, all right, from his job as a drug dealer, and he wrecked because he blew a stop sign at seventy trying to evade the squad car he thought was going to pull him over. You wonder if this still meets the definition of tragedy.

Perhaps in some loose sense.

A traffic collision has you stuck in traffic on the freeway and you're fuming. Now you're going to be late to work or to your appointment. But it's good to keep in mind the title of the classic children's book by Margo Zemach, based on a Yiddish folktale: *It Could Always Be Worse*. How about you're on the interstate and a big rig filled with live chickens has toppled over, blocking three lanes of traffic, and the even bigger rig needed to get it right side up is also stuck in the same traffic jam? Or what if another large commercial truck spills its load. Its cargo? Nails. I have encountered both of these incidents on my morning commute.

Things could always be worse.

8

The Corner

Not Yo Wifi, Bitch
—One of the available wireless connections on my phone while standing at the
corner, October 2015

Not all city corners are the same. But what's described in this chapter will sound familiar to officers from coast to coast and to anyone who knows the grittier part of their hometown. In San Francisco, it's places like 3rd and Palou. In Milwaukee, 35th and W. Fond Du Lac. In Baltimore, I'm told, it's Rutland and Federal. The corner is where crime, commerce, and urban despair all mingle, with an undercurrent of street theater. There's often a guy passed out in the coin-operated laundry, his teeth ground to nubs. Watch your step on the corner because the sidewalk is lined with broken beer bottles, Moonpie wrappers, feces both human and animal, and the occasional 9mm shell casing that the cops missed in their search last night when someone emptied a magazine at two rival gang members with the street names of Sleepy and Cuervo.

On the corner, you won't just find a Discount Liquor Store but a Super Discount Liquor Store.

On the corner, a guy in a wolf mask will roll by on a unicycle. And you hardly even blink—that's not even the weirdest thing you're gonna see today. No, he's running second to the shirtless man in ragged drawstring pants wearing a Cat in the Hat hat leaning against an ATM like it's a chaise lounge and furiously dry-humping the air.

On the corner, you'll see rats scurrying away. Even the vermin want out.

The police spend a lot of time there.

It is a working cop's playground.

Folks get plenty riled up on the corner for reasons ranging from a contro-versial police use of force to the home team winning the title. If things really get rolling, they will riot. But riots are by no means exclusive to the corner. Anyone who thinks riots originate only in lower socioeconomic neighborhoods should check out the history of Madison, Wisconsin, on Halloween, where the primary source of violence and bedlam has been Chads. (For a definition of Chad, please refer to Chapter 4.)

As a cop, you are required to be hard on the corner. If the situation calls for you to hit someone in the mouth, you let fly with your best Sunday punch and you don't apologize. But you can't walk around all rough all the time. Because the corner has seen that before and it isn't impressed. I'm not talking about being meek. The meek are gulped down on these streets. I'm talking about being able to roll with it. For the corner calls for flex-ibility. You must know how to sidestep. Which verbal challenge to deflect. When to give someone something they don't expect. What situations call for mild goofiness. So when some corner lifer scowls and steps up to you with "You think you're pretty tough, don't you?," instead of flexing on him, you might respond with "Yep, I am tough. You should see what I did to the crabgrass in my yard last summer." If the short but oh-so-loud drunk gal in front of the convenience store curses you up and down, ask her, "Why so unfriendly?" Then tell her not to give up on you and cheerfully predict the two of you will be fast friends by the end of the month. If the best you get in return is a reluctant grin, that's still more than you had before. You're just an urban Johnny Appleseed out there trying to lay down some plants that will come to fruition.

Have an adventurous spirit? On a tight budget? There are hotels available near the corner with quite reasonable rates. They may not be heavy on accoutrements and the bathrooms are often shared, but you can still get a room for $50 in San Francisco where the average one-bedroom apartment goes for three grand a month. One seedy establishment on the 6th Street corridor, ground zero for lawlessness in San Francisco, prominently boasts a sign that says Students Welcome. Another on the same stretch proudly advertises COLOR TV. It's 2018, man. People have color televisions on their wristwatches.

Most corner hotels feature grated exterior doors you have to be buzzed through. The acrid smell of urine hits your nostrils as soon as you pass the doorway, and as you ascend the stairs to the front desk, you will step over empty baggies of meth and discarded condoms. The hallway lighting is a sickly institutional yellow. Some folks live in these hotels full time and have taken to plastering their doors with signs ranging from Keep Fuck Out to helpful tips on which guy on the floor has a supply of Narcan, which can revive someone who has just overdosed on heroin. Because it takes a village.

Even the corner of the corner is its own neighborhood. I was at the northeast point of 16th and Mission a few years ago talking to an old-timer who was sitting on a milk crate watching the world go by. I was relatively new to the district then and he broke down the demographics for me.

"This here is Africa," he said, gesturing to the black males around him. "Over there," he said, pointing to the northeast corner of the northeast corner, "is the Hispanics. You cross the street, I don't know."

"That there's ISIS," one of his compatriots said helpfully.

Romance is far from dead on the corner. I once investigated a stabbing where a twenty-two-year-old woman was slashed by an acquaintance on the rooftop of a flophouse motel after a drug dispute. I asked the woman if she had dated the suspect, which would make the whole thing fall under domestic violence, which would allow me to turn the investigation over to the Special Victims Unit and continue to pursue the sub sandwich that had yet eluded me that day.

The woman thought about that for a minute. "He has tried to court me," she professed. Court her. The suspect was a heroin addict with prominent neck tattoos and the street name of Monkey. I wondered how Monkey commenced his courtship. One glass of iced tea with two straws on a porch swing in the waning twilight?

Monkey isn't the only character on the corner. There's also the guy wearing a fur hat with ear flaps on an 85-degree day. (The proper police response is to point at his head and tell him, "That's a great hat.") Or the elderly woman with chin whiskers wearing a 1950s shawl panhandling with a dirty fast-food cup, eyes closed, swaying from side to side. Or the man you remember primarily because he once ripped a pigeon in half in front of you. Many people are in wheelchairs, although a few use them as cover for their corner hijinks and can walk just fine, which you find out when you approach with the intent to get into their business and they spring out of the chair and sprint away from you, calling to mind Eddie Murphy's "I can see! I have legs!" epiphany from *Trading Places*.

You will get to know many of these folks, but you must be careful when you address them in public. If you use their Christian name, they often scowl and reply, "Don't be putting me out there like that." Because on the corner they are known just by their first name or nickname and they would like to keep their real name on the down-low so as not to compromise whatever street hustle they're currently working. You respect that. Mostly. If some repeat offender really bugs you, you might see him, roll down your window as you pass and call out, "Henry Johnson, holding down the block!" What's the worst Henry can do? Complain to your supervisor? "That officer referred to me by name—I'm going to sue him for all he has and I'll be living in his house by sundown."

On the corner, wound care can take interesting turns. I investigated an incident where a man named Rory was stabbed by his live-in girlfriend in the thigh and face with a steak knife. I found Rory a block from his house sitting near the pay phone where he had called 911. I looked at the facial wound. It would need a number of stitches to seal.

"Let's call you an ambulance."

Rory shook his head at my overreliance on Western medicine. "I'll just put some Vaseline on it," he said.

Vaseline. Like old-time boxers used to slip punches in the ring. Despite Rory's faith in petroleum jelly, I convinced him to go to the hospital, where I interviewed him further. He had been with his girlfriend for ten years. She had just been acquitted of homicide, and, Rory observed, it made her feel invincible. They were still together, despite her transgressions and tendency toward stabbiness.

I went back over Rory's account of what happened. The chronology struck me. The girlfriend had slashed him in the leg after arguing about how he had prepared the ground beef for dinner. He punched her in return and walked away. She caught up to him in the living room and cut him again, this time in the face. He sat on the porch and smoked a cigarette. She left in a huff. He stayed on the porch for a time until a man walked by. He asked the man to come over and look at his face. The man suggested he go to the hospital. Rory, taking heed of this stranger's counsel, called 911 from a pay phone. There was a decided lack of urgency about the whole affair.

"I don't care if she's messing around as long as she don't give me no diseases," Rory said. Then he added, "I love her. But that [the stabbing] was wrong."

I nodded because it seemed wrong to me too. But it seemed right for the corner.

Your desire is to keep the peace and improve the quality of life on the corner. But you can't arrest your way out of entrenched social problems that predate you by decades. Some elements you have little control over. You watch the truck pull up and unload fresh pallets of cheap beer in front of the mini-mart. Hey, how about some fresh vegetables up in here, pal? Don't think we need any more booze. Or you see a woman, high and unfocused, squat and take a bowel movement between two parked cars. You recognize her because she gave birth on that same corner two years ago and left her baby for dead in the rain. Now, as she stands, hair unkempt, flecks of spittle on her lips, it looks like she's pregnant again. (By the way, who is the miserable SOB who put another baby in this woman?) There's humanity in her, there has to be, doesn't there, but she presents as a walking, talking sack of animal urges. It would take some kind of magic trick to change things for the better out here. And you can't pull a rabbit out of a hat if you don't have a rabbit to start with.

People languish on the corner because they lack the two things that adults need in order to thrive:

1. A stable living situation.
2. Full-time work, school, or child care so the bulk of your day is taken up with something positive. Even if you wanted to commit crimes, you've been working all day and you're too tired at the end of it to get in much mischief.

For many of us, these two things are a given. We graduate from high school, perhaps earn a degree, get in a relationship, begin an occupation, live in a decent home in a decent neighborhood, maybe start a family. We expect this. In short, we enter healthy, independent living like slipping into a warm bath.

Not so with the denizens of the corner. You run into a lot of them who don't work. Who have never worked. I'm talking about guys in their forties who have literally never held down a real job. And a lot of them don't know anyone else, besides you, who is gainfully employed. That's why it's refreshing to encounter the working man during your tour of duty. You are inclined to give such a fellow a little room to operate. "To hell with the kings," the mayor of Milwaukee once said when told the king of Belgium was planning a visit. "I am for the man who works." Cops feel that way too. A job isn't some kind of shield against police action. But it counts for something. The guy is at least out there trying to be legit. And you respect that. Moreover, you want to help him sustain what he has. You don't want him hanging on the corner. That's why if you don't have to arrest or cite the laborer, you tend not to. You pull a guy over and he has paint-spattered pants or he's wearing a polo with a company name on it or there's a hard hat on the seat next to him, maybe he gets a break on that license plate light citation. Because it could be his family is one ticket away from not being able to pay rent. Fines pile up and turn into warrants, all of which can threaten a man's employment. And you know that if you take someone's job away, you essentially take them away.

If the man on the corner does happen to work, it's likely part time with Dickensian wages. You ask where he stays and he points to the bench right behind him. He doesn't have to go anywhere; he's already home.

Drug dealing is robust on the corner. The dealers are typically a loose circle of young men in hoodies. If you roll up in a marked car, the whole group starts the slow drift away with the occasional backward glance to see if you're following. You leave and come back in five minutes and they'll have returned to the same spot. They're out there all day to the point where sometimes you encourage them to pursue a hobby between customers to make the best use of their time. Like Hacky Sack.

Listen to narcotics cops and you'll hear tales of the last time one of them tried to buy dope at the corner in an undercover car. He pulls to the curb and five different guys come up to him, ten hands in his open window trying to make the sale. When he gets the product, he's gotta follow that hand up the torso to the face so he can remember which of the five guys it was who he bought from.

On the corner, people sit on stained mattresses and cajole passersby. They eat dry ramen noodles, drink swill from brown paper bags, and roll their own cigarettes, because a man has to have a craft. If you have time, you take their booze away to protect them from themselves, so the next contact the two of you have isn't when they're bathed in blood from the drunken brawl they committed or provoked. Kids are out on the corner even when school is in session. Maybe they're not skipping—maybe it's a half day. But you look at your watch and it's ten in the morning. Half a half day. The corner is filthy and will stay that way unless the mayor is touring the jobs center down the block, in which case the street cleaners will give it an extra hose down and it will look semi-habitable for a few hours. From time to time, a community center will sprout up near the corner. It's often a dismal affair—an apathetic staffer presiding over a few slouching teens gambling with dice underneath a sign announcing anyone who enters can be searched for weapons.

One of the frequent public critiques of law enforcement from the corner is "Y'all doing too much." You put a meth dealer in handcuffs. "It's just dope, y'all doing too much." You chase down a teenage auto burglar. "He's only a kid, y'all doing too much."

Conversely, some of the folks on the corner will loudly proclaim the police aren't doing enough. That they don't do anything at all. Don't do anything? We do so do stuff. Depending on the size of your jurisdiction, you may have anywhere from a few dozen to a few hundred people booked in your county jail every single day. Who do you think puts them there? They don't just turn themselves in out of a crisis of conscience. The police nab them, these murderers, robbers, rapists, and thieves. If the police actually did nothing, you know what that would look like? The film *Escape from New York*.

You'll see folks on the corner who don't quite mesh with the surroundings. I thought of this when I was at the corner walking behind two hipsters. One of them had a yoga mat slung over his back. The other had fingernails painted black.

"I just had this new peppermint chai tea," Yoga Mat said.

"Oh my God, that sounds amazing," Fingernails replied as they stood near an intersection where just last week a man with no teeth and a dreadlock wig had attempted to murder a prostitute by repeatedly knifing her in the chest over a $150 debt. Or you watch the gawky twenty-year-old who just left a fantasy gaming convention and is walking over the viaduct straight into gangland territory wearing plastic chainmail with a toy broadsword. Attention, young paladin, your mystic blade might be +2, +6 versus ring wraiths, but you're heading in the direction of some guys who won't necessarily impress. You can warn the kid all you want, but the right to move about freely is one of the main tenets of democracy.

Some nights on the corner when it's warm and lots of people are out, you get the unsettling sensation that someone is going to die violently tonight. You are often correct. Things get so bad in the summer that cops sometimes jokingly refer to the corner in the most antiseptic of ways: ah yes, the intersection of Louis and Whitman, I'm told we are experiencing some instability in that region.

Most people who get shot on the corner utter precisely the same thing. They say, "Agghhh, shit hurts." I have heard this so many times that if I am ever shot, my guess is that's exactly what is going to come out of my mouth too. It's what one says when one is shot. The shooting victims who don't make it are remembered by street corner memorials complete with teddy bears or small bottles of gin. The chalked messages on the sidewalk range from the heartfelt (We miss you Derrick) to the vengeful (We gonna get them niggas).

If there's a playground near the corner, the swings will hang perpendicular to the ground from a single chain. If there is a basketball court, the net will be torn off the hoop or the hoop will be missing altogether. If you take your gun out while searching backyards for a suspect, a neighborhood kid will gleefully shout, "Hell yeah, 5-0's got out his nine!" The dining options in this place are limited. There's often a Chinese restaurant with sticky floors and a quick mart with chili dogs and jumbo dill pickles. Neither establishment is Zagat rated. That one hip hamburger joint that just opened, buoyed by city tax incentives, shutters within the year. The corner fights gentrification like Ali fought Frazier.

There are a number of things you must have if you wish to belong on the corner. The low-slung pants are a given; don't even show your face on the block unless your pants are pooling at the soles of your shoes. And designer jeans with an elaborate logo on the back pockets, like flaming stallions, are allowed and even encouraged. Neck and forearm tattoos are standard, as is the plain black or white T, preferably extra-large. Do-rags aren't as popular as they once were, but their donning is still acceptable. Do you have a gold grill? Silver rope chains? You're in, welcome. Everyone, but everyone, moves in the Can't Say I Care saunter. And the prevailing attitude toward police is that of aggressive indifference, like that bumper sticker that says How's my Driving? Call 1-800-EAT-SHIT.

In days past, cops used to clear the corner of thugs by telling them to move along, often accompanied by a kick in the pants or a prod of the nightstick. One old-time cop I know used to tell a guy on the corner "Come here, kid" solely for the purpose of then telling him "Now get the fuck outta here" when the guy trotted over. You mayn't do that anymore. Not just because you now must essentially write a police report every time you make physical contact with someone or because a crowd is recording you on their cell phone, but because this isn't North Korea. People have the right to assemble and they don't have to move just because some uniformed cop tells them to. It's right there in that pesky U.S. Constitution. Sometimes the corner will clear by itself as soon as you show up, because the drug dealers don't want to talk to you, and the guys buying stolen cell phones will respectfully relocate down half a block. But if you're going to tell someone to move, you need a lawful reason to do so. You need a plan of attack. There are a few minor or obscure laws you can employ to this end, like the one that prohibits smoking within fifteen feet of an operable door or window of a building, or the ordinance against sitting on a fire hydrant because it obstructs fire operations. Littering is a good one. You can use these things as leverage to encourage some of your undesirables to take a walk and not come back for a while. So parts of the corner can still be cleared. It just has to be done properly. Eternal vigilance, as they say, is the price of liberty.

But while the corner demands considerable police attention, it's also important to take the occasional break from urban blight. Good to mix it up, be among regular people. Your squad partner tells you, listen, a drunk hooker told me to blow myself and I just stepped in gum. Can we go now? So you agree to a brief foray somewhere that's the opposite of the corner. Like the command van. Or, I don't know, Whole Foods.

The two anchor businesses of the corner are the quick cash joint and the convenience store. At the instant cash storefronts, day laborers wire money from the city to their families back in Mexico, El Salvador, or Guatemala. They send $500, and $400 arrives because of the exchange rate, wiring costs, and fine print fees. The names of these businesses are variations on a theme: Cash Gram, Manda Express, Kwik Send. They are rarely robbed because of the bullet-resistant glass separating customer from teller that runs from counter to ceiling.

The corner convenience store sells single cigarettes, although it's against the law, and cheap flowers in short glass pipes; addicts buy them, dump the flower, and use the pipe to smoke crack. Some of the folks working the corner store are responsible businessmen trying to make it in a tough climate. They'll feed you information about crime in the neighborhood. They do their best to discourage people from loitering outside, and if something goes down in the street, they'll give you their surveillance footage without you even having to ask.

Others, well, don't do any of those things. They're in league with the criminals, buy stolen property from them, and couldn't care less that they're dealing dope because the dealers keep coming in for sodas, smokes, and lottery tickets—they're some of the best customers. Take them away and whaddya got? Just the sixty-year-old alkie shopping for a ninety-nine-cent beer whenever his panhandling allows.

A traditional police weakness is to write off an entire neighborhood as lost. You'll hear cops mutter "Someone should napalm this block" and every so often, that cop is you. But solid citizens live near the corner and they deplore it as much as you. Parents pack their kids' lunches and send them off to school where they're promptly robbed at the bus stop. A family scrounges up enough money for pizza night, putting the coins and dollar bills in a glass jar, but their apartment is burglarized for the seventh time in the last three years and now the pizza money is gone along with their small TV. Plus the suspect took a giant steaming dump on their kitchen floor for good measure just as another way of saying screw you.

When I was living near the corner in Milwaukee, an elderly couple named the Coles lived below me. I remember seeing them one night sitting on their front steps dressed in bulky layers to fight the cold. Mrs. Cole wore an oversized Kraft Macaroni shirt with a picture of a dinosaur called Cheesasaurus Rex. Mr. Cole wore a faded security guard's uniform, his gray hair plastered to his skull, a can of nitro spray close by to combat his frequent heart trouble. They were living on the kind of razor-thin margin where a single parking ticket would set them back weeks. They used to sit out there, quiet mostly, watching the street, as if awaiting a promise made real.

Some make it out. It's a long road, but it's been done. Oprah Winfrey, George Soros, Sonia Sotomayor, who grew up in public housing, professional basketball player Caron Butler, Starbucks' Howard Schultz, San Francisco's own Chris Gardner. Folks who rise from humble beginnings to make their mark. How do they manage that when so many falter? Persistence no doubt, help from friends and family, getting an occasional break here—the same formula most of us rely on. Some of it just comes down to choices. One resident of the corner broke it down to me in stark biblical terms: "You can either follow God or you can follow Satan. And I know Satan, cuz I done sucked his dick for a long time."

It isn't all gloom and doom on the corner. It's not uncommon to see a kid surfing down the street on a garbage can lid, which is dangerous but riveting. Some of the old-timers will tell decent jokes although they veer toward the obscene and scatological. If someone plays music, others will spontaneously dance. And on the first of the month when government checks roll in, it's party time where those on the corner are drunk or high or trying to get there. You are the uniformed police presence, the party crasher, the killjoy, knifing your way through the crowd assembled for this mini Mardi Gras as guys unbutton their shirts to the waist and women cackle and sway, bottles of Royal Gate vodka in hand, just a few more voices in the human choir.

But you'll also have those dedicated souls who use the corner as their base of operations to evangelize with vigor. They're trying to bring light into some dark places, and even if the message is sometimes delivered a bit off-key, it deserves your respect. I spoke with a middle-aged woman once at the corner of 3rd and LaSalle, which, if you know San Francisco, you understand that to call it a hellscape would be kind. She was in her Sunday best asking for directions and I gave them to her. Then she got out of her car and clasped my shoulder. She closed her eyes and blessed me fervently for several minutes. She asked the Lord to be with this officer. Normally I don't let strangers put their hands on me in a familiar way, but I went with it—seemed absolutely wrong not to—and we both left, I think, better off for the encounter.

If you are smoking a cigarette and about to enter a place of business on the corner, no need to toss it. No, you carefully place your smoke on the top of the entry door to be retrieved upon exit. On the corner, people wear T-shirts emblazoned with their philosophy toward cooperating with local law enforcement, Don't Say Shit, and kids have only one roller skate. On the corner, they'll tell you that all the police do is enforce the conditions that keep the poor and minorities down. You may be confused by this statement as you strain to remember the last time you passed out booze and cocaine to the locals, handed working firearms to all able-bodied males, and blocked children from attending school. In this place, it is a pedestrian habit to nonchalantly cross in front of moving vehicles against the light. The law of the land is that oncoming traffic slows and waits. To honk would be bad form and also an invitation to have your car vandalized or to get an up-close look at a handgun. On the corner, dirty diapers are stuck in trees. Around here, the neighborhood wisdom is that if you're ever in trouble, don't go to the police; find an old black woman and ask her for help. She'll know what to do. On the corner, local artists will put up a peace mural after a spate of senseless neighborhood slayings. It will say something like "Stop the Bloodshed" or "Creativity will prevent violence through the restoration of the artist in everyone." As a street cop, you will laud these artists' intentions. They're trying to make things better out there, just like you. But such endeavors will also lend themselves to cynical quips among your coworkers like "Sweet, we can all turn in our guns and bullets and go home. You know. If there's a peace mural going up."

On the corner, there are so many people just hanging out throughout the day and deep into the night, so many folks fighting and gambling and drinking, so many residents with no job but seven kids whose names they can't keep straight, so much consistent chaos and dysfunction that seem like such a natural lifestyle that every so often, you wonder if they're right or you're right. I mean, it's gotta be you. There's no question. You have a sensible mortgage and umbrella life insurance and pants that aren't spattered with your own vomit. Those are all things you should have. But why are the numbers on the corner so high? Do they have some insider's view you don't? Are they on to something? They can't be. Can they?

The police have a complicated relationship with the corner. You love it. You hate it. It beckons and repels. Kensington and Somerset drove you half crazy, but that overtime from those warrant arrests helped put both your children through private school. A sense of perspective is helpful on the corner. It's grim, but it could be grimmer. There's not much chance of stepping on a land mine or getting hit by mortar fire. Children go hungry, but they're not starving. It's the corner, sure, but it isn't quite the corner in Aleppo.

But when it's all said and done, the temptation, and it is strong, is to give up on the corner. You take one hardened criminal away on a solid case and he's replaced by two others. The corner just keeps reloading, as formidable as before, like the Connecticut women's basketball team. There are more of them than there are of you, and they're looking at you right now, all cocky and unvanquished. And because of this, some cops say why bother? The corner is eternal. There were robbers and dopers before you got there and they will remain long after you're gone. You're not going to reinvent society here. So why not just trudge through your work shift, phone in your performance, and leave early so you can catch *Monday Night Football*? What's the point of it all?

But, you suppose, you do what you do for that brief window when all is calm on the corner. Order has been restored, or at least the appearance of order. You savor that moment. You try to stretch it out as long as possible. And when the corner starts heating up again, you elect not just to wring your hands in despair. You are paid to stop criminals. You are imbued with considerable power by the state to enforce the law and arrest its violators.

So let the corner do its worst.

You are a cop battling for a foothold.

You will not yield.

9

Safeguards and Dangers

Avoiding danger is no safer in the long run than outright exposure. The fearful are caught as often as the bold.
—Helen Keller

The field of law enforcement requires you to be well versed in all manner of threats, not just those posed by suspects with weapons. So you are trained not to park over a vault or manhole during an electrical emergency because they can blow up and you're taught that it isn't just metals that become energized—so can trees, wooden ladders, and rope. If you arrive at a residential gas leak, you know not to step on the doormat, which could cause a buildup of static electricity that will spark, and you know better than to ring the doorbell, which could act as an ignition source.

Lots of nots and don'ts in this job. Another one is don't let someone get chewed up in an escalator. All escalators are state mandated to have two kill switches, one at the foot of the stairs and one at the top. This is vital to be aware of because commuters have gotten everything from hair to scarves stuck in the escalator's metal teeth and been scalped or asphyxiated as the stairs kept grinding interminably away. So if need be, look for the bright red button and push it as hard as you can.

Don't use a fire extinguisher if the fire you're facing is larger than the extinguisher itself. Otherwise, you've bitten off more than you can chew and the fire is just going to spread as your extinguisher putters out and you squander valuable time you should be using to flee.

If a building or structure does become engulfed, you'll sometimes see cops run in there without any protective gear. Firefighters call this the blue canary effect. If the officers pull someone to safety, they will be lauded as heroes. But more often than not, the police rush in, save no one, and emerge with serious lung damage. I came close to the latter category once when I charged into a burning house in the Ingleside district after a woman screamed out, "My mom is still inside!" I got as far as the front hallway where I was met with stifling darkness and a wall of smoke and heat. I staggered right back out, coughing, gulping in air, hands clutching my knees in the classic tripod position. I had been in the building for around two seconds and I felt like I was already clinging to life. There was no way I was saving anyone inside—I just would have become another body the fire department would need to step over. And, as it turned out, the mother wasn't in the building at all. She was waiting for her family a half block away. Remember when you were a kid and your parents would do a fire drill and have an agreed-on meeting spot so everyone would know where everyone else was? I don't think people do that anymore.

If someone falls or jumps into the water, you, as a uniformed cop, have to do the same kind of clinical risk assessment you'd use during a fire. Do you go in after them? If you make the leap with all your gear on, your ballistic vest and wool uniform will take on water. Unless you're a strong swimmer, you'll sink like someone just lashed an anchor to your boots. But you can't just hand your equipment belt, gun and all, to the homeless guy on the pier and ask him to please watch it for you. You also have to figure the body of water you're about to enter is likely cold with poor visibility and spotted with everything from needles to human waste, as urban waterways are not known for their pristineness. And you know that drowning people, in a frenzied panic, sometimes drown their rescuers.

Belonging to a profession with a motto like Protect and Serve means you can't very well just stand there and watch someone die. Maybe you look for a branch or a pole to extend to the person in the water. Or you cross yourself and take the plunge despite the substantial risk. Whatever the case may be, you want to avoid becoming part of the problem, unless you don't mind a Marine Unit fishing two corpses out of the water instead of one.

If you're about to go hands-on with a suspect, hopefully you've been able to size him up and notice if he's already got his arms apart for counterbalance or is wearing a Regional Tae Kwon Do Ultra-Champion T-shirt. Because if your potential arrestee is a trained fighter, it's liable to be a long day for you. Experienced martial artists can deliver kicks upward of ninety miles an hour. Like a big league fastball. And they aren't kicking you with their foot, which is comparatively soft. They're using their shin, which isn't nearly as forgiving.

Even more dangerous than the karate man is someone who knows what they're doing with a knife. They learn on the streets or in prison that you don't show your opponent the knife, but you make sure he feels it. They deliver a salvo of quick, surgical strikes. And one of the primary but unorthodox targets they choose is the anus, which is potentially a killing strike for two reasons—that area both tends to gush blood and creates a wound that cannot easily be sealed. Because, as a self-defense instructor once pointed out to me, you can't very well put a tourniquet on a guy's ass.

You're a cop out there, not a physician. But you need to show up to work with some game and recognize medical emergencies for what they are, because you'll see plenty. Like shock, which author William Giraldi once pointed out looks like a cross between surprised and sleepy. Or AMS (altered mental state), which often presents itself when a suspect goes from a hundred miles per hour straight down to zero after a struggle. Or delirium tremens (DTs) which stems from sudden alcohol withdrawal and causes chills, fever, and hallucinations, which is why many heavy drinkers need medically planned detox to avoid lapsing into a coma.

You are trained that if someone passes out on you and then comes to with a distinct color change to their face, it's likely a cardiac event. Don't let them stand up. Standing up could kill them.

You know that there are only two situations when you should give food or water in a medical emergency. The first is for diabetics. The second is for heat exhaustion.

If an infant's pulse is less than sixty beats per minute, start CPR. Infant pulses should be over a hundred.

If you think someone is having a stroke, you look for an uneven cast to their face and listen for slurred speech. But the best test is to have them put their arms out straight like the Mummy. If one arm lags, it probably is a stroke.

And finally, there's the woman in labor. Oh boy. If you're in a major metropolitan area, the ambulance will probably get there soon, but until then, it's all you. If mom's water has broken and contractions are less than two minutes apart, that kid is coming and coming soon. You tell mom to breathe and push, just as they do on television. You want to apply gentle pressure to the baby's head to stop it from shooting out. Once the head is through, you're more or less in the clear. You hold the baby under the arms and dry him, especially the head, and keep him warm. If it's been over thirty seconds and he hasn't breathed on his own, start rescue breathing. And praying. After about twenty minutes, the placenta arrives. If the ambulance still hasn't shown by then, it's because the firefighters, sprawled out on love seats playing Fallout 4, don't understand what the word *labor* means.

Pulled over by the police? Do yourself and the officer a favor and don't get out of the car unless asked. It isn't just because stepping out near oncoming traffic can be dangerous. It's because police officers have been murdered by people who have gotten out of their cars during traffic stops. As a cop, you want to contain the occupants of a vehicle. You want to control their movements, so you might instruct them to keep their hands on the steering wheel while you talk to them and not to reach into any purses or bags unless specifically requested.

Now, as a citizen, you may think, wait a second. Hurt a cop? That's madness. Not you. You're a pillar of the community. In fact, you're the head of the Junior League and you're wearing a respectable sweater. And to that we say great, keep up the good work, and you're right, that is a notable sweater. But we just met. You are a complete unknown to us. And murderers don't always look like murderers just like thieves don't always look like the Hamburglar. Plus it's dark out. And it's the hands, and what's in them, that will hurt a cop. Until we run you up for warrants and see for ourselves what kind of record you have, we will be on high guard. So get back in your car please and stay there unless otherwise prompted. Do this and we will get along famously.

It is true that police officers overreact to danger from time to time. In fact, you know what this job does to you? If a citizen offers you lemonade on a hot day, you'll say thanks for the thoughtful gesture, but you won't take it unless it's an unopened bottle or can. Because you'll fear it's been doctored. With spit or urine or a roofie. Maybe Costanza slipped you a mickey. Danger is afoot.

On some basic level, this reaction is insane. I've never heard of a cop poisoned by a beverage given to him by a citizen. It's the kind of thing that happens only in Miss Marple novels. But your guard is always up. This same approach is why many police officers won't shake hands. With anyone. It's a hazard of the profession. You're taught that if your hand is occupied with a handshake, you're compromised. Someone could pull you off balance or go for your gun. So you give 'em a fist bump or a curt nod. Your gun hand remains eternally free.

I stray from this philosophy on occasion, especially with crime victims, witnesses, and even some suspects. Because at times it strikes me as wrong not to shake hands. At times it seems a handshake is exactly what's called for. And I figure the high commercial value of the public seeing a cop shake hands with a citizen is also worth considering.

That being said, every so often I extend my hand and think, "Well this could be a mistake." Want to know why cops are on edge? Perhaps it's the Kill a Cop challenge you just saw on Facebook. Or the phone call from the prison guard who just found your name on the hit list of a street gang during a cell toss. Or the morning lineup where the warrants list includes a man wanted for two counts of armed robbery and one count of felony assault. This suspect, you are told, is a three-strike candidate and has told relatives that he will not return to prison and will shoot any officer he sees. Or the last brawl you were in, where one suspect said to another words that speared you through with dread: "Get his gun." Or people like Lawrence Wallace Jr., who hid a small knife in a bandage and stabbed Mobile police officer Steven Green to death in February of 2012 while Wallace was being transferred to county lockup. Or the afternoon you spent in a hospital room waiting to hear how much of your partner's intestines the surgeon would have to remove after he was gutshot on Halloween night by an auto thief.

Things like that.

It's easy for the public to cry out Stop Overreacting. But when you're a cop and you overreact, maybe you get a citizen complaint. Underreact and maybe you're all kinds of dead.

The danger doesn't boil down to a simple numbers game. According to the U.S. Bureau of Labor Statistics, it's more deadly to be a fisherman or logger than a police officer. In fact, law enforcement routinely fails to make the top ten most dangerous jobs in the U.S. in terms of casualties at work. But those figures can be a bit misleading—deaths in those kinds of professions often stem from heavy equipment accidents and rough weather—as far as I'm aware, people tend not to murder loggers on the job. And these figures don't include injuries, which cops are subject to after knock-down fights with suspects or high-speed vehicle accidents. You don't work with fish. You work with people, who are twitchy and unpredictable and have weapons and don't like jail. So when you're on the street, danger hangs over you like a shroud. You do a job that punishes you and the public when you're careless. So you don't give many folks out there the benefit of the doubt. Like, for instance, that special kind of adult idiot who trains a laser pointer on a cop because he think it's funny—that guy's subsequent arrest report will read something like this: "I observed the red laser dot cross my chest, which caused an immediate concern for my safety because I believed a weapon was being pointed at me. Due to my training and experience, I commonly associate a red laser as the target acquisition tool for a firearm."

These various hazards are why you will never see a squared-away cop with his hands in his pockets on the street, even if it's cold. You keep your hands out and free, preferably above your waist, ready to block or throw a punch. Or return fire. Or munch on an apple fritter or deliver a baby.

But some days you run through the tools on your belt—gun, stick, spray— and realize none of them are quite going to cut it. If time permits, you need to think beyond the use-of-force manual. One of the very best examples of this was a 1997 incident in Seattle where officers faced off with a deranged man wielding a samurai sword on a downtown street. The situation was resolved when the police knocked the man down using water from a high-pressure fire hose, pinned him with a ladder, and took the sword away without serious injury to anyone on scene. The hose-and-ladder approach wasn't found in any department guide book. But it was a thing of beauty, belonging in the pantheon of excellence alongside Kim Novak in *Vertigo*, the throaty blues of the Reverend Gary Davis, and desserts with a graham cracker crust.

In *400 Things Cops Know*, I remarked on how bad of a shot criminals often are. Cops aren't always much better. We react well to danger, but police aren't immune from the stress that accompanies the use of deadly force. No one is. So it's not uncommon for three cops to dump, say, ten rounds each on a suspect at reasonably close range and only hit him a handful of times.

This errant aim comes up much more commonly in vicious dog encounters. Dogs are smaller and quicker targets than people, and when police elect to shoot them, they frequently miss. Prevailing wisdom is that if a dog hasn't attacked you yet, it probably won't, but regardless, you want to get big on a dog you think might be dangerous, which means standing tall and holding your hands out. Shout "Sit" and "Stay" so he knows who the Alpha is. If you turn your back and retreat, that mutt is going to be all over you. Some cops claim that if a dog charges, they'll give it their forearm and will only fire if it latches on; the dog is more of a stationary target then anyway. Others in the business say forget it, give a dog your forearm and those popping sounds you hear will be it vigorously chewing through your tendons. There goes your racquetball game forever.

When it comes to evaluating danger, nothing is more common than the threat complaint. It's a familiar assignment for police officers. Threats come in person, on the phone, online, and via third parties. They usually stem from some relationship gone bad or neighbor trouble or gang-related malarkey. They often take one of three forms:

1. "I'm gonna burn your house down."
2. "I'm gonna blow your house up."
3. "I'm gonna kill you."

People often ask you what you're going to do about this threat. The answer can vary wildly. First you have to identify the threatening party. When I worked in Milwaukee, such a threat would typically amount to a $167 disorderly conduct citation. In California, it falls under the category of Criminal Threats, which is a felony but is usually charged as a misdemeanor. So you can make the arrest, but nobody is going to stay in jail very long. The follow-up question is, What if this person does try to kill me or burn/blow up my house? Well, as my first FTO, Gilbert Gwinn, once pointed out, the police can't arrest someone for what they might do. This isn't *Minority Report*. What you usually tell people is that your department takes thousands of complaints involving threats to burn or blow up homes, and very few of those result in a house actually been burned or exploded. As for death threats, it's mostly just talk. "The death threat is among the threats least likely to be carried out," writes Gavin De Becker, author of *The Gift of Fear*, who studies violent behavior for a living. Most death threats, De Becker points out in his book, are mere intimidations, especially if they contain words like *if, until*, and *unless*.

"But what if this is the time it actually happens?" is the typical follow-up question. To which you respond that if you have unobligated patrol time, you'll make extra passes by their house and keep an eye out. You recommend a restraining order. Other than that, they're on their own. People don't like to hear that. They want, I think, to have the police detailed to their house on a 24/7 protective detail, ever vigilant, with the ability to mobilize in seconds. But nobody gets that treatment, except for the president and maybe Kylie Jenner.

If your partner is driving and you're the passenger and you come upon a wanted vehicle, it's instinctive for your partner to move in and block its driver's side doors with the passenger doors of your squad car. Then your partner will run around the back of both cars to cover the occupants of the suspect vehicle at gunpoint. The upside to this approach is that it seals in the driver, preventing him from fleeing on foot. The downside is that the police car is parked so close to the suspect vehicle that you, the passenger, cannot get out. And if the driver of the car you are six inches away from is armed, you are trapped right in the middle of the kill zone. Given these tight quarters, this seat position is called the Grey Poupon spot, named for the venerable mustard TV commercials that ran in the '80s.

I've been in the Grey Poupon seat before and once nearly tumbled into the lap of the driver of a stolen car while I was trying to crawl out the passenger side window. Awkward.

When the dust had settled, your partner, who has Poupon'ed you, is required to do two things.

—Apologize.

—Buy you coffee and a baked good of your choosing.

When a suspect pulls a gun on you, you will shoot him; cops don't do warning shots. Maybe this particular gunman had no intention of using the gun. Maybe he was going to throw it away or politely hand it over to you for safekeeping. Perhaps his adrenaline was pumping so hard and his brain was so addled from stress that he had no idea what he was doing. Could be he's socially and academically disadvantaged and comes from a fractured home or was just about to do something positive in his life—get a job, marry his pregnant girlfriend, reenroll in school. It's possible the gun isn't loaded, or is just a replica firearm. None of that enters into your considerations. You are willing to take significant risks as a police officer. You do so every time you put on the uniform. But you are not some kind of sacrificial lamb waiting your turn to die. Pull a gun on a cop, whether it's real or fake (the police aren't trained to stick their face near a suspect's gun barrel to examine it for workability), and you have punched your own ticket. You will be shot and you will likely die. Expect that.

Upon receiving a 911 hang-up call from a residence, you and your partner don't automatically call for the command van, burst through the door, and tactically somersault into the living room with your hands in the ready position. There could be an actual emergency, but there could also be quite a few innocuous explanations. Crossed wires on the phone line. Kids horsing around. A plain old misdial. If someone comes to the door, you let them know why you're there. If they say they don't know what the 911 call was all about, you might tell them you don't care if they have a few blunts on the table or overdue DVDs from the library—you're just there to poke your head in all of the rooms to make sure nobody is dead or dying. To make sure all is well. And it often is. But you have to check. And if someone comes to the door and tells you that you can't come in, that's when you give them one fair warning to open up and if they don't heed it, well, just standing around hoping for the best really isn't enough. So you plant your size eleven tactical boot just underneath the doorknob and kick that mother open, order everyone down at gunpoint, and see for yourself what's up. Because you're not going to be the cop who walks away from a house where a parent is bound in a closet, or a child is dying in a bathtub. Doors can be repaired, explanations and apologies can be offered. But that's all later. This is now. And now, you must make sure.

Regular viewers of the evening news might think it's too dangerous to venture onto the streets, which constantly seem to be on the verge of either a pandemic or a hostage situation. You are well versed in the perils of microwaved plastics, swine flu, and ecoterrorists. But you have to get out of the bunker here and there. So don't skip the symphony just because you have to walk through a somewhat dodgy neighborhood to get there. Don't take a pass on the farmers' market because some alarmist said the skateboarders in those parts are particularly aggressive this year. And even though tonight's breaking news story is Man Stabbed on Subway, don't forget that your last thousand subway rides have been entirely without incident. This is your city and you are supposed to play in it—you pay enough in property taxes.

   None of this means you put the blinders on. You cannot eliminate risk. But you can reduce it. Listen to your gut. If your instincts tell you to cross the street because you don't like the looks of the trio of young people coming your way, then cross the street. If the warning bell in your head sounds when the ostensibly nice stranger offers to carry your groceries into your house, don't ignore it. Maybe you fear you'll come across as skittish to the youngsters or rude to the helpful fellow, but that's just common sense at work. And all the while, look up from your smart phone. Know what's going on around you. Don't be a soft target. And live your life. No one is going to live it for you.

If Helen Keller can do it, so can the rest of us.

10

Death and Dying

Moss: Is Carson Wells there?
Chigurh: (Looks over at Wells, who he just shot dead.) Not in the sense that you mean.
—Javier Bardem, *No Country for Old Men*

A fall from a great height makes the human body come apart like a wet paper bag. It's the medical examiner's job, with your help, to locate and recover any and all body parts—every appendage, every scrap of skull and brain. You must do this because it's part of a thorough investigation. Also, it is truly poor form if a pedestrian steps on an eye or ear on the sidewalk the next morning and Major Crimes gets called in and they trace the whole debacle back to you and your inept search.

While a leap off the postcard-friendly Golden Gate Bridge may seem like a serene way to go, and perhaps is for the few seconds the jumper is in the air, it's all pain once you hit the water. When you drop from such a height, around 250 feet, water has no give. It's basically concrete. The impact unfastens your organs. Broken ribs become skewers that can penetrate the heart. And if the blunt force trauma from the fall doesn't kill you, the mighty current often sweeps jumpers miles out to sea. So you're looking at searing agony coupled with an aquatic surge followed by drowning. They don't put that part on any postcard.

If a body has been in the water awhile, it turns bloated and waxy and it's an uphill battle to figure out who the deceased was and how they died. So a police department will send out an all-points bulletin that will read something like this: On 01/04/2014, at approximately 1716 hours, the partially decomposed body of a male was found along the high tide line at the Bay Shore Marina in Newport Beach. An autopsy revealed the body to be that of an adult male, unknown race, approximately 40 to 60 years old, 5'8", 140–150 pounds, with a 34-inch waist. No scars or tattoos were visible on the nondecomposed portion of the body. The male was missing all but two of his upper teeth and had only five bottom teeth, which were in poor condition. The male had alcohol-related liver damage. There was no trauma to the body. Fingerprints are unavailable. The male is estimated to have been in the water for approximately two to four weeks. The male was wearing blue Lee jeans and no underwear, shoes, or socks. Inside the jeans was a silver bracelet with a broken clasp.

And that's all you have to go on. The agencies receiving these bulletins check their Missing Persons files for anyone fitting that description. If there's a possible match, that's where dental records and DNA come in for confirmation. Otherwise, the body stays in the morgue for a few months as a John or Jane Doe and is ultimately disposed of in accordance with state law. In some jurisdictions, this means cremation. In others, a pauper's grave.

Performing chest compressions often doesn't work. In some cases, like when a victim has multiple bullet holes, your compressions make more blood spurt out—you're just pumping him dry. But you do them because there's an outside chance you'll save a life and because they look good to onlookers. It's also good practice. Pumping on the chest plate of an actual human being is worlds apart from CPR on a dummy. You need to know what it's like to hear ribs creak.

But no matter how bad someone looks at a death scene, how obviously and graphically deceased they are, you still call for an ambulance. The ambulance doesn't necessarily have to rush in lights and siren, but it still needs to show. Because as a cop, it's not your place to pronounce people. A doctor does this, often via a remote link with the medics on scene. The only real exception to this rule is if the victim has been reduced to a skeleton or has been decapitated. Then you can skip the ambulance and just call the medical examiner. Because no one has ever bounced back from either of those two conditions.

If you've been in a house with a person who has been dead for some time, you often get the eerie sensation that you're taking some part of him with you when you return home. So you scrub mint-scented shampoo into the roots of your hair when you shower. The uniform you wore that day stays outside in a bag to be dry-cleaned. Your work boots remain on the front porch. You eat your food covered with spices, piquante, anything to try to flush the stench of the dead out of your mouth and chest and skin.

As for the family of the deceased, they are left with a bloated corpse that has taken on bacterial gas and is emitting dark fluid from all orifices. The medical examiner will take the body away if an autopsy is to be done. Otherwise, removal is handled by a private funeral home. But regardless, it is up to the homeowner or property manager to clean what remains after everyone has left. There are private companies that specialize in this kind of cleanup, but most of what they do is what you'd do if you took on the job yourself. Which is spray and mop.

There are two primary ways suicidal people slit their wrists. Some cut horizontally across the wrist. Others cut vertically down the length of the arm. The latter is far more deadly because it severs the radial artery, making blood rush out more rapidly. Both approaches are excruciatingly painful, so much so that many people committed to ending their lives will cut one wrist and then be unable to bring themselves to cut the other. But even if the cut is vertical and deep, there's a chance the victim can be saved if they get to the hospital on time. In fact, one of the main reasons the U.S. homicide rate has dropped steadily over the years is that ER docs are so proficient at patching up the wounded. And they're only getting better. Back in the day, a guy took a bullet or a knife on the street and often died on the table. Just grist for the mill. Now gang-bangers get blasted nine times and live to bang some more with the added street credibility of having survived a shooting.

One homicide detective I talked to had another theory: "They use cheap ammo now," he said. "It's a recession."

One of the deeply ingrained traits of law enforcement is to tell dark jokes at death scenes. I'm talking pitch-black. Obsidian. If three men are murdered while sitting in a vehicle, someone will inevitably ask if this will show up on the Carfax. Deep cut to a victim? "Look at that marbling. That could be sold at Costco." Rookie cop steps in a recently murdered victim's brains at a crime scene? "Hey," a wiseguy will say. "He was just using that like two minutes ago."

What is wrong with us as a profession that we say these things? Maybe quite a bit. But the gallows humor is a way to keep horror at arm's length. You don't do the public any favors by becoming emotionally invested in a death scene. This is a problem to be solved and it's your job to solve it, not be caught up in it.

If you have a murdered body in the street with no ID on him, you'll figure out who he is soon enough via a friend or family member and through fingerprints. But you want to know about this person right out of the gate. Is he local? A working man? A transient? All of this will help guide the investigation. One barometer is checking the dead man's socks. If they're filthy, he's likely on the streets. If they're clean, he's probably got a home.

If you come across a murder victim whose pockets are inside out and is likely missing valuables, you could be looking at a robbery that slid into murder, but you may not assume that the person who killed this man also took his belongings. As a cop, you will look at surveillance video after surveillance video showing a homicide victim sprawled out on the sidewalk or inside a business. And then people will walk by the body or come in the shop and see the obviously dead man. Some run right back out, fumbling with their phones to call 911. Others, seeing an opportunity, test the waters a bit. Perhaps there is an opening here for some free shit. I watched one such video where a woman moved in on a dead man in a diner, and in eleven seconds, she had his wallet, watch, phone, and ring, like a piranha stripping meat from the bone.

Such light fingers at homicide scenes aren't just limited to those people taking advantage of the dead. I recall being at a double homicide scene in San Francisco's Bayview neighborhood where the defibrillator from an ambulance was stolen right out from under the medics while they tried to save the victims' lives. I'd like to think the thief is still out there somewhere, a roving Good Samaritan, properly applying the defibrillator to save the lives of people in cardiac distress, but it was probably sold that night at the corner for fifteen bucks.

A man is murdered in the city and the victim's family demands to know why there haven't been any arrests. You understand they're in pain. You'd crave answers too if you were in their place. But answers will be elusive in this matter because this man was shot late at night in a dirty alley. There's no ballistic evidence, because the bullets in the victim's body are too fragmented to test and no casings were found at the scene because the shooter either picked them up or used a revolver. No video surveillance. No witnesses. No fingerprints. No hairs, fibers, or DNA. The victim had no enemies, or perhaps everyone was his enemy. Maybe it was a robbery gone wrong or he was an unintended target. Homicide will still work every angle of the case and any patrolman worth his salt whose sector this particular shooting occurred in will own it and hit the streets to see what they can find. But say this killer acted alone and is especially taciturn. And he's from way out of town. How would you ever solve this crime unless the suspect decided to turn himself in just for kicks? The victim might as well have been killed on an outer ring of Saturn.

In movies and on television, cops will at times consult psychics to help solve such arduous murders, some swami types who draw on astrology and tarot cards and claim their gift is to sense the killer's life force because, you see, it vibrates at a level that differs from that of the rest of us. The mentalists will profess to have a vision of the murder: "I see a body in a lake." Well, it's going to be either there or on land so you had a 50 percent shot at that one. But it's all hokum to drum up business and they're frauds, every last one. In real life, the only reason some homicide detectives might talk to psychics is that they haven't had a good laugh in a while.

Because the psychics don't come through, you'll see signs advertising rewards for information leading to the arrest of homicide suspects. They usually feature a picture of the deceased, often in their Sunday best or wearing a cap and gown on graduation day. The reward amounts vary but typically range from $1,000 to $75,000—the more heinous and high profile the murder, the higher the reward. Where does this money come from? It can be a patchwork affair. The local Crime Stoppers agency, a nonprofit funded by donations, will put up a few thousand. The family of the victim might contribute, often raising money online. If the victim worked for a large company, the business itself may post an award. The city and state will also pitch in, using revenues from police auctions often slated for such rewards. And sometimes the feds will get involved—ATF, FBI, U.S. Marshals—even for nonfederal cases, although law enforcement may wait until the case has been cold for at least a year before releasing any funds.

Some cold math can be involved here. Justice for this particular human life is worth $10,000. That other one? More like $50,000. Perhaps this is why some jurisdictions, like Philadelphia, offer a set $20,000 reward for information on each and every homicide, whether the victim is Lenny the Dope Fiend or Sebastian the Paragon of Civic Integrity.

Many such rewards, even the sizable ones, go unclaimed. Maybe no one knows who did it. But more likely, witnesses fear the cost of providing information and then having to live in fear of violent retaliation from the suspect's people. Police departments can take measures to protect witnesses by making them confidential informants and sealing search warrants. But while the reward money may be guaranteed, anonymity is not. And municipal witness relocation programs are limited, even in big cities. Even if a witness decides to testify and then be relocated, what kind of life will you have? Sure, there's an extra sixty grand in your bank account, but you have to spend it all in Blowpatch, South Dakota, where you've moved under an assumed name to avoid being murdered yourself. You have a studio apartment, no friends, and a part-time job at a carpet store. Plus you still live in a state of constant dread. Was it all worth it?

Murders place a tremendous strain on police departments because of the sheer amount of resources required to properly investigate the case. A single homicide can take up the entire shift of every cop in the district. When homicides are up in your sector, you feel it in a visceral way. Once the scene is secure, the real work begins, or as former Glasgow detective John Carnochan once said, "The clever stuff gets done." Blood spatters are measured, rough sketches of the scene are drawn, evidence is collected in coin envelopes and vials and cardboard boxes. Investigators write down the temperature outside, the color of the victim's clothes, the way he was sitting in a chair, all the details that might seem indiscriminate to a layman. Anyone that might know something is interviewed. And reinterviewed, because maybe something was overlooked the first time. The postal carrier. The victim's coach. The Meals on Wheels deliveryman. Homicide detectives hear street whispers about killings and have to figure out if someone actually witnessed the killing or heard about it secondhand, or if it's just loose murder talk that someone plucked out of the air and adopted as their own. If investigators find a baseball cap at a scene that doesn't look like the victim's, they'll send out an email blast to all officers in all counties, even if the hat isn't all that distinctive, even if the evidence in this case is so thin you can hardly see it. Maybe someone saw that hat on someone. Maybe it will lead to a witness. Maybe it will lead to the killer. Maybe. If all you have is a long shot, that's what you go with.

Diligent homicide investigators often return to the scene of the crime to take a second look. A third look. A fourth. Detectives hope to be the recipient of a lucky break or engineer their own lucky break.

Working with the victim's family in a homicide is probably one of the most enervating parts of the job, and a homicide detective ends up managing them as much as the case. Some are needy and demanding, the most human of responses to having a loved one murdered. Others lie about the victim's past. Some of them develop a friendship, for lack of a better word, with the investigator over the months and years. One thoughtful homicide investigator I know calls the family on the anniversary of a victim's death. He lets them vent. It goes a long way. He doesn't tell them he's going to catch the killers, because that's giving them false hope. He only promises he will work as hard as he can to solve the case.

There is no one case file on a homicide. It's files, plural. Binder upon binder, pages and pages that show here's what we did and here's where it got us and here's what we plan to do next. It's a project that never goes away. Not every cop is built to carry that kind of weight. With that in mind, I once asked a Homicide investigator if there were any perks to working the unit.

"Well," he mused, "I never have to interview another victim again."

If the trail leads nowhere, a cold case unit may pick up the investigation at some point. Cold case units are typically only for homicide and sexual assaults, owing to the statute of limitations, which varies state by state. There is no statute of limitations on murder, but Wisconsin, for example, has up to six years to prosecute a general felony. California has three years.

DNA evidence is the primary path toward solving an aging murder. But other cases become unfurled because people like to talk. And many of them aren't used to or good at keeping secrets. They also aren't used to people closely listening to them when they talk, so when given a chance, they tend to let it all out whether they want to or not. If you are sociable enough, pick your spot, and the stars are aligned, you can get someone to tell you just about anything. Time cuts both ways here. It works against you because people's memories fade and the proverbial trail has grown over. It works for you because as the years pass, relationships change. Marriages unravel. Friendships sour. Allegiances shift. Kiki knows her man was the shooter but didn't say so in order to protect him but now that same man is stepping out with her best friend, so fuck it, whaddya want to know? Phillip was sworn to secrecy about the rape and murder he saw right in front of him, but now he's in jail on something else looking at ten to fifteen years and he knows he won't last doing that kind of time. So he's taking another look at your business card.

One thing about trying to erase the past is that there's always someone out there who remembers.

The investigation of homicides also illustrates how crucial it is to be decent and civil to people whenever possible. Maybe some lady on the corner knows who murdered Chuckie at S. Halsted and W. 77th last night and is thinking about sharing this information with the police. Problem is, her last police contact was some uniform stopping her for loitering and calling her a scabby bitch. She remembers that, and will act accordingly. My former partner Rolf Mueller used to give even the gamiest hooker tissues when they got teary. He treated them with quiet deference, like gentle ladies of a bygone era. And they would tell him things. A lot of smart police work comes down to being professional. To simple human decency. Even putting decency to the side and looking at it clinically, there's still high value in treating people right. Like the old CIA saying, everyone is a potential ally or asset.

Periodically, you'll have a guy come into the district station and confess to a homicide. A handful of these confessions are legit, an unburdening of conscience or the weary act of a person worn out from being on the run. As they say, not getting caught isn't the same as being free. But there's something about death that draws in the mentally ill, and such walk-in confessions are typically complete delusion, the ramblings of a diseased mind. There are many stories in the city and only some of them are true. But you have to sit down and listen to the confessor on the remote chance that he's for real. One fellow showed up at my workplace to somberly report to me that he'd killed a man. He presented fairly well at first. Seemed sane and coherent. He reported how he set the victim up, shot him, and dumped him in the bay. So he got handcuffed and led to a cell while I ran up the alleged victim's name. He was dead all right. But of natural causes and on dry land. I came into the cell and showed the man a mug shot photo of the deceased. He nodded that I had the right guy. So I told him the good news. That he hadn't in fact murdered this man. He seemed a little put out. I asked him if he had any mental health problems and he replied quietly that he was paranoid schizophrenic. I asked him why he thought he had killed this man. He told me he wasn't quite sure. I let him know he was free to leave. He seemed even more disappointed. When an officer leaned in to take the cuffs off and show him the exit, he promptly punched the cop right in the face. This man was going to jail for something, and if he couldn't get murder, he'd take assault.

We ended up obliging him.

Determining the motive for a homicide is fine and all, and juries seem to like it, but it isn't always a crucial part of the case. Legally, the prosecution just has to show Person A willfully and maliciously caused the death of Person B. Not why. The "why" is just a nice bonus. Like when you're at a restaurant and you get an after-dinner mint with the check. As Al Pacino's homicide detective explains to a murder suspect in the film *Insomnia*, "You're my job. You're what I'm paid to do. You're about as mysterious to me as a blocked toilet is to a fucking plumber. Reasons for doing what you did? Who gives a fuck?"

11

The Law

Teenager: Are you going to take me to jail for car theft?
Fletch: Why, did you steal the car?
Teenager: I sure did.
Fletch: Well, I'm not even sure that's a crime anymore. There have been a lot of changes in the law.
—Chevy Chase, *Fletch*

I'm told the justice system in other jurisdictions moves with more alacrity, but in the two cities I've policed, your subpoena says show up in court at nine but the judge doesn't even sit down until closer to ten. Maybe she's got a putting green back there in chambers. Even after the judge materializes, the court day trudges along. You wait as cases other than your own are called and then disposed of. It's a long, dull slog with few theatrics or laughs. You hear a lot of lawyers start sentences off with "If it pleases the court." You endure droning on about legal fees—thirty dollars for the security fee, fifty bucks for a Needs Assessment. You watch a glum, steady procession of prisoners who look like Dreamsicles in their county jail orange come up to the podium, nod that they understand whatever the judge or their lawyer is saying, and then trudge out of the courtroom. That's why you perk right up when you see a defendant representing him or herself for a legal proceeding, because here, now, is vast, almost unlimited potential for amusing courtroom antics. A coworker told me of a case he was on where the defendant, a diehard member of the Aryan Brotherhood, decided to go at it alone without counsel. Then this white supremacist found out his judge's name was Silverman and promptly showed up to his next court appearance wearing a yarmulke. *Judge me, if you must, your honor, but know that I am one of you.*

Some cases never seem to end. They feature pretrial conferences. Hearings on the admissibility of evidence. Requests by the defense to examine the disciplinary records of the officers involved to look for any sustained complaints that could affect police impartiality. Motions to suppress. Motions to continue. The defense, and sometimes the prosecution, keep shuffling, postponing, drawing things out. The accused has the right to vigorous representation to be sure, and it shouldn't be rushed. But if you are of a cynical bent, you might suspect the defense is hoping these extensive delays will cause the victim and/or a key witness to slowly lose interest in the case. Or they'll move out of state. Or be hit by a commuter train. And there are sitting judges who will allow this type of legal farce to continue, which is why I once found myself on the witness stand in 2015 testifying in an attempted homicide case from three years ago, even though the suspect was arrested the same night of the incident. Three years. It was long enough ago to make me nostalgic. Yep, 2012 was good to me. I was working Street Crimes then, and my partner and I were arresting grimy felons by the handful. The Lumineers were on the radio and the Milwaukee Brewers were burning up the NL Central. Ah, sweet 2012.

When you do make it to the witness stand, you will be asked a barrage of questions, and every now and again, you won't quite be sure of the answer, especially if the incident took place a ways back. The defense will ask how many of your fellow officers were in the suspect's house with you that night. How long did it take you to find the body? What was the temperature outside? For these types of questions, it is okay to estimate. But you may not guess. Guessing has no place in a courtroom. Guessing is essentially filling in the blanks in your memory and is the close cousin of embellishing. And if you embellish on the stand, that will cost you. But not much; just your courtroom credibility forever.

Folks will ask me if they should bother going to court to fight a traffic ticket. I tell them it's worth a shot. Not because they didn't commit the violation, because they usually did in exactly the manner described on the citation. No, it's because sometimes the issuing officer doesn't show for the court date. Maybe he forgot about the subpoena, or worked a double shift the night before, or is, frankly, hung over. Or perhaps he doesn't keep good notes and has no clear recollection of the circumstances under which he pulled over Doug LeFlure of 123 Oak Grove Drive, Chico, California, on 04/12/2018 driving a teal Toyota Yaris in the unit block of Folsom Street. Which means when Doug LeFlure comes to court and the officer doesn't show or has submitted a declaration stating he doesn't remember the facts of the traffic stop, LeFlure is given an official slip of paper dismissing the case outright. LeFlure fought the law and LeFlure won.

LeFlure showers regularly, but you get some mangy characters coming to court. Some of them are wearing hats. Hats are forbidden in court so any bailiff paying attention will tell the person to take it off. But you don't want him to take it off. You want that hat to stay firmly in place. In fact, you'd love it if he took out another hat and put it on top of the first hat. Reason being, you've taken a hard look at this guy and you know the hat is the only thing protecting the courtroom from the lice and the bedbugs.

If you want to do this job right, you need a solid working knowledge of the laws of the land. Problem is, there's a slew of laws with exceptions and shades to them. Moreover, every year, the penal code is amended and enlarged. Police powers are expanded in some ways, diminished in others. Not long ago, a smart, competent sergeant I worked with mistakenly advised an officer to search a car incident to arrest, a search that the *Arizona v. Gant* case stopped the police from doing three years prior. I'm no exception—when a new patrolman discussed a robbery arrest with me the other week, I told him to throw a burglary charge on the suspect, as he had no money or means of payment and thus we could show he had entered the store with the intent to steal. The cop looked uncertain. New kids, I thought. Gotta spell everything out for them, lead them by the hand. When he left the office, I recalled that with the advent of California's Prop 47, you can't automatically charge commercial burglary anymore unless the value of the theft is over $950. No wonder the officer looked confused. He was just too polite to correct me.

Because you must wade through this legal swampland, sometimes you find yourself asking a reasonable question vital to the foundation of your criminal case, and not one of your coworkers knows the answer. Or you get three different answers from intelligent sources, each of whom seems eminently confident in their response. So you take the same question to the DA's office and they don't do much better. How can this be? How can no one know this? Someone must know. But where is that person and how do I access them? These are trained professionals with degrees and courtroom experience. The Supreme Court can't even agree on most things and they are steeped in jurisprudence. If the Robes can't pull it off, what chance is there for the rest of us?

The presiding judge is supposed to be a keen expert on the law. The Master of Motions. The Count of (Habeas) Corpus. And many of them are sharp, focused, and fair. Many, not all. I once took a Ramey warrant to the duty judge, and after some hemming and hawing, she admitted to me she had no idea what a Ramey warrant was, which is a little like an NBA power forward not knowing what "the paint" refers to on the basketball court. Another judge confidently signed my search warrant on the line where I was supposed to sign. I was in court once where a judge seemed to have considerable difficulty understanding the difference between brandishing a weapon and actually using that weapon to assault someone, a distinction most sixth graders with at least a B average can follow.

But these folks still have a grave manner and a framed degree in their office from a renowned legal institution that deems them a juris doctor in flowing script. As you might imagine, this can invite some cockiness. A bit of ego. Judges will throw their weight around just because they can. I once watched a DA tell the judge, "Your honor, I'd like to just take a moment to sort out some victim issues."

"No," the judge snapped. "Call your first witness."

It's not just the judges. We're also talking some prosecutors with haughty airs. Detectives decked out in pinstripe suits who don't even try to hide their disdain for everyone who isn't them. And defense attorneys, oh the defense attorneys. "I cannot make that court date, your honor," I heard a defense lawyer intone, stretching each word out for maximum effect, "for I will be attending a homicide seminar." He could have just left it at seminar, without the modifier, but he wanted to sound like hot shit.

Come to any courtroom in the United States and you'll get your fill of legal bluster from the defense. You'll have a case where the evidence against the suspect is damning. He did the crime in front of multiple witnesses and an HD video surveillance camera. He still has the proverbial smoking gun on him when arrested. Then he gives a full confession. And you wonder how the defense is going to spin this one. There's always the ever-faithful "This is a witch hunt" declaration. But sometime it's just this from his lawyer: "Mr. Radner is very concerned about these allegations, and he is looking forward to his day in court when more of the facts will come out. For now, he just wants to get back to his family." I'd be concerned too if I were Radner. In San Francisco, a man was arrested in 2015 for attempted murder during a drive-by shooting. His lawyer's take? "My client could not be more shocked and saddened that what began as a simple car ride turned into these charges." Turned into. Sort of like how nice weather can turn foul. Not his client's fault, you see? Hey, nobody can control the weather. And if the defendant is convicted, you get more legal puffery prior to sentencing. "My client has already paid a heavy price for his errors in judgment," the lawyer will proclaim, as if to suggest any formal penalties from the court at this point would just be plain mean.

Ask most cops what they think of defense lawyers, and they'll grimace and give an answer suggesting they see them in about the same light as gonorrhea. But it's the job of the defense to represent their clients to the best of their ability and, if the case goes to trial, to generate reasonable doubt in the minds of a judge and/or jury. To make the prosecution prove their case. We have an adversarial criminal justice system in this nation, and you need both sides scrapping with each other to truly have adversity. If you will allow me a personal note, my cousin Victor is an excellent defense attorney. He's also a profoundly good person who is active in his church, bikes against MS, and believes in law and order as much as I do. That "profoundly good person" and "defense attorney" can go together so easily may be surprising to some, both in and out of law enforcement. Defense lawyers also have laudable insight into the human condition, like the veteran attorney who told me of his affinity for strippers as clients. "They're always getting into trouble," he said, "and they always have money."

What can give defense lawyers a bad name are some of the tactics they employ in the courtroom, many of which reek of desperation, which, as Mr. Homer Simpson once noted, is a stinky cologne. They're looking for something, anything, to put their client in a more favorable light. That's why you'll have the defendant's attorney ask you if you saw his client stab anyone and when you say no, because you hadn't yet arrived on scene when the stabbing happened, the attorney will look triumphant. Ah hah! Sure, three other witnesses already testified they saw the stabbing, but this officer here, he saw no such thing! Points to the defense! This approach is akin in spirit to 2012 presidential candidate Herman Cain's response to reports that he sexually harassed women, two of whom later received cash settlements: "For every one person that comes forward with a false accusation, there are probably thousands who will say that none of that sort of activity ever came from Herman Cain." Way to show 'em, Herm.

Another practiced defense move is for the lawyer to put his or her hand on the defendant's shoulder in court. Sometimes the lawyer will give the shoulder a simple clap. Sometimes the lawyerly hand lingers and turns into a tender squeeze or even a brief nurturing rub as if to indicate to the judge and the jury and to all assembled here that this man, although accused of a grave offense, is worthy of affection, entitled to respect and love. Is he so different from us? "Christmas, why don't you just make out with him already," a cop next to me in court once muttered during such a blatant show of affection.

Prosecutors, of course, are not afforded any countermeasure to the defense's show of affinity. The DA may not, for instance, recoil in mock horror as soon as the defendant walks into court.

The best defense attorneys are cagey and make you work for it, which is as it should be. Say you stop a guy and he starts sweating and fidgeting, wiping his brow, and stammering when he talks. Some cops will put in their report that this man appeared nervous, especially if the encounter leads to an arrest. This is because nervousness implies guilt and knowledge of, say, the contraband later found in his car or on his person. But a defense attorney who is paying attention will jump on that. How do you know his client was nervous? That's a subjective observation. Maybe this man always looks like that. Perhaps he is just a sweaty, flushed-face kind of guy. Police reports are to contain facts and expert opinions, not lay opinions. Calling someone nervous isn't an empirical observation. It's a biased observation by someone, namely the arresting officer, who has skin in the game.

There is, however, no problem with noting the suspect's heavy perspiration, halting speech, and shaking hands without officially deeming it nervousness. Let the judge/jury make that connection. Or you can simply ask the guy if he's nervous. One time I did this at a traffic stop with a particularly shaky fellow and the guy replied he sure was nervous. I asked why and he said because of all the dope in his car.

Sometimes a crime victim will retain a defense lawyer. Sometimes he needs one, especially if he's on the cusp of evolving into a suspect. But other times a victim will hire a lawyer because, well, I don't know why. I had one guy who was the victim of a brutal, unprovoked street assault. He got knocked out, and when he woke, he was down a few teeth. The drunk suspect was arrested on scene. The victim had no criminal record, and surveillance video from a nearby bar showed there wasn't even a hint of malfeasance on his part. When I attempted to interview him, he hemmed and hawed and then asked for a lawyer. Sure, I said, generally mystified, but you understand that you're the victim, right? The DA is your lawyer. He'll explain things to you. He'll appear in court on your behalf. Lawyerly stuff like that. And it's all free. The victim wasn't sold. He later explained to me he genuinely thought this situation required a lawyer because nothing like this street assault had ever happened to him before. I found this comforting. Despite the stack of violent felonies on my desk, maybe people weren't getting their teeth knocked in as much as I thought they were.

Most of your cases end up in either municipal court, which handles traffic tickets and infractions, or superior court, which processes state misdemeanors and felonies. But now and again, you'll get a federal case, often a gun crime where the suspect is a repeat violent offender. You'd love it if all gun cases went federal because that's the court where they really lower the boom—the last one I had, the guy got sentenced to 15 to 20. Federal court is also where prosecutors will actually discuss the case with you ahead of time and prep you for the kinds of questions they'll ask you on the stand, as opposed to state court where the assistant DAs shoulder a crushing workload, and show up to court with a stack of files, few of which they've really had time to look at, and most of which they may have just inherited from some other equally harried prosecutor. "My breakfast this morning was instant coffee and Cheetos," an ADA once confessed to me before completely winging a preliminary hearing. In federal court, you walk down burnished halls where one has the sense that people are behind closed doors quaffing Earl Grey infused with just a whisper of bergamot orange. The lawyers wear ties suggestive of the intersection between power and accountability. The bathrooms are immaculate. All the elevators work. Whereas in San Francisco's Hall of Justice at 850 Bryant Street, one elevator is nearly always down and the other one smells periodically of piss. But other than those things, what's the difference between the state and the feds? As one sergeant explained to me, "Federal court is just like superior court except everyone takes themselves a lot more seriously."

People will sue the city for reasons ranging from frivolous to serious. The City Attorney's office will often settle with the plaintiff, even if the suit is entirely without merit, in order to spare the cost of a lengthy trial. It's not always about what's right. It's about what's financially prudent. That's why a murderer who flees the police and is subsequently bitten by a K-9 might receive a check for five grand. Was the bite unwarranted? No. It was the most warranted dog bite in the history of dog bites. But city lawyers know that if a civil jury sees a photo of that flayed-open skin, it might shock them into a higher judgment. Hence the check for 5K. Here you go, sir. This is your reward for not obeying the clear instructions you were given by the dog handler.

There's a philosophy among some staff in the City Attorney's Office that the police should be wary of apologizing for anything. An apology speaks to guilt and culpability, which will color any pending litigation against the city. But sometimes, as a cop, you're going to bungle it. Because you are an imperfect person doing a challenging job. So you apologize anyway. Because you were wrong. Because human decency calls for it. The City Attorney didn't misread one digit on a license plate and hold all the terrified occupants of a car at gunpoint because he thought it was the kidnapping vehicle from the morning's crime briefing. You did that. So you own it.

The ACLU is an organization dedicated to defending people's individual rights and liberties against governmental overreach and abuse, a laudable goal. They took on the 2017 White House for a hasty and ill-conceived executive order on immigration, which I admire. They are also dead wrong on some things, chief among them their protest against gang injunctions. Freedom of assembly is a fine thing, but it has limits—otherwise there'd be no such thing as a restraining order. Gang injunctions, which prohibit documented gang members from associating with each other within a defined geographic area, fall into a similar camp. Such injunctions need to be vetted judiciously—you don't want to deem a kid a gang member just because he was seen shooting hoops once with some hard-core bangers, and there can come a time and a place when you can remove some members from the list. But I have seen the positive, even transformative effects such court orders have had on inner-city blocks. The loudest critics of gang injunctions often seem to be people who have never spent any meaningful time in the kinds of communities that gangs torment with everything from drug dealing to drive-bys. They often seem to be people who want to say how things should go in neighborhoods they never have to enter. Easy to fight for the unfettered movement of the 18th Street Crips from your safe, lofty perch miles away on 100th Street. I would recommend that all ACLU adherents imbed themselves deeply in gangland territory.

Actually live there for a spell. Give it just six months, which should be long enough for abstract notions of justice and constitutionalism to turn concrete. Experience this the way the gang members' neighbors do. Feel it on a daily basis, this life under siege. I would suggest earplugs for the nightly gunshots, a throwaway wallet for the inevitable street robbery, and a sound home security system. After six months, if the ACLU aficionado remains convinced gang injunctions should be done away with, his position will still be wrong but at least he'll have earned it.

When you're assigned to patrol, you tend not to deal with search warrants much, as they don't typically fall under your area of responsibility. You know detectives and investigators are out there somewhere writing them, and if you're new to the job, you may think that putting together a search warrant affidavit and then getting it signed is some mythical process involving a wizened sage on a mountaintop with a quill pen. But they're actually a pretty routine affair, just like any old police report really, except a few more clerical vagaries and some boilerplate legalese. And they can put a smoking crater in the life of a bad guy.

One of the best things about search warrants is that they're gold plated. The courts presume they are legal and reasonable. The burden of proof shifts over to the defense to prove the warrant is defective. And you know who presides over any effort the defense makes to show the warrant is faulty? The same judge who originally signed it. Unless you're dealing with a judge who has crippling self-doubt and wishes to publicly express in open court among the very people who elected him what a colossal blunder he made in approving that warrant, you're probably good.

Sometimes you try for verbal or written consent to search a suspect's residence to save the time and hassle of getting a warrant. Some cops will say, look buddy, if you don't give me consent, that's fine; I'll just get a warrant and come back here and search the place anyway. Either way, I'm in your house tonight. This may seem like a reasonable approach for the police to take. But you need to mind your word choice. Your goal is consensual entry, but if you tell the person that if he doesn't grant it, you're going to get a warrant and go in anyway, a crafty defense attorney will argue that this negates the consent, which must be freely and voluntarily given. My client was assured by police that a search warrant was a foregone conclusion, the defense attorney will say, and that's the only reason he consented. Instead you want to say you will *seek* a warrant, which doesn't imply the warrant will automatically be granted. It's a bit of a semantical dance, but there's a fair amount of that in police work.

Sometimes you don't have a warrant, but you still want to get into a house to follow up on some leads and perhaps make some arrests. But in the absence of any exigent circumstances, you gotta play it straight. No tricks. You may not go to the door and say you're there on a report of a gas leak. Or looking for an abducted child. Or show up in plainclothes and pretend to be a deliveryman and then whip out your badge once you've crossed the threshold. The U.S. Supreme Court said it best in *Bumper v. North Carolina*: "Where there is coercion there cannot be consent."

As a police officer, you are to be an objective fact finder. You aren't for the victim or the suspect. You aren't against him. That's why it's your legal duty to include exculpatory evidence in your reports, exculpatory being a big fancy word for evidence that favors the defendant's case and could potentially exonerate him.

In reality, human nature being what it is, it doesn't quite work out that way. If you have a credible victim who is injured and afraid and you have a parolee suspect with eighty prior felony arrests with the shakiest of alibis, you're going to root for the victim and try to clothesline the parolee. But you still have to include any exculpatory evidence. Here are some examples, all from cases I've worked:

—The victim claims she bit the suspect hard on the hand in self-defense during the assault, but the suspect has no such injuries on him when arrested that same day.

—A witness was highly intoxicated during the offense. He was so fall-down drunk, if you cut him, Pabst would leak out. Such people make both awful houseguests and witnesses, and everything they say has to be closely examined.

—The victim lied about his name, perhaps to conceal his felony warrant.

—A key witness wasn't wearing her glasses when the incident went down, and without them, she sees like Mr. Magoo.

—The victim was a prostitute who was stiffed on her payment. Hell hath no fury . . .

Laws are a funny business. At the time I left the Milwaukee Police Department, the theft of any domestic animal was a felony. On the other hand, $2,500 was the threshold for felony theft. So if you stole $2,499.99

from a victim, you'd be looking at a paltry misdemeanor, even though for many people in poor neighborhoods, that amount of money would be triple their life savings. But get convicted of pilfering Lucky, the anemic cat with the bad leg someone got for free at the shelter, and you'd be looking at hard time.

You also still have laws on the books that are lingering vestiges of a time gone by, when kids bought penny candy and rode bicycles with playing cards in the spokes. Laws governing how balloons are filled. Regulations on fluoroscopic shoe machines. Adultery is still a crime in many states. In Wisconsin, it's a felony. This caused a minor stir in 2000 when then-married Milwaukee mayor John Norquist publicly admitted to an affair with a staff member, begging the question, is anyone going to be taking hizzoner into custody? The answer turned out to be nope. Perhaps the thinking was, if the police arrested everyone who committed adultery, there would be no one left to run the local, state, or federal government. And I assure you, half the police department would be behind bars.

As a street cop, you will become wearily familiar with hearing the suspects you arrest on warrants swear they were going to turn themselves in tomorrow. Or they'll insist they were actually on their way to take care of the warrant when you stopped them coming out of the club with a mixed drink in hand. Both bright, shining lies of course, but what does hold true is that many of these offenders don't think they should be arrested on the warrant. They think they deserve a second chance. But suspects with warrants already had three chances before they even cross paths with you. Their first opportunity was to not break the law in the first place. Their second chance was to appear in court when they were supposed to and face the music. Their third chance was to take care of the warrant by turning themselves in or showing up in Intake Court to get put back on calendar. But they failed on all three counts. Now they want a fourth chance with you. As I sometimes ask people, how many chances do you think you should get? Six? Eleven? Forty? Maybe we should abolish laws altogether just for you, good sir.

What's more, you'll encounter suspects who are on their third bench warrant for failing to appear on the same case. Their fifth. Their eighth. And at that point, you stop being disgusted with the suspect, because he's a criminal and that's what he does, and you refocus your ire on the court system that keeps letting this man out with yet another future court date rather than keeping him locked up or at least tied to reasonable bail until the case is resolved. This fellow here has firmly established he isn't going to show up for his case unless he is brought there in handcuffs. He could not make this more clear if he hired a skywriter to stencil it in the clouds. He's telling the court through his clear and definable actions that he doesn't respect the police or the judge or the whole damn system. Is anyone listening to this man?

This same legal system does not allow for the police to go out of state to pick up certain violators, especially those who have committed only misdemeanors. Even some felony warrants are limited to surrounding states. So you'll run a guy up and he comes back with a drunk driving warrant down south, but there's no extradition. You gotta let him go. It seems unfair that you can escape justice as easily as hoping on a Greyhound, but municipalities don't have the resources to extradite on every misdemeanor or nonviolent felony. Justice ends at the border.

After you make an arrest and work up the case, you lay out all your evidence for the DA. You're impressed by it and, frankly, you're impressed by you. But sometimes she looks at what you've assembled with only mild interest. Like she's examining a novelty car mat. Because while your standard for arrest is probable cause, which means, more or less, that the suspect probably committed the crime, her standard for charging the case is being able to prove it beyond a reasonable doubt to twelve jurors. Meeting that threshold isn't easy, especially in a liberal stronghold like San Francisco where some jurors give off the impression that not only are they more than capable of finding reasonable doubt in the most unlikely of places but that they desperately want to press violent criminals to their nurturing bosom and tell them it wasn't their fault. All of this means it's not really about what happened; it's about what the prosecution can prove. He said/she said cases without additional corroboration go nowhere.

Even if your case has legs, the DA might still take a pass. If every case that could be charged was charged, the courts would be more preposterously overburdened than they already are. There are several official dispositions that cover this Let's Punt approach, such as Violation Does Not Justify Expense. Or Discharged for Future Bundling. Or the generic catchall that drives cops nuts—Dismissed in the Interests of Justice. It's all shorthand for Nobody Feels Like Dealing with This.

And if you do manage to get your case in front of a judge, it can still be routed away from standard criminal court to a diversion program. Like Drug Court. Community Court. Veterans Court. Behavioral Health Court. Now there's something in San Francisco called Young Adult Court. These venues emphasize counseling, community service, and rehab over prison time. All worthwhile endeavors. But the perception among working cops is that such alternatives lack bite, to the point where they are collectively deemed No Consequences court.

It's easy to get disgruntled about the justice system. You come to work and get served with a subpoena for a case that concluded yesterday. Or you show up on a current subpoena and the DA looks surprised to see you. You're here on the Braxton case? That pled out last week. A guy will commit eight armed robberies but only be charged with three. The other five just get read into the court record. When he's sentenced, the sentences run concurrent. So he essentially gets five free armed robberies. Judges put violent defendants on probation and electronic monitoring in lieu of the state pen. In San Francisco, you'll encounter people on double probation for two different crimes. You'll run into guys who are on both probation and parole. You could have sworn you just read an article about prison overcrowding, but it's all enough to make you ask, wait, we still have jails right? Anyone in 'em?

But when you look at how some other countries are doing things, the U.S doesn't come out looking half bad. In 2013, a sixteen-year-old was gang-raped in Kenya, suffering severe injuries, and then tossed into a latrine. The suspects were caught. Their punishment? They had to cut the grass near a police station. On the flip side, they're still stoning folks in Saudi Arabia and flogging them in Singapore.

If you give it some thought, flogging doesn't sound too unreasonable, especially if the defendant is given the choice between flogging and jail. It cuts down on lockup costs and provides a painful but vivid reminder for the suspect to walk the straight and narrow. Do I sound out of touch? Maybe. But I'm not alone—for more, see criminologist Dr. Peter Moskos's book *In Defense of Flogging*.

It is a rare thing indeed to feel like a suspect in your case is getting a raw deal. That he didn't do it and got railroaded by the system. But some defendants are factually innocent, which is often revealed when key witnesses recant their testimony or DNA test results point to someone else entirely.

Maybe a cop screwed something up along the way out of incompetence or malice. Perhaps the victim just plain got the suspect ID wrong or a lab tech botched test results. Some of these suspects are lifelong felons who have committed a multitude of crimes, and the time they spent in prison for the one crime they didn't do may have actually protected society from a host of offenses they would have done if they were free. But be that as it may, the question remains, did this man do this crime? That's how the law works. If he did not, and was wrongfully accused, the proper reaction to this set of circumstances is sorrow. My father, a Protestant minister and theologian, addressed this issue as well as anyone during the 2000 Opening Convocation at Calvin College called "On Truthfulness as a Vocation." "You will grieve for this man," he said, "and for his family, and you will grieve for yourself, because you will see that a decade ago you had fought not for the truth, but for a disastrous falsehood, and now nobody can give back to an innocent man all the years that the locust has eaten."

Amen, Dad.

12

The Kids

Fresh: I have this dream.
Chuckie: Yeah, like what?
Fresh: Nothing. Sometimes I have it, that's all.
—Sean Nelson as a twelve-year-old drug dealer, *Fresh*

Cops don't want to deal with juveniles. I heard of one SF officer who kept seeing an 11-year-old driving his family's car through the neighborhood. "Just park it, man," the cop pleaded, no doubt anticipating the typhoon of police reports, babysitting, and notifications that would accompany a juvenile arrest. The kids, they don't make any sense. One youthful offender I know took off his felony ankle monitor, which automatically triggered a warrant for his arrest. His reasoning? It didn't look right with his shoes.

Best-case scenario, juvenile criminals don't grow up to be adult criminals. Because you've seen that before. Seen the kid who started out snatching purses and, a few years later, graduated to full-on murder. So you put some work into connecting with the kids, to make your relationship with them as positive as it can realistically be. But it's a prematurely weathered crowd, and some of them are so angry and distrustful of authority that they treat your efforts as part of some larger conspiracy, or receive you with an attitude that oscillates between stony nonchalance and outright hostility.

"Why the fuck you even *talking* to me," one teen from a tough block asked in exasperation when I attempted to strike up a conversation about something other than his lengthy arrest record. He was shot dead on the same block a few months later.

For others, you don't even try, because you have to be able to recognize a lost cause. Like the teen rapist with the spiky hair who is always sniffing wood glue—that kid is probably on his own.

But if it looks like there's an opening, sometimes you'll take it. Pick a youngster as your personal project and keep tabs on him. Encourage him. First you need to separate the kid from the pack, so there's no more audience to impress, no more show to put on. What follows varies depending on the officer. My former partner Rolf Mueller arrested a fifteen-year-old once after the boy's struggling single mother called the police because she found drugs in his room. The boy admitted to the possession. He was respectful and doing well in school. In the war on drugs, he didn't quite seem to be the face of the enemy. Rolf wrote him up for the dope, took him home, and wrote out a Code of Conduct for him to follow:

I will abide by my mother's rules.
I will respect myself and others.
I will not hang out with thugs.

Rolf had the boy sign it and gave the signed copy to his mother. A Code of Conduct. It was something only Rolf would have thought to do. Maybe it would take hold.

I've had a standing offer with many teen offenders. If they can go a year without an arrest, I'll buy them lunch. And not fast food either, but a halfway decent place. If they make it to college, I'll pay for their first semester of books. Over the course of my career, I have given out a number of business cards with these pledges and promises written on them. Haven't gotten any calls back yet, which means no one has made it that far, they lost my card, they didn't believe me in the first place, or maybe all three. But I'll keep trying. A lunch or some books isn't going to magically transform someone's life, and if the only thing I've accomplished is to show them the police aren't quite the opposing force they thought they were, maybe that's something. And I probably do it more for me than for them. And my wife likes it too, which counts for a lot, like a better chance of there being blueberry pancakes for breakfast on the weekend.

But one of the reasons my phone isn't ringing is the rotten company these kids keep. The broken school they go to where as long as they aren't fighting, the teacher doesn't care what the hell they do. It's the bleak neighborhood they're mired in. The father they don't know and the mother they wish they didn't. This city is killing them. You want to scoop them all up and plop them down on a ranch in a place where they can work with their hands and learn discipline and fortitude and all those other rustic values that people like me want to impose on people like them.

The kid that Rolf tried to mentor? Some months later, we would see him standing outside a known crack house in the company of some other slouching teens in hooded sweatshirts and baggy pants, a freshly minted gang tattoo on the side of his neck. He had not, in fact, turned his life around. Rolf recognized him and pointed him out to me. I remember there was a catch in his voice.

Doesn't mean you don't hand the next youngster a Code of Conduct. You always work for the future. I keep giving out the cards to kids who are consummate question marks. Maybe they'll always be hustlers. Maybe they'll join a youth choir. There's no way to know. But I'll give them out even if they don't work, even if they don't mean much of anything. Because if I'm gonna go down, I prefer to go down swinging. I was a Big Brother in Milwaukee's Big Brothers Big Sisters program for five years. After I moved to California, my little brother was sent to state prison for reckless homicide. I visited him the last time I was in town. We still write. I still send him food and clothing. You don't give up on people when they're family or close to it. Maybe you're not allowed to.

But at the same time you realize there are no guarantees.

You want to do all you can to avoid arresting a parent in front of their children. No child should have to see that. But sometimes you'll have to. If possible, you let the arrested parent talk to their children for a minute before you lead them away. Let them give assurances that both they and their kiddos are going to be okay. Depending on the timbre of the situation, I've told children that their parent was coming with us because "Your dad is giving us a hand with something." Or I've told them their mother isn't a bad woman, but she just needs some help. I'm not sure that's always the right way to go. But I'm reminded of something my mother once told me. She said that sometimes you have to shield children from the way life is.

Until they're strong enough to face it.

As a patrol cop, you will be called to the maternity ward of a hospital to assist Child Protective Services (CPS) when an infant has tested positive for opiates—usually meth or cocaine. CPS typically places a 72-hour hold on the child pending an assessment because of the substantial risk that the infant could suffer harm if left with the mother. Your department's Special Victims Unit will start a child endangerment investigation, which typically involves a blood draw warrant. You tell the mother she cannot leave with the child. Some give you pushback. Others accept this news with a shrug. Under California law, you are also obligated to tell the parent that a written statement is available explaining her rights in this investigatory process. This statement is available at all public schools, probation offices, and welfare departments. I'm not sure how far an informational brochure goes in fixing something this broken, but the law is the law.

Whether this mother is arrested depends on jurisdictional factors and the best interests of the child; arresting new parents still in their hospital gowns, recovering from recent labor, isn't always the best way to go. And, as I write this, the effects of opiates on newborns are still not well known. *The New England Journal of Medicine* published a study in 1985 that suggested cocaine babies would have birth defects and developmental disorders, which touched off a firestorm of outrage about "crack babies." But it used a small sample (twenty-three women) and has since been widely called into question, especially because it's difficult to separate the specific effects of drugs on babies from the effects of the general poor prenatal care that many addicted birth mothers practice. And prenatal exposure to opiates is nowhere near as potentially damaging as, say, fetal alcohol syndrome. Pediatricians will tell you that many addicts give birth to healthy babies.

But that's still not quite cause for rejoicing. Psychological effects aside, the cold truth here is that you're still looking at a newborn whose mother chose to ingest a corrosive street drug while pregnant. That living environment is just one of the many hurdles the child is going to have to clear if they are to make it in this world. The main goal of child welfare agencies is to preserve the family unit whenever practical, but some families need to be split up, for the good of the child and, further down the line, for the sake of public safety, because damaged kids who remain in damaged homes get older and damage others. Around and around we go.

Back at the station, you write your police report, which will have a vague and antiseptic title like *Aided Case* that in no way reflects the enormity of this situation. What the report should be titled is *Mother Damns Newborn* or *The Police Will Be Seeing a Lot of That Kid Starting in Around Thirteen Years*. And when you get to the place in the report where you are to write the name of the child, you call them Baby Boy or Baby Girl and add the last name of the mother because most of these children haven't been named yet. It makes you ponder how you would have fared in life if you had such a beginning. Would you still be a cop? Or would you be slumped next to a shopping cart of your belongings, a needle deep in your arm? Are drugs still a victimless crime? Not today. So welcome to the world, little one. It's going to be hard for you out there. You're going to have to be stronger than you know. Good night, and good luck.

In an effort to end this chapter on a more upbeat note, here are some Halloween safety tips to keep kids safe during trick-or-treating:

—Stay bright. I read of one mother who suggested telling your child there is a secret order of ninjas who wear only yellow. Use reflective tape and have your kid carry glow sticks or a flashlight.

—Keep costumes short so they don't trip.

—Institute a no running rule. Know that it will be broken frequently.

—Go with your kids until they're at least ten and stay in a familiar neighborhood.

—Check all candy. The razor blade in the apple is an urban myth, but kids under three are at higher risk for choking so remove hard or gummy candy and bars with nuts.

—When my older daughter was three, she dressed as a "policeman girl" for Halloween and called her handcuffs her "handcups." What does that have to do with safety? Nothing. I bring it up because it's empirically adorable.

13

Police Culture

I come from an Irish family in Brooklyn, a few stockbrokers, a smattering of intel-
lectuals, and 40 percent of the New York police force. My uncle the cop used to read
me bedtime stories: "Humpty Dumpty sat on the wall. Humpty Dumpty fell, or
was pushed, from the wall. The perpetrator has not been apprehended. Three male
Hispanics were seen leaving the area."
—Comedian Colin Quinn

Police culture is macho, crude, sometimes childish, and fiercely loyal
and features some of the best jargon you'll ever hear. A hard-bitten
sergeant I had in Milwaukee used to look at any given horrific crime scene
and muse, "Broken toys," a kind of catchall grim sigh in the face of urban
madness. Another cop who was constantly getting in trouble would enter a
room and be greeted with a cheerful "What's up, Conduct Unbecoming!" It
is not at all unusual to hear the regular police use of obscenities in even the
most unnecessary of circumstances, as in "Hey, any of you fuckfaces want
to get coffee?" Most cops also don't mince words. I once asked a coworker
why a certain common gun charge wasn't on the department cheat sheet
for firearm offenses. "Because," he explained patiently, "the person who
drew up that list is a booger-eating moron." Another one of my coworkers,
Lt. Sean Perdomo, a relentless detective who is my go-to guy on questions
ranging from sealing search warrants to managing informants, tells me
on occasion, "Standing closer to me won't make you a better investigator,
Plantinga." I laugh but remain where I am. *Just in case he's wrong.*

If you're a newer cop struggling to keep up with the demands of the
job, and you see an older cop sizing you up as a tailor might, you aren't
imagining things—that's exactly what's going on. He's taking your rough

measurements because he wants to have your uniform for free if you fail Field Training. This will help him continue the proud police tradition of spending his monthly departmental uniform allowance on craft beer and salted meats.

New cops start buying all the extra work accessories they think they need as soon as they get their first paycheck. They'll go to the police supply store and pick up the cool monogrammed duty bag with all the pockets and straps. An oscillating flashlight. The $200 tactical boots. But all the new gear in the warehouse won't compensate for their lack of street miles and their unformed instincts. Police instincts can be taught through training and firsthand experience, or at least honed to a degree. It isn't like bat speed on the baseball diamond where either you have it or you don't. That's important, because rookie cops tend to have lousy instincts. They go to a holdup alarm at a tavern and see that the place is empty except for a man standing behind the bar. Ah, the bartender, they think, and instinctively lower their gun. Gotta be a false alarm. But how do they know that guy is the bartender? Because he's standing behind the bar? Maybe he's standing on top of the real bartender, who he just shot dead during the holdup. Need to make sure first. You learn.

Every station boasts that one cop you want to emulate. He's an unequivocal badass, the kind of guy who will walk through the projects and when one of the locals shouts "Dead man walking," he'll stop, look at the guy and say "Was that for me or for you?" He's aggressive, unflappable, and cunning. He's got a phone full of confidential informants and knows how to cultivate the ones who have just the right amount of wrong in 'em. He exudes grit. He probably smokes. You want him to teach you his ways. He's the one always strolling in a little late to roll call, coffee in hand, but the lieutenant never says anything because he and his partner bring in more gun arrests than the rest of the shift combined. He boasts a sticky memory, and if someone asks him what car a certain suspect drives, he'll tell you the guy used to have that white and red Lexus with the custom rims before he sold it to Arthur Tucker. Now he drives a gray Monte Carlo with a bad exhaust and keeps it parked in front of his girlfriend's house on 22nd and Wells. He's kind in a gruff Han Solo way. He won't step foot in the command van because he's a worker, not a watcher. Out on patrol, he's got the magic eye. He sees the street the way a movie director sees in images. He can recognize a suspect by the back of his head. Spot the hand-to-hand drug sale a block and a half away. Sense when a crook is about to run from him by a subtle shift in body language or demeanor, like the slightest of tremors along a fault line, the micro-observations only a natural cop picks up on. He knows that if you're outside searching for the handgun the bad guy just shot off and discarded, a good pair of night vision goggles will pick up the thermal signature of the recently fired weapon and help the cops find it. He dispenses hard truths to citizens and criminals alike. He's polite when it's called for, but also a student of human violence who knows that good manners don't always carry the day. On the Milwaukee Police Department there were many like him: Al Morales, Jon Osowski, Kim Lastrilla, and Karl Zuberbier. In San Francisco, it's cops like Matt Mason, Kelvin Sanders, Carla Hurley, and Derrick Lew. If you had a squadron of this caliber, you could send them into the most crime-ridden neighborhood, give it a week or two, and then confidently withdraw, all your objectives achieved.

The men and women I've described above are cops. There is a vital distinction to be made between police officer and cop. Police officers take the assignments they are dispatched to, back up their fellow officers, and make the occasional stop of a suspicious person or vehicle. They do what the job requires—nothing less, nothing more. They're competent and steady. Every department has them and every department needs them. But a cop digs deeper. A cop unpeels things. Ask a police officer if he's ever solved a murder and he'll say, "Well, no, but I haven't been sent to one in a while." Ask a cop the same question and he'll think back to the homicide with suspect unknown that occurred in his patrol sector on his off-day. He'll tell you he and his partner returned to work and took it upon themselves to look at the surveillance video up at Major Crimes. Then they hit the streets, asked around, arrested some guys, found someone who knew something, dragged his happy ass over to Homicide, and gave them the lead that broke open the case. You ask a police officer who's the 6'3" cronk with the lazy eye robbing elderly women up and down Leavenworth Street and he doesn't know, but he can quote the union regs on overtime verbatim. You ask a cop that same question and he knows exactly who it is. Where he hangs out. What his street name is. In fact, he's on his way to arrest him right now. *And* he can quote the union regs on overtime. Overtime is sort of important, no matter who you are.

In the law enforcement world, just like any other workforce, promotions are sometimes given to the undeserving. Like the supervisor who finally gets his stripes and now demands the kind of proactive policing and enduring excellence that he himself never once displayed as a line cop. "He got reborn hard" is what his coworkers will say of this mystic transformation.

Or the lieutenant who claims to have an open door policy, but either he's not in his office or he's in there all right but the door is locked and the blinds are drawn. Then the guy goes to a 40-hour Leadership and Effective Executive Communication course and now takes every opportunity to bloviate, turning what should be a 10-minute roll call into a half-an-hour windfest. He is the opposite of coffee and illustrates the principle of physics that writer Joseph Epstein liked to point out—gas expands to fill time.

Or the haughty captain with his sights set on deputy chief who asks you to go to hell and back for him on a weekly basis, but although you have worked at his station for years and have made commendable arrests and show up to work on time with a can-do attitude and a clean, pressed uniform, you are certain he does not know your name and can't be bothered to look down at your name tag to even speak it. To him, you're a piece on the chessboard. You'll still put in the work. Still do all the good things you've been doing. But you're not doing it for him. You're doing it despite him. For he is a dipshit. And you hope, at some level, however deep down it may be, he knows it.

Or the senior deputy, just transferred in from Personnel, who asks for your stats at the end of the shift. You tell him about your arrest, the gangbanger wearing a ballistic vest who had a Tec-9 with an extended mag, and sixty rocks of crack cocaine.

"Okay," he sighs in the tone of voice that suggests you are talking about something worthy but rather obscure, like defending the habitat of sea turtles. "But did you write any parking tickets? Captain's had a lot of community complaints about illegal parking."

These are the kinds of supervisors who move through life lightly, for they are unburdened by genius. The only thing they have to teach you is how important it is not to be like them. But how mad can you get at these people? It isn't their fault. They were promoted past their abilities. You learn not to expect much from them. Like houseplants.

So what does a good police boss look like? You can tell him exactly what you think. He's a student of the game and puts in the effort to keep up on case law and department procedures. He strives to make your job easier but isn't afraid to set the bar a little higher. He throws his weight around only as a last resort. He'll still be the first through the door on occasion. At a hot scene, he knows to plan for the what-ifs. What if the suspect drives right through that plate-glass window? What if he jumps onto the roof of an adjacent building? What if he takes a hostage? A good boss will bring you food and a hot drink at a critical incident where you've been holding the same corner for hours without relief. And he probably doesn't have a picture on his wall that says something like Leadership Is the Capacity to Translate Vision into Reality. He doesn't need crap like that to remind him what the brass should be doing. He just remembers that stuff on his own.

I remember returning to work one New Year's Eve after a long layoff due to back surgery, jumping behind the wheel of the patrol wagon ready to once again ferret out evil, and promptly backing the wagon into the front of the shift lieutenant's personal vehicle. An audible crunch was heard followed by a very bad word that was said by me.

The damage sounded worse than it looked, but I had definitely scraped the front of the lieutenant's ride. I told the lieutenant, a grave but fair man named Wayne Jensen who had been a machine gunner in the Vietnam War and favored a pipe. He came out, looked at his vehicle, looked at me, and was silent. Then he shrugged and said, "The sun will come up tomorrow." He could have written me up for it, but he watched out for his people. He told me to get back out on the street. "But he drives," he told my partner. Sort of a get-back-on-the-horse approach. I thanked him, resumed my position behind the wheel of the wagon, and painstakingly navigated out of the narrow garage like a kid on his first day of driver's ed.

Now that's a good supervisor.

When cops are transferred to a new station, a thinking sergeant will introduce them to the plainclothes team, because it can get confusing out there in the heat of it and it's important to separate the good guys from the bad to avoid friendly fire. What helps is that most plainclothes cops look like cops and wear the standard plainclothes outfit of ball cap, cargo pants, and the hoodie with the home team logo. The criminals know this too, which makes it hard for plainclothes officers to sneak up on people. In fact, in some neighborhoods, if your face is free of oozing sores, everyone will suspect you're the law. So for an actual undercover operation, some plainclothes guys will don costumes. Wigs. Heavy overcoats. They'll push a shopping cart full of cans. It's always Halloween.

There can be some mild to moderate animosity between patrol and plainclothes. The latter affect some swagger. They have their own office and aren't beholden to dispatched calls on the radio and may turn up their nose at the humdrum of taking assignments because they've got bigger things going on. They're all about pistols and kilos. This attitude can rankle uniformed veterans because some of these plainclothes guys just got off Probation a few months ago. Okay, hotshot. When you're booted off the team because you don't know anything and aren't producing and have to trudge back to Patrol, I'll show you what you missed.

Cops tend to be more patriotic than most. They're good about giving up their seats to the elderly on public transit. They're avid hunters and know how to fix boats. Many officers coach youth sports teams and are elders in their church. Few cops are Democrats, what with the Republicans purporting to be the law-and-order party and all. Lots of cops are car guys, and you'll often hear a debate about what kind of vehicle has just been featured in a Crime Bulletin. It's a Ford Escape, someone will say. No, someone else offers, it's a Lincoln MKX, their crossover SUV. The headlights are wider than those of an Escape, you see. And the first guy will nod. Good point.

City hall is not always held in the highest regard among the law enforcement ranks. For instance, if an officer is seriously hurt on the job, the chief of police and probably the mayor will visit you in the hospital. Most cops are okay with the chief coming. But the mayor, now that's another story. In fact some cops explicitly tell their spouses or partners that if they are injured or killed on duty, they don't want the mayor at the hospital or at their funeral service. Especially if your mayor is some handshake phony with a reputation for cocaine use who can't be bothered to learn the names of his police protective detail, opting instead to call them Hey You. A visit from him? Nah. That slickster d-bag can wait in the lobby.

The law enforcement community isn't always so keen on social programs, because the last midnight basketball game, called Peace Hoops, exploded into violence and a cop's nose got busted. And don't get a police officer started on the city-sponsored needle exchange. You'll see plenty of NRA signs on police lockers along with stickers that say "Keep Working. Millions on Welfare Depend on You."

Like most professions, law enforcement battles a culture of mediocrity. Some officers are doing just enough to get by. When the lieutenant tells you in lineup that he wants Patrol to fill out Field Interview cards on all street contacts, you know it's a good idea, but half the time you can't get guys to flush the toilet in the men's locker room even after they've dropped a deuce so you're pretty sure some of those FI cards ain't getting done. Or you're just off FTO, ready to rock the criminal underworld and you find yourself saddled with a partner with a spongy work ethic and permanently affixed with an amiably dull expression reminiscent of how Elvis Presley looked in most of his movies. A look that says Just Filling Space Over Here.

But perhaps what's really going on here is a wariness of specialization. In a large police department, if you show yourself to be only okay at your various job tasks, people will leave you alone. Show a talent or affinity for something, say, electronics, and you will quickly find yourself in charge of the Computer Forensics Division with enough regular work for eight people but a staff of two.

But on the other end of the spectrum are the officers who take on-the-job dedication to extreme levels. They have three different radios playing in the car so they can listen to all district channels, neighboring agencies, the Highway Patrol, and probably Fish & Game in case there's a report of a salmon poacher. They are eminently plugged in. Maybe too plugged in.

"Be advised," you'll hear such an officer say when a suspect description is broadcast on the radio. "That man stole a Ford Yukon in the spring of 2003." Okay. That was thirteen years ago and this current incident has nothing to do with a vehicle but thanks, I guess.

I take no pleasure in saying this, but some cops are thieves. Not many, I don't think, but more than any of us would like. There are locks on officer lockers in police stations for a reason. My tactical boots have been on top of my locker unsecured and unattended for years, but coworkers will tell you the occasional tale of their own boots being snatched right out of their duffel bag. You take an expensive flashlight and drop it at lineup and, the joke goes, it will never hit the floor. Leave a nice pair of sunglasses in the side pocket of a police car overnight and maybe you'll see those glasses again and maybe you won't. Cops write their initials or badge number on their equipment with a permanent marker or an engraver, but it still doesn't always ward off the larcenists. Maybe part of this pilfering is cops punishing cops for making themselves easy victims, as in "You should have been smarter, dum-dum." But that's just a wild guess. The bottom line is I don't understand it and I never will. I've never stolen anything. Not even candy from a store when I was a kid. It never occurred to me. Why would I take that? *It's not mine.* An officer at a station where I once worked stole all the hot dogs designated for an all-shift summer cookout and tossed them over an adjoining fence to later retrieve for himself. He was caught in the act, and one cop spoke for the entire cosmos when he demanded, "What the fuck, Al?"

So if any of you thieving cops are reading this, the rest of the police force has a message for you. Resign already. Resign because you suck and you make us all look bad. And we have enough of that going around as is.

Part of police culture is having a job where you must watch the unwatchable. Internet Crimes Against Children (ICAC) units do this on a daily basis. When working a child pornography case, investigators also have to figure out whether the illegal file was downloaded or showed up accidentally. They need to know how long the file has been there and, if it's a video, how long the suspect watched it for. And in order to build a criminal prosecution, they need to reasonably conclude that the persons featured in the video are actually underage, which is done by anatomic analysis. The whole process can take months, because it often leads to other suspects. Fish in a barrel, anyone in ICAC will tell you of their efforts. And suspects don't just crave the child pornography as an end in itself. They revel in the very idea of doing something so taboo that if they are found out, they'll be ruined. That kind of danger is, for some, the ultimate aphrodisiac.

ICAC investigators take on a burden that many others in law enforcement, including myself, are incapable of bearing. I claim no special religious insight, but I know that everyone with ICAC will be on the express train to heaven, and when they get there, they will be provided with the downy pillow of their choosing. Some departments have a written or unwritten rule that you can be in ICAC for a maximum of only two years, for sanity's sake. The work leaves scars.

There are other hard-driving units from Homicide to Domestic Violence that can lead to early burnout. Just the ingrained weariness of pushing a radio car for decades can make one ponder what work life would be without all the blood and screaming. When you've done your time in the muck, sometimes you want to switch gears. You're tired of having to strip off your uniform in the garage to keep the gore, smashed roaches, and rat turds out of your home. You want to step off the line and try something else. And if that's the case, there is still a place for you on a large urban department. Backgrounds, Admin, Youth Engagement, Academy instructor. You are still contributing to the department's mission, but you are doing so far from the madding crowd. I was reminded of this once when I saw a property clerk salute a lieutenant.

"At ease," the lieutenant said.

"I work Property Control," the officer said. "I've been at ease for six years."

After yet another police incident where the officers acted wrongly and may have even committed a crime, the chief or a department spokesperson will trot out the usual platitudes that this malfeasance represents only a fraction of the department, that it is not a sign of an endemic problem, and that the vast majority of police officers are decent and hardworking and do what's right. They say this because it sounds good but also, more importantly, because it's true. But a week later, you open the paper and read that a press conference has been scheduled to announce federal indictments of officers at your station. A colleague has just been arrested for sexual assault, two more are under investigation for a murky shooting, and yet another was just charged with drug trafficking. It's enough to make you ask, Wait, we're still the good guys, right?

Problem is, the good guys don't get ink. Nobody pays much attention to you as a police officer until you screw up. Like an NFL long snapper. So let me tell you about some folks you'll likely never hear about: the SFPD Bayview Station plainclothes team made up of Sgt. Sean Griffin and Officers Gabriel Alcaraz, David Johnson, Ali Misaghi, Carlos "Moose" Mustafich, Erick Solares, and Eduard Ochoa. Why am I bringing them up? Because in the Bayview District, between January 1, 2014, and October 8, 2014, there were twelve homicides, fifty-one shootings, seventy-nine calls of shots fired where ballistic evidence was discovered, and numerous additional calls of shots fired where no evidence was found. These numbers would be far higher if not for the remarkable efforts of Bayview plainclothes. During that same time frame, these officers seized sixty guns and made forty-seven gun-related arrests, the majority of which were arrests of convicted felons and/or documented gang members. Even factoring in vacations, off-time, and periodic special assignments that took the unit out of the district, that's still an average of well over one recovered gun and one gun-related arrest a week. And the unit considered this a slow year—in 2013 they made even more gun arrests. How impressive is this? I'll give you a comparison. It's like a ball player hitting a grand slam a week.

How did they pull it off? By knowing the violent and dangerous criminals in the district. By skillful use of informants and tech-savvy social media investigations. By relying on keen observational skills, including how the weight of a firearm will cause a prominent dip in one pocket of a jacket as well as "gun retention" movements where suspects will engage in a series of pats, pulls, and tugs to ensure their firearms are in place. And by repeatedly putting themselves in harm's way to engage suspects they knew or suspected to be armed.

I watched these cops operate during my time in the Bayview. Saw their unwavering work ethic in helping keep the most violent part of the city safe. You'll never hear about them because they'll never tell you about themselves. They went about their duty quietly without fanfare. They sought neither awards nor recognition. That's called honor. And there are units like this on departments across the country. They are an example of all that is right in police work. Especially in recent years, law enforcement has lost ground to both criminals and criminal cops.

Units like Sgt. Griffin and his team are winning it back.

There's a popular rap song by Public Enemy called "911 Is a Joke." Can't say I agree, at least not anywhere I've worked. Upon hearing a hot call, officers will routinely run out of the assembly or dash from the kitchen leaving sandwiches half-eaten and cups of coffee still steaming on the table. I recall two Milwaukee cops sprinting from the station to respond to an emergency rounding the same corner at the same time and colliding heads, nearly knocking each other unconscious.

Problem is, on a busy summer night when people are out and misbehaving, it is not unusual for there to be more emergencies to respond to than there are responders. The number of officers is not unlimited. You can't send a patrol car to an A-priority assignment if there's no cop inside of the car, so officers are constantly breaking from lower-priority assignments to go to hot calls. That's the nature of the business. So the report of the broken flowerpot with a known juvenile suspect is going to have to wait in the queue because a man is attacking another man with a hatchet downtown and he's already chopped off most of one arm and is going for number two.

In these pages, I use the male pronoun to refer to police officers, in part because alternating between he/she/him/her can get unwieldy. But I have questioned the appropriateness of that decision. Many of my colleagues are women. I've had female chiefs in Milwaukee and SF. I expressed these concerns to a female coworker. "Don't worry about it," she said. "It's a male-dominated profession." So I'm not worrying about it. But despite the abundance of tough, competent women on the job, references to female officers still can run toward the dismissive. "She's just some chick in a ponytail and Skechers," I once heard a lieutenant say about a fellow officer to everyone at lineup.

If I may paint with a broad brush, women are traditionally better communicators than men out on the street and have a better chance of defusing a family crisis or smooth-talking a criminal into handcuffs than their male counterparts. Which is important, because there's a lot more to the job than just bludgeoning people. But if it does come to bludgeoning, female cops may be quicker to go to their pepper spray or baton because the suspect they're facing off with may be larger or stronger than they are. And that's okay. You use the skills that you have and the tools on your belt. Female officers also capitalize on male suspects underestimating them—just like someone who doesn't follow the fight game might think Laila Ali is just another pretty face or some lowlife looking to snatch a phone may assume that slender gal is an easy mark when in fact she just graduated from Marine Corps boot camp. Some guys must find things out the hard way. And when that happens, it's really fun to watch.

I heard a radio call not long ago where officers were sent to check on the welfare of a woman who had been reported missing and was possibly suicidal. The cop came over the air stating she had been located and was fine. "She's healthy and happy," he added. Healthy and happy? It made me want to get on the radio and ask what her secret was. Sounds like she's doing better than most of the police force. Depression is commonplace in law enforcement but often goes untreated because of the powerful stigma attached to taking anything that could be deemed psych meds. You'll know about the cop on your shift who has stopped wearing his ballistic vest. Because he just doesn't care anymore. Or the one who regularly lets anger make decisions for him and seems right on the verge of coming loose.

Many years ago, I saw one of my police academy classmates at HQ. His name was Greg Braun, a rugged Army Ranger who had just returned from a military deployment and was working a rough patrol sector. I hadn't seen him in a while. He was usually a high-energy guy, but that day he looked exhausted.

"How ya doing?" I asked.

"I feel like shooting myself in the head," he told me matter-of-factly.

I clapped him on the shoulder the way men do. Said something like "Hang in there." What he said didn't register with me any more than if he

145

had commented on his lunch plans. Because I knew Greg. He was made of iron. He used to lap me on the academy track even back when I could run a sub-six-minute mile. This was just macho bluster. Cop gun talk. I knew it wasn't unheard of for an officer to jokingly put a gun to his temple in protest of some crap sandwich of an assignment or a preposterous new police regulation.

It wasn't long after this conversation that Greg shot himself in the head with his own service weapon. He died alone. When I heard, I remember shaking my head. Just continually shaking it as if I could shake the news away. He told me he was going to do that. He went right up to me and told me. And what did I do? I hit him on the shoulder and I walked away.

At Greg's funeral, his tactical boots were laid out underneath pictures of him in uniform. Pictures of his family. During better times. Times that made sense. He had been a natural police officer. Smart and efficient. Fearless. A guy you'd go through the worst kind of door with because he'd have your back and could handle anything that came at you. I would later learn that while he was on Ranger patrol, extended combat missions in the kill zone had left him with PTSD, chronic pain, and insomnia.

I will never know if I could have prevented this tragedy. Maybe I wasn't the only person Greg told. Perhaps there were others who let him down when he needed us the most. But I am not responsible for any of those people. I am only responsible for my failure, and my failure has stained me. I can only vow to be ready the next time. And given the darkness that shadows this profession, there likely will be a next time.

In *400 Things Cops Know*, I wrote about the police code of silence, where officers are traditionally reticent to report wrongdoing by their fellow cop. I wrote about this but probably didn't write enough. The code of silence is the exact opposite of how it should be, of course. The corrupt cop should fear the honest cop, not the other way around. To combat this code, some departments are tightening up hiring procedures and others are emphasizing ongoing ethics-based training. But maybe the most important change that needs to take place is for police officers to collectively support truth tellers, not ostracize them. The blue wall of silence has been around for a while, which means not everyone is going to be on board with efforts to break the wall down. Not everyone is going to like it. But that's okay. "Being responsible," General Colin Powell once said, "sometimes means pissing people off."

14

Predators

For us to live any other way was nuts. To us, those goody-good people who worked shitty jobs for bum paychecks and took the subway to work every day, and worried about their bills, were dead. I mean they were suckers. They had no balls. If we wanted something we just took it. If anyone complained twice they got hit so bad, believe me, they never complained again.
—Ray Liotta as mobster Henry Hill, *Goodfellas*

What is a predator? Someone who's decided they're over this whole basic humanity horseshit. They'll murder a Special Olympian for his wallet and high-five each other afterward. They'll make a woman drink drain cleaner and then videotape her vomiting for their sexual pleasure as her stomach sprouts holes. In 2016, Dwight Boone-Doty, a reputed gunman for a local Chicago gang, lured a nine-year-old into an alley by offering him candy and shot him in the head in a revenge murder stemming from a dispute with the boy's father. Then he bragged about it in a rap. If you're holding out to see if there's a line these people won't cross, get a comfortable chair because you'll be waiting awhile.

Predators' criminal histories boast carjackings, kidnappings, and brutal assaults. They have records in multiple states. For some of them, the only crime they haven't committed is something relatively uncommon, like arson. And that's the really best thing you can say about them—they haven't burned anything to the ground yet, or at least haven't been caught for it. Their rap sheets will cycle through an entire ream of paper with the only significant spaces between arrests occurring when they were confined to state prison. Or when you try to run their criminal record, your computer screen will say "Record too large for transmission. Request mailed transcript." They are committing crimes every single day. You go to work each morning. Unofficially, predators do too.

Some predators follow a familiar pattern. Felon by age fourteen, drop out of school by fifteen, a baby or two on the way by sixteen, right on track. They have a cool hundred felony arrests before they've turned thirty. Some are so steeped in the criminal justice system that they'll quote the proper penal code section when they talk to their investigator. "This here is more of a 212.5 situation," a parolee once announced to me. And he was exactly right. He was familiar with that law, having broken it many times before.

Predators don't always see themselves as predators. Some see themselves in a more noble light. You see the tattoo on the murdered drug dealer that reads "Live a solja, die a solja." Exactly what cause was he fighting for? A more equitable distribution of heroin? Maybe we can go ahead and cancel the 21-gun salute for this fallen warrior.

For a predator, going to lockup can also be a time of reunions. "I'm in here with a nigga I went to elementary with," one felony assault suspect cheerfully told a relative on a jail call I listened to. But he wasted no time wondering how the victims of his violent crimes were faring, opting instead to focus his attention on the quality of institutional meals. "They're giving me some bitch-ass cheese and bread," he groused. Then he complained he was bored. I looked at a crime scene photo that showed one of the four victims of his baseball bat assault, a petite twenty-two-year-old whose arm he shattered and whom he hit so hard in the skull that it created a fissure deep enough to see the soft tissue of the cerebrum. I was betting she wasn't bored. She was busy trying to process the extent of her brain damage and wondering if she'd ever be able to use her arm the same way again.

Predators aren't looking to get rehabbed in jail. They go inside to enhance their street cred and learn from their mistakes so they can become more effective offenders upon release. It's Crime College with an open enrollment. Some predators are looking to give the prison guards their money's worth—one of their more revolting practices is to fill a Styrofoam cup with a cocktail of urine, feces, and semen and call a guard over to pose an innocuous question. When the guard opens his mouth to respond, the inmate tosses the contents of the cup in his face. Feel free to check out www .prisonjobs.org for correctional hiring opportunities in your area today.

Some folks view the Hells Angels as the last of a vanishing breed of outlaw patriots. They got the outlaw part right and hopefully the vanishing part right too. Don't be fooled by the toy drives and the stories of Angels helping stranded motorists. Their civic exterior is a façade. The Hells Angels aren't merely a motorcycle club. They're a predatory criminal street gang. And don't just take my word for it—ask any gang expert across the country. The Angels shoot their rivals at casinos. Carry daggers and chains to stab and bludgeon their enemies or just crack off the side view mirror of a motorist who annoys them. Sure, they tend not to commit street crime in the same obvious fashion as the Crips or the Latin Kings, but they're no less dangerous. They're not just sitting around debating the best weight of motor oil for their bikes. They're debating whether they should murder their rival by detonation or knife.

Another group whose viciousness can be woefully underestimated is the Sovereign Citizens (SC), a collection of survivalists thought to number in the hundreds of thousands who are comfortable with firearms and violence. Officers most frequently contact them on traffic stops, where the SC will, in lieu of his driver's license, hand over a document with some poorly spelled blather about government corruption. The Sovereign Citizens counted Oklahoma City bomber Terry Nichols among their members. They're the kind of folks you'll find in possession of hate literature and instructions on how to phone-bomb public officials. They like to gum up the works by passing bogus money orders and putting faux liens on the property of people who cross them. Their origins hail back to the colonists, a part-time amateur army that showed up for training with cornstalks instead of rifles. They're typically made up of lower- to middle-class peevish white men in rural areas who claim to be exempt from their governing body's rules. Some burn their driver's licenses because they represent an unethical contract with a corrupt government. SC groups speak a good deal of the constitutional and biblical right to do as they please.

It can get confusing to track such groups because some folks will try it out for a while, like a bowling league, and then quit. Or they'll disband and rename themselves; today's Sons of Liberty are tomorrow's Freedom Fathers. They'd be the kind of groups you'd chuckle at if they weren't such a threat. Their brand of anarchist philosophy was seen at Ruby Ridge in 1992 and in Waco, Texas, a year later. The Southern Poverty Law Center lists them as an extremist group. The FBI has labeled them a domestic terror group. And in July of 2010, Sgt. Brandon Paudert and Ofc. Bill Evans of the

West Memphis Police Department conducted a drug interdiction traffic stop along I-40 on a minivan occupied by what turned out to be a father-son pair of SC members named Jerry and Joseph Kane. While Jerry was being questioned, sixteen-year-old Joseph emerged from the van with an AK-47 and murdered both officers, an act caught on one of the squad car's dash cams. The Kanes fled and were killed ninety minutes later in a gunfight with pursuing deputies.

Robert Paudert, now the former chief of the West Memphis PD, educates police departments across the country about the dangers of the SC movement. Like the shooters, Robert Paudert was also part of a father-son pair. Sgt. Brandon Paudert was Chief Paudert's oldest child, and the father found his boy murdered on the freeway that July day, Brandon's service weapon still clutched in his hand. Law enforcement is at its finest when members can absorb unspeakable tragedy and, in time, turn that sorrow into something that will help others. Chief Paudert both understands and practices that philosophy.

Contrast his approach with that of Jerry Kane's widow, who sued, claiming her family members suffered "torture killings." She demanded restitution in the form of gold, specifically $38 per troy ounce (Sovereign Citizens believe the United States went bankrupt when it abandoned the gold standard).

She received absolutely nothing and was lucky to get that.

Predators are quick to tell you they just can't catch a break. They like to blame others, like the police, or just general universal forces that conspire against them. A gang member in one of my cases lamented, "Every time I try to do good, something comes and messes it up." Darn that rotten luck. What was this "something" he referred to? A wicked case of stomach flu that prevented him from making that promising job interview? A lost wallet that contained his rent money? No, the "something" in his case was his arrest for bludgeoning his middle-aged aunt in the mouth and head with a handgun after a drunken argument and then fleeing the scene, but not before tossing his loaded gun under a parked car where any curious child could have found it. But what's a fellow to do? "Something" just came along. Messed it all up.

Predators will claim to suffer from mental illness, and many do, but you'll have a running conversation with your coworkers about whether they're actually crazy or just putting on a show in hopes of being referred to the softer sanctions of mental health court. Looking bug-eyed and dropping reference to wet work for the CIA does not impress you. Now, on the other hand, a predator who enthusiastically gobbles up his own feces? Okay. Now you have my attention.

But chief among the whiners is the sex offender. Get into his business a bit and he'll claim you're just harassing him because of ancient history. The system is keeping him down. If he's a day late on his offender registration, a jailable offense, he'll insist on a break. But as I regularly tell sex offenders when I arrest them, "If I give anyone a break, I promise it is not ever going to be you."

If a sex offender spins you his hard-luck tale and then starts to cry, it could be genuine or it could be a desperate ploy for sympathy. But it doesn't really matter to you. You want those tears to keep coming. You figure the victims of all his inhuman crimes, the ones you know about and the ones you never caught him for, had some tears of their own at one point—perhaps this is one infinitesimal step toward restoring the balance. You are emotionally, intellectually, and ecumenically incapable of feeling sorry for a sex offender. You draw strength from his tears. In fact, ask a cop what he'd do if he found out he had cancer and had only three weeks to live. He'd spend some quality days with the family, sure. But he'd also walk down the street and throttle every pedophile in sight. It would be an appropriate use of his remaining time on earth.

Predators don't always look like predators. Many look utterly innocuous. The kind of folks you'd ask for directions or chat with while waiting in line. But it has been my experience that a disproportionate number of sex offenders look exactly like what they are, as if their sickness has soaked into their pores and sallowed their features.

Predators will use any weapon available to them. Like lit cigarettes that can put out an eye. One guy I dealt with carried a sock full of shattered glass that he'd use to split his victim's skin. Do predators possess any redeemable qualities? Sure. Some are tidy. You search a parolee's dresser drawers and you often find his socks neat and organized, rolled up in balls just as they would be in prison. Others are tough as roofing nails. I was at a shooting a few years back where the victim, a stone-cold felon who had just been shot in the face, sat on the curb with casual athleticism awaiting the ambulance and making a point to crack every one of his knuckles as he surely plotted revenge. And then you have those who are ingenious in the worst kind of way, like the suspect who pretends to be deaf in the hopes that the police will handcuff him in front so he can use his hands to sign. This makes it easier for him to try to grab an officer's gun to shoot his way out of custody.

Predators use guns not just because they are effective but because many of them don't know how to fight and, even if they did, aren't willing to endure the physical harm that comes along with it. They wish only to inflict pain, not suffer it. That's what the guns are for.

You'll see whole family trees of predators. Maybe it's the Tolliver family, Jarrell, J'Paris, and Jerome, who have been keeping municipal law enforcement employed for decades. Or the Sassets with their hockey hair and frequent bouts of drunken violence. They boast four brothers, who are hard to tell apart, especially with all that facial grime. They remind you of the inbred farmers from that one *X-Files* episode. (Tolliver and Sasset are names I have invented to represent the real clans I have based them on.) You wonder if these family matriarchs are done having kids, or might there be someone else you'll need to worry about. You fervently hope they don't keep passing on their sad legacy to their offspring. And then you'll see him, on one of the Tollivers' phones. A picture of a child posing with his lip curled up, one hand making the shape of a gun or his neighborhood gang sign (this is called "throwing the hood up") and the other hand giving the camera the middle finger. He's wearing a T-shirt that says Get Cha Money. The photo already has a hundred Likes and rising.

Cops like to use these types of families as developmental yardsticks. Have you arrested a Tolliver? Brawled with a Sasset? No? Then you haven't quite earned your badge yet.

The Tollivers and the Sassets in your city can be found up on district station photo boards along with their fellow predators. These boards are typically labeled something like MVPs (Most Violent Persons) or Top Offenders. The suspect photos will include a fact sheet that indicates whether they're on probation or parole, what car they drive, where they hang out, and what their weapon of choice is. Such boards often have a color-coded key. One red line through the face might mean the suspect is in custody. One black line means the suspect is deceased. If a suspect, say, burglarizes a business by sneaking in through the ceiling and accidentally trips the ventilation fan, crushing his neck, this will touch off a spirited debate about whether Death by Ventilation Fan should merit its own color-coded icon.

On one such board I have seen, someone push-pinned a wilted daffodil on the face of a recently deceased and particularly reprehensible gang-banger. I won't say which department was involved or what district was home to this flippant memorial, because it will probably generate a citizen complaint. But I'm pretty sure it's still up there.

If a bunch of crooks are hanging out in public, the most dangerous one isn't going to be the mouthiest. It's the quiet guys you need to watch for. Smart predators know there isn't any upside to getting lippy with the cops. All that does is make you memorable, and that's not what you, a lawbreaker, want. A shaggy-haired fellow named Steve found this out several years ago when he entered a café near 7th and Market where my partner and I were running surveillance on a stolen property operation. Steve loudly identified us as the police. Then he took out his guitar and strummed a little ditty, the chorus of which went like this: "Fuck those cops, fuck 'em in the face." I remembered that song and I remembered Steve. So when I saw him out and about a few months after he played his little antiestablishment ballad, I ran him up and, low and behold, he had a felony warrant. So Steve went to jail. I saw him again about a year later. Another felony warrant, this one extraditable to Los Angeles County, some 380 miles away. Steve returned to the clink. He seemed rather crestfallen by these developments.

"You played that song because you wanted our attention," I explained to Steve. "I can assure you that you have it."

Predators know their terrain better than you and are ready to run at all times. They have familiarized themselves with escape routes, short-cuts, recesses, and dead ends. Turn your head for just an instant and poof, they disappear into a project house they know to be friendly. One predator in the Bayview neighborhood of San Francisco had a series of buckets set up behind a fence off a blind alley behind his house. If the law came, he bailed and used the buckets to jump the fence to the adjoining block. Next logical step for this enterprising fellow—a zip line.

Consider the case of a man convicted of a violent felony and currently wanted on a parole warrant. Factor in that this man's own family admits he is a pimp and that DNA evidence recently linked him to the rape of a twelve-year-old girl. Add on that the man is driving around town with a loaded handgun in his car, yet another felony. Now, not for nothing, include in this set of facts that this man murdered four police officers in one day. Wouldn't that make him an obvious predator? Prima facie evil? There's no way he'd have supporters, except for perhaps the sort of lost soul who proposes marriage to the Charles Mansons and Scott Petersons of the world. Right? Wrong, wrong as hell. Welcome to East Oakland, California, where a march was held in support of cop killer and suspected child rapist Lovelle Mixon. On March 25, 2009, a crowd estimated at sixty to seventy-five people walked MacArthur Boulevard wearing T-shirts with Mixon's picture on them, chanting, and holding up signs that said Stop Police Terror. Mixon even had a shrine built to cherish his memory outside the apartment building where a SWAT team killed him after he opened fire on them with an assault rifle. One local journalist, if you are willing to use the term loosely, sounded a note of snarky triumph when he wrote, regarding Mixon, "How does it feel when the rabbit has the gun?" Various indie blogs deemed Mixon a "ruthless street warrior" who took "rightful measures." Here you have a small but vocal segment of the city lamenting Mixon's death and outright rejoicing at the murder of the police officers. Score one for their column.

The fact that Oakland Police, who had just lost four of their own, didn't tear down this shrine or clash with the protestors is testament to their restraint and professionalism. There's a lot of talk, and important talk at that, about how the police need to reach out to the community. Lots of speeches about restoring the public faith. The police need to do this, the community says. The police need to do that. But it's a two-way street. Which begs the question, what does the community in East Oakland need to do to uphold their end of the bargain with law enforcement? And when are they going to do it?

Predators don't hang out with people who try to keep them on the right path. Who tell them, "Hey, maybe you shouldn't do that," when they contemplate a gas station robbery or a stomp-down of a crime witness. They also have their enablers. On one of my cases, a drunken hood savagely beat a family member and then shoved a gun in her face. She didn't wish to prosecute, she told me, because he was family. But, she added, his behavior "was uncalled for." Uncalled for. As if he had merely raised his voice to her.

Other enablers include the parents who hid their fugitive children in the basement and girlfriends who provide wholly false alibis ("What night you need accounting for, officer? Whichever it is, he was with me that evening.") But not all predators' families follow suit. I listen to jail calls where mothers, grandfathers, and uncles urge them to do right. Pray with them. Plead with them. Get plain sick of them. They won't harbor Shithead Tommy, because they've been fed up with him a lot longer than you have. And they know that if he's in jail, he'll be a lot safer than he is on the streets and so will the community. Maybe he'll be able to kick that drug habit. Incarceration is the best place for him. And they will hope against hope that he will come out of this reconstructed in some way.

Among the most terrifying predators is the school shooter who seemingly can strike anywhere, anytime, in neighborhoods both prosperous and poor, in award-winning schools and institutions struggling to keep their doors open.

But the signposts are there if you watch for them, and many students and faculty have been discerning enough to stop these murder plots and save lives. They spot a disturbing comment on a website. Hear the prospective shooters boast about their plan, or try to recruit the wrong classmate who doesn't really want to cover that exit. Teenagers struggle to keep secrets, and if someone warns them ahead of time to stay out of school that day, they may tell an adult and that adult may tell a police officer and the madness can be cut off at the pass.

But shouldn't we also keep close tabs on that sophomore loner who is preoccupied with violent songs and video games and wears all black? The FBI says no, there is no real profile and the stereotype of the teen brooder who one day just snaps is a myth. School shooters come from all races and social strata. Many live in stable homes and most have no violent history. The vast majority of school shootings are planned in advance. And preoccupation with violent songs and video games could just be a kid blowing off steam. I remember in high school writing stories filled with guns and knives and all manner of mayhem. I watched every blood-soaked action movie I could get my hands on. And I turned out halfway respectable. So did my friends.

But there will be warning signs that go unnoticed or unheeded, by both school communities and the police who are supposed to guard them. And there will be yet another heartrending news story about students who want nothing other than to inflict maximum carnage in a place that everyone thought was safe.

As a parent, you take care of your children. You guide and nourish and discipline them. Navigate potty-training and broken bones and first crushes. Chuckle at how your little one says tornado when she's trying to say tomato. You pay for piano lessons and shin guards and summer camp only to have your loved one ripped apart from bullets by a boy she was always nice to.

As a cop, you steel yourself for a school shooting. You will go in and head straight for the sound of gunfire and screaming. You have trained to be the right officer for that call. The one that is going to fix that situation as much as it can be fixed. Gunmen don't just sit around and wait for you. If you look at the average duration of Virginia Tech, Sandy Hook, and Roseburg, Oregon, from start to bloody finish, you know you have to move fast.

You have about eight minutes.

Apologists will claim some predators can be saved. They say these offenders have limited education and come from abusive homes—they need our help, not our jails. Just give them another chance. A do-over. A mulligan. More opportunities. More government-backed programs. They are works in progress. They can be redeemed. In San Francisco, there are people who apparently believe the most effective way to combat violent crime is via a nurturing circle of folksingers.

Redemption? Maybe. A few predators will get an honest job. Some gang members become gang counselors. Inmates can make significant progress working with prison chaplains. But in a cop's book, that's a pretty distant maybe. I don't pretend I would have achieved much in this life if I had been born a Tolliver or Sasset. I drew a good hand growing up as a Plantinga and I don't take it for granted. Save for sporadic fistfights with my older brother, my house was a safe haven of familial warmth and intellectual curiosity. My father taught me both the difference between jealousy and envy and how to jump-start a car. My mother was a model of fairness and deportment while also demonstrating it was wholly acceptable to shout "Holy shit" if you accidentally lit your apron on fire while cooking over the stove. We lived in a neighborhood where people didn't shotgun each other over drug debts. Classical music filled the rooms of our home. There were expectations of college and an honorable vocation and a life lived in community.

But wrecked childhood or not, predators make a choice to get involved in crime. They may claim their hand is forced out of economic necessity. But that's an insult to everyone who grew up as they did and was able to make it. No, true predators commit crimes because they want to. Because they like it. They belong in prison because they have proved time and time again that they should not be among people. They hurt people. It's all they know how to do. "Even God gives up at some point," Charles Dean says in the play *The Sunset Limited*. "There's no ministry in hell."

I have devoted most of this chapter to felons who commit violent crimes. But some of the worst predators among us have never physically assaulted anyone or lifted a weapon in anger. Like notorious stockbroker Bernie Madoff, who took the Ponzi scheme to new heights. Kenneth Lay of Enron, who sold millions of his own tanking stock while reportedly encouraging his employees to buy more shares. Former CEO Dennis Kozlowski, who filched around $100 million from Tyco International while using company money to throw lavish parties, one of which featured an ice sculpture of Michelangelo's *David* urinating high-end vodka. These criminals stole enough money to surpass the annual gross domestic product of some countries. They bilked shareholders and gutted worker pensions. Just because they had $500 haircuts and wore respectable suits while inflicting their wrongs doesn't mean they belong in jail any less than the murderers and the rapists.

But do their white-collar stature and high social standing give them any consideration in lockup?

They sure do.

You'll make sure all their magazines get forwarded.

15

The Station

Captain Connolly: Let's see about getting this place painted.
Heffernan: Well that's kind of a problem, painters won't come up here.
—Two cops discussing sprucing up the station, *Fort Apache, the Bronx*

If you're worried that your tax dollars are being squandered on police luxuries and accoutrements like indoor bike paths and rooftop gardens, let me set your mind at ease. Sure, headquarters might have just gotten a sparkly new building, but the outlying district stations and facilities look like the set of *Assault on Precinct 13*. I'm talking flypaper. Buckets in the hallways for leaky roofs. Bathrooms you're guessing haven't been remodeled in a while because they still have ashtrays built into the stalls. Bullet holes in lockers, some decades old, remnants of times gone by when cops were making questionable decisions while armed. At San Francisco's old Southern station, the first thing you were taught as a new arrival was not to drink the water. The second was that cancer was medically presumptive because of the heavy presence of asbestos in the building. The third? The rumor that the one-way bullet-resistant glass protecting the cops working the front counter was installed backward.

Beyond aesthetics, police stations have their own distinct character and lore. There's always the one district that has a reputation for arrogance, but the best kind of arrogance—the kind backed up by performance. They have slogans on the wall like this: "75 percent of the earth is covered in water. Our station will cover the rest." At one SF building, the cops got into the habit of throwing pencils up at the soft ceiling tiles to get them to stick but had to stop when a pencil fell and landed on the lieutenant's head during roll call. At another station I know, a strapping police stalwart once broke his long baton in half on a violent protestor's leg. It is said that the shards of this weapon are on display noon to four on weekdays. No flash photography is permitted. See the docent for further details.

In most cities, there is a venerable police station every cop wants to go to. Where people wave at you and you can get your coffee without any rush. In San Francisco, it is Central Station, which covers the north end of downtown and, to a lesser extent, Northern, which incorporates the Marina District, where there are a lot of attractive people jogging. In their down time, the cops try to watch them, but all the best spots have already been taken by the firefighters. The wait list to transfer there is as long as the list for Packers season tickets. You get to a place like Central or Northern, you stay. You burrow in like a tick.

But no matter where you work, you'll see some of the same things in police stations. Signs for blood drives. American flags. A Junior Police Officer sticker affixed to a vet's locker. An overtime pagoda filled with small porcelain gods. Occasional misspellings, like the copier that has a digital folder for "Serteants." Shelves with toys, coloring books, and stuffed animals for kids who come to the station as victims or witnesses. Bumper stickers that say "Sig Sauer: To Hell and Back Reliability" and "We, the unappreciated must do the unimaginable and see the unthinkable to protect the ungrateful." Plaques to honor those officers killed on the job. Crime maps with dots to indicate violent felonies—in some sectors the dots congeal into one brightly colored blob. When you're searching for much-needed supplies at your station, you won't be able to find any medium-size binder clips or USB drives, but you'll have a whole crate-load of blank videocassettes, even though no one has watched anything on a VCR since 1996.

You tend to stay clear of the station when you're off duty, unless you heard someone brought in free food. A guy might show up to make copies of his divorce papers in order to save money he'd otherwise be spending at Kinko's. This is against department general orders, but nobody cares much—divorce is hard enough without sweating someone for using work copiers for personal documents.

If you work for a large metropolitan police department, it can quickly become onerous to keep all the different divisions straight and what they do and where they are in the station. It doesn't help when the names change. The Criminal Intelligence Division (CID) becomes the Behavioral Investigative Unit (BIU). The Violence Reduction Team is now the Patrol

Bureau Task Force, which is what it used to be called before it was the Fugitive Recovery and Enforcement Team. Internal Affairs becomes the Professional Performance Division and then morphs into the Office of Professional Conduct and then evolves into Management Control. Then it changes right back to good ol' Internal Affairs. The Fraud Unit transforms into White Collar Investigations, but now it's Financial Transaction Crimes! (Why all the name changes? I'm not sure. It's like painting racing stripes on your car in the hopes that it will drive faster.) When I worked investigations, I'd receive phone calls asking if I could appear at a school to give a talk or speak to a wayward youth, which I found confusing until I realized my desk number was the same as the main number for the Juvenile Division, which hasn't existed since 2010. You call Comstat to get crime figures so you can write a commendation for the plainclothes guys and you get a busy signal all day. You call next day, still busy. The office has moved, you see, but nobody told anyone. Other offices relocate to a spot where there's no sign outside the door.

If you have trouble navigating this bureaucracy as an insider, think how difficult it can be for citizens trying to do the same. They have to go to three different offices to pick up their car that was towed for evidence. Fill out forms that they don't understand. Slog their way through administrative inertia. "I went over There," they say, "and they sent me Here." You try to be helpful, but sometimes the best you can do for them is a rueful smile as you send them back over There.

The station is where stories are spun and recrafted. In fact, legends abound on police departments to the point where it can be difficult to separate fact from fiction. Did you hear the one about the hulking Samoan who got really mad and threw half of the San Francisco Ingleside swing shift into a dumpster? They kept coming up trying to handcuff him and he kept tossing them in. He gave up only when some smart cop called his mother, who was able to calm him. You look into this story but cannot quite confirm it, although that doesn't mean you're not fond of it.

Or consider the tale of the pregnant prostitute in the Tenderloin who made a deal with an undercover, and when the arrest team came for her, she took off on foot and gave birth right in the middle of being chased. The baby was hanging from the umbilical cord, the story goes, flopping between the mother's legs as she ran. "Dude, it happened," a cop will insist. "I saw it. I was there." Someone points out that medically speaking, this whole scenario seems rather implausible. "Okay, so I talked to a guy who was there," the cop says defensively.

But how about the transient frequenting the Central district whose claim to fame is that he pulls a small cart containing a mouse sitting on top of a cat sitting on top of a dog? That guy's one hundred percent real. I last saw him in the spring of 2009.

Another story circulating around the station has to do with how the police do their absolute best but sometimes still fall short. I've been told this account of a man in San Francisco on a ledge threatening to jump. An officer tried to talk him down, but the guy wasn't responding. So the cop talked to his sergeant, who mulled it over and then mused that maybe the guy couldn't hear. Armed with this information, the officer returned to reengage the man and concluded that the sergeant was right, the man was deaf. So the sergeant called for another officer who was an American Sign Language interpreter. A short while later, the ASL guy came back down from the ledge.

"I can't help you, Sarge," he said. "This guy's from Munich."

It ain't always easy being a lawman.

On the other hand, sometimes cops don't do much and still come up aces. In the Bayview some years ago, after negotiations with a murder suspect broke down, the department brought in a different SFPD negotiator, who was a little more direct and was also the same color as the suspect.

"Get your black ass out here," the negotiator said.

The suspect immediately complied, the standoff resolved with those six words.

16

The Projects

Housing projects are a great metaphor for the government's relationship to poor folks: these huge islands built mostly in the middle of nowhere, designed to warehouse lives. People are still people, though, so we turned the projects into real communities, poor or not. We played in fire hydrants and had cookouts and partied, music bouncing off concrete walls. . . . The rest of the country was freed of any obligation to claim us. Which was fine, because we weren't really claiming them, either.
—Jay-Z, *Decoded*

If you seek to do meaningful police work, you have to be dialed in to the public housing in your sector, which can vary from old military barracks to semi-nice apartments to decrepit towers where Gollum would be at home. Subsidized housing is designed to be temporary, but many families have stayed for decades, seeing the projects not as a temporary way station to a better life but as a final destination.

To live in public housing, your income has to be below a certain line. Then the city takes around a third of your paycheck for rent. If you are unemployed, you live rent-free. Residents of public housing will tell you there's no point in working because they'll just have to pay more rent. And some folks who do have jobs don't want promotions or better jobs, because that, too, would make their rent go up. So what they're looking for is side work with tax-free revenue. That's why public housing features underground businesses. There's always a candy house where someone with a Costco card buys sweets in bulk, brings it back to their apartment, and sells it at a profit because their customers rarely leave the block. Others offer cigarettes or pirated DVDs. Sometimes you'll see a mini barbershop. And then there's always good old-fashioned street crime to make ends meet; after an armed robbery, at least one responding police unit will break from the pack and head right to the nearest housing project in anticipation of the suspects' return.

The waiting list for public housing swells, but projects make up some of the most violent and depressed spots in the city. Sure, the rent is subsidized, but no one is living the high life. The apartments themselves are often in disrepair with holes in the ceiling, pervasive mold, and inoperable smoke detectors. You have to mind bringing heavy weapons inside, as an AR-15, the standard patrol rifle for many departments, can punch right through a thin project wall and kill an innocent person three rooms over. It would cost millions to make the projects more livable, money the city is reluctant to pay. There is no post office in the projects. No gym. No florist. The lone neighborhood business boasts a large sign that says "Here to Win, Here to Stay," but it's long since closed down, with graffiti scrawled across the front door that says "Enrique is a bitch." After dark, some motorists treat red lights like stop signs to avoid having their car stolen at gunpoint. Some seniors are so frightened, they won't go outside alone even though they need their blood pressure meds. In 2005 in San Francisco's Visitacion Valley projects, a new children's playground was built to signal a kind of renaissance, bolstered by a $250,000 donation from the Dave Matthews Band. The renaissance didn't last. The jungle gym was set on fire. Twice.

It's instructive to take rookie cops on a tour through the projects. Show them the alcoves and recesses where danger waits. Advise them that suspects fleeing the police often toss their gun on a rooftop to come back for later; a thinking cop will rouse the fire department from their deep palatial slumber and soft-serve yogurt to bring their ladder truck to check those roofs. Teach them that if you're chasing a suspect and he goes over a fence, avoid blindly going over it in the same spot the bad guy did; move to a different location on the fence and pop just your head over the edge in case he's on the other side waiting to shoot you. If you go past a house where music is playing loudly, you let the new cops know that doesn't always mean someone is home. Folks in the projects keep the music on so burglars will think the house is occupied and leave them alone. The rookies might point out that this is a waste of electricity.

"This is the projects," you explain. "They don't pay for their electricity. You do."

Officers who regularly work public housing know that in the projects, it is an encouraging sign that no one has been beaten unconscious since the day before yesterday. They are accustomed to project lingo; if someone is hurt and is gushing blood, an onlooker will note, matter-of-factly, "You leaking, man." When housing police are on patrol and see a couple of guys working on a vehicle with the hood up, their first thought won't be car trouble. It will be *stolen* car trouble.

Project dogs like to rumble with each other, because they aren't raised right. So you often find yourself looking to break up a dog fight. A bucket of water is good. Pepper spray is better. You can grab a dog's hind legs, but you may become the focus of its ire. If you want to pry a dog's jaws off the person he's biting, you pull the dog's collar straight up and push his mouth right in the direction of the bite. It'll cause a gag reflex and he'll unclamp.

But while the projects can be both lethal and chaotic, some of the dangers are overblown. Like the rats you'll encounter. Yes, they are nasty, disease-ridden critters, but are all the stories surrounding them true? Are some as big as cats? Do they bite sleeping babies? The answers are no and some-times, though rat bites can come if there's an odor of food in the crib. Cold comfort to be sure, but in public housing, you'll take any kind of comfort you can get.

As a cop, you won't always have a lot of fans in the projects. If you lose your handheld radio, which can happen during a foot chase, it often falls into the wrong hands—the standard battery life is only about ten hours, but that's ten hours of everyone on your radio channel having to endure sporadic on-air giggling and periodic taunts of "Po-po ain't shit." Make an arrest in the projects and everyone spills out to watch you, curse you, or intervene on the arrestee's behalf. So you try to expedite things. No need to stir up the hornet's nest if you can avoid it, and heaven help you if you get on the PA and order the crowd to disperse because that guarantees the crowd will triple. So you get your arrest in the back of the car and whisk him out of there. Some working cops bristle at this fast-track approach, seeing it as akin to retreat; we should not adjust to them, they should adjust to us. And there's something to that. But one of the fundamental goals in urban law enforcement is riot avoidance.

When you have a serious crime, you conduct a canvas of the block. This involves knocking on doors to ask people if they saw, heard, or know anything related to the case you're investigating. Such efforts often flounder in the projects. Ask some public housing residents if they heard anything and they'll tell you they heard screaming. You ask why they didn't call 911 and they tell you the man next door beats his wife and the woman down-stairs beats her kids. There's always screaming, they explain. There's always cars peeling out. There's always gunshots.

Some folks won't even come to the door, although you'll see movement at the peephole or someone peering out at you from the curtains. Or they'll talk to you from behind the door without opening it, or from an upper balcony without deigning to come down—you're just a cop trying to solve a violent felony; you aren't quite worth descending ten steps for.

Others will answer the door and be angry from the jump for reasons having nothing to do with the matter at hand, demanding instead to know where you were when their son got shot on the basketball court last winter. Or they're so paranoid about being seen as the snitch on the block that they tell you they don't know nothing before you can even tell them why you're there. And they tell you not to come back. *Because you know what people gonna think.* Or the door opens and you are hit with a plume of pungent weed from some doper who struggles to lash together a coherent sentence.

"Guy just got robbed outside. You see anything? Hear anything?"

"I don't know," comes the long, drawn-out reply. "There a *re*-ward?"

"Yes," I said once. "The deep internal satisfaction you get from doing the right thing."

At the time of this writing, that particular case remains unsolved.

Wanted felons dot the projects, which means you're giving quite a few guys you pass by second looks. Is that the man from the wanted flyer, or do you know him from another case where he was a suspect/victim/witness?

There are those in the projects who resent your prolonged eye contact and demand to know if you've got a problem. You don't much care if you've ruffled their feathers—you're the cops and it's your job to do some occasional feather ruffling. But there are still ways to downplay such an encounter. When someone asks you what your deal is, maybe you tell them you were just talking to your partner about how much they look like a local sports hero. Hunter Pence or Draymond Green. No matter what the race of the complaining party, I periodically claim I thought they were my cousin from upstate. If they ask the cousin's name, I say Ned.

17

Being Off Duty

There is no such thing as work-life balance. Everything worth fighting for unbalances your life.
—Alain de Botton, writer and philosopher

The rules for a cop getting involved in an off-duty incident are pretty simple; you're encouraged to be a good witness, nothing more. You are not expected to swoop in and save the day, especially not by yourself. If you were on the job in uniform, you would think twice before making a solo arrest, and that's with a gun, vest, handcuffs, and radio. So why would you try the same thing when you're away from work with no police equipment, wearing flip-flops and your Bluth's Original Frozen Banana Stand T-shirt? And with two kids in the car? Plus anytime you put yourself on duty, you have to call your lieutenant afterward and write a memo. Who wants that? You're on your weekend and there are salmon steaks to be grilled and ale to be quaffed.

But each officer does some cost-benefit analysis and ends up making his own decision about such matters. I've managed to squelch a few street fights over the years and have made a handful of off-duty arrests for offenses ranging from drunk driving to auto burglary to carjacking. Each time I did so, I was well aware I was rolling the dice and things could go awry. Sometimes your better half makes that call for you before you can advise her against it. "It's okay," my wife, the ultimate peacemaker, once loudly proclaimed when we came upon a group of people in a moderate sidewalk squabble in which I had no intention of intervening. "My husband is a police officer."

When I say things can go awry, I'm thinking about the time Rolf Mueller, a mensch if there ever was one, stopped at a gas station for fuel and a newspaper after a long shift and encountered one Thurmon Ataurus Williams, who was in the process of shoplifting. Although in plainclothes and unarmed, with only his badge in his rear pocket, Rolf identified himself as a police officer and attempted to stop Williams, a 6'1", 240-pound career criminal some thirty years Rolf's junior. The fight was on. Rolf called for the clerk to dial 911 and tried to get Williams in a headlock, but Williams elbowed Rolf in the chest while yelling at the store clerk to "get this crazy motherfucker off me." He shoved Rolf into a shelf, tipping over a full pot of coffee, which left first degree burns on Rolf's left hand. Then Williams reared back and delivered a head butt to the front of Rolf's skull, a blow that Rolf would later describe to me as "devastating." Williams delivered the same head butt three or four more times and ran out of the store. Rolf picked himself up and, through the haze of pain, chased Williams on foot. While he was running, Rolf heard something that sounded like footsteps crunching on loose concrete. He looked down. No loose concrete there. He later told me he thinks that sound was the creaking of the bones in his face from the man's vicious blows. When Rolf lost sight of Williams, he returned to the store and directed the responding units to where he'd last seen Williams. Then Rolf sat down. The battle had lasted about four minutes, which in fight time is an eternity. Another officer found Williams several blocks away, sweating and out of breath, with fresh abrasions to his elbow and his pockets stuffed with stolen gas station food.

Williams's total take from his theft amounted to $17.55. He stole beef sticks. Some dip. A Little Debbie snack bar. It was a low-rent offense, one usually handled with a municipal theft citation. Many off-duty officers wouldn't have bothered with it, especially not at five in the morning, unarmed with no backup facing a younger, larger man. But Rolf had bothered. Because he didn't like it when people stole. After identifying Williams and giving a statement, Rolf went to the hospital, where his face had swollen like a bruised balloon. After being treated, he was given a ride home by another officer. He had the officer stop at the same gas station.

Rolf still owed them $9 for his fill-up.

In a telling twist of fate, Rolf would arrest Williams a few years later on open warrants. Rolf recognized Williams right away, but Williams didn't remember Rolf. The potential was surely there for some payback, but that wasn't what Rolf was about. It turned out to be an uneventful arrest where

Rolf treated Williams courteously as he would anyone else, demonstrating professionalism and self-restraint that too few of us have and some of us don't even understand.

If you take off-duty police action, the onus is on you to identify yourself as a cop to the responding officers. You may be in a position to call the police yourself, in which case you can give your rank and department name and a quick self-description so the responding officers don't tackle you by mistake. But if you are in the middle of a fight, you may not have a free hand to dial. That's why if you're going to carry your gun during your days off, you are also required to carry your badge and police ID. When uniformed officers arrive on scene, they may not have any idea who you are, especially if you aren't in your own jurisdiction. And if you have your gun out, you better pray they spot your badge because:

1. The badge can be seen from only one direction. If an officer approaches you from the side or rear, they might see only your gun.

2. The police aren't going to automatically assume you're one of the good guys. And if you try to explain it to them, they may not hear it because they're already screaming at you to drop the gun.

That's why best practices call for keeping your gun holstered unless absolutely necessary and even putting your arms up and/or proning yourself out when the on-duty cops show. Basically, you do everything the responding officers tell you to do. You expect to be treated like a suspect until you can definitively establish you're all on the same team. Because friendly-fire shootings are the stuff of nightmares.

When it comes to carrying a firearm off duty, everybody's different. Some officers have it with them all the time. Some don't want the bother. Others just pack it when they're going to be in the city; I won't enter Oakland or SF without at least fifteen rounds. But you can't have it on you if you're going to be drinking, so Friday night with the fellas is out. In the summer, handguns are hard to conceal with just a T-shirt on and that fanny pack you bought to hide your firearm is the object of your wife's consistent ridicule. Plus you figure you can survive a Wednesday lunch at a suburban Cheesecake Factory without a piece. But these are uncertain times. Maybe your waitress's ex-boyfriend shows up to her work with a .38 because if he can't have her, no one can. Perhaps today is the day that odd duck on the corner who's always muttering to himself takes a knife out and slashes the next person who walks past. A host of very bad people with the worst of intentions have been stopped by an off-duty cop with a keen eye and a gun.

It's nice to be off work. You walk out the station door and see a police car with lights and siren heading one way, but your shift is over so you head the other way. Go get 'em lads. But when you're in law enforcement, your life is not quite your own—some days you're just renting it. The department can and will cancel your off-days for demonstrations, or Halloween, or for the aftermath of a World Series or Super Bowl win. It drains a little joy out of your team taking the title when you know you're going to have to deal with the boozy exuberance, looting, and late-night violence that follows, all the while being booed by the crowd whenever you take police action, as if you represent the opposing team. And because the planning for these events is sometimes a bit haphazard, notifications are often last minute. You may have audaciously made plans on your off-days and not wish to come in. That scenario has led to exchanges like this:

> Lt.: "I need you in right now, Jorgensen."
> Jorgensen: "I can't come in. I . . . am drunk."
> Lt.: "Really? It's ten in the morning on a Sunday."
> Jorgensen: (Fakes hiccup.)

A few guys decide not to answer their phones, which is weak but effective; they can't make you come in if they can't reach you.

If you work investigations, you'll get called in on your off-day if they arrest a suspect on one of your cases. I once interrogated a guy for a serious felony, and when I was done, I went to the bathroom and took note that my face was streaked with transfer glitter from having played with my little girl and her princess dolls earlier in the day. The suspect hadn't mentioned a thing. Maybe because it was San Francisco.

When you're driving off duty and see the police have someone pulled over, you automatically slow to watch if the cop needs help, especially if there's only one officer, because backup could be a ways out. And if they do need you, you will stop your car, jump out, and help as best you can. You won't think twice. The officer you are helping would do the same for you. It's a brotherhood.

But it's funny, when you're in your car and you see a cop right behind you, you often have the very same thoughts a civilian would. Despite the fact that he is your brother and you would fight to the death at the side of the road to help him, you find yourself asking, what, did you make an illegal lane change? Are your tabs expired? Why is he all up on you? Back off, Johnny Law.

Because you have a job where you make enemies, you adopt a watchful readiness and take care to guard your privacy. You keep your name out of the phone book and your kids' school directory and go through a process of sending certified letters to opt out of public databases (although you have to start this process all over again if you do anything like refinance a mortgage). You recognize the perils of Instagram and Facebook. Some officers I know take different ways home in case anyone is following them. A few wear their gun while mowing the lawn. *My foes are all around me.*

When you're at a restaurant, you sit with your back to the wall watching the entrance. When I first met my wife, she asked me why I always chose that seat and I told her. Then I said I did an individualized threat assessment on everyone who entered. I wasn't entirely kidding. I also wanted her to think I was sort of tough.

If you live in one of the tonier towns in your county, you may relax this tactical seating policy a bit, but if you're on your game, you won't relax too much. Because look what happened to Wild Bill Hickok the one day he broke tradition. My older daughter understands. That's Daddy's seat. My younger one struggles with the concept, and if there's enough crying, I might relinquish the chair. Okay, young one. Seat's all yours. But I want you to visually screen every person who comes in. Or I guess you can just eat that hot fudge sundae.

If you take public transportation, there's a reasonable chance you will see some of the same drug dealers and hustlers you butt heads with on a regular basis now heading home. They put in a full shift today like you, just in a different enterprise. You see them and they see you. And usually nobody says anything. Sometimes civil nods are even exchanged. A truce. Because the cat-and-mouse game is done, at least for now, and there's nothing in it for either of you to start it back up prematurely. See you at nine tomorrow morning, gentlemen. We'll do it all over again.

It's no fun being sick or hurt, but it's a little worse when you're a cop. It's not the pain or discomfort so much, although you aren't too high on either of those things. It's the sense of vulnerability, of operating at a quarter speed. You are coughing incessantly. You're drained and listless. I can't feel this way, you think, I am society's protector. But right now a ten-year-old could dribble you like a basketball. If you saw a crime in progress, you wouldn't have enough energy to stop the suspect; you'd just have to point with a rubbery arm and say, "Hey, cut it out." You feel weak, exposed, unequipped. Like going to an armed robbery in progress without your ballistic vest or shotgun, armed only with your sense of irony.

The weekend was nice. You took your kids to the park and it had the fountain on. You had a pleasant evening out with your wife at a restaurant with mood lighting and key lime pie. You even found time to clean out the garage. Now that's all over with and it's time to step back in the netherworld. Yesterday you were rolling around in the yard with your six-year-old play-wrestling and today you're on the sidewalk wrestling for real with a drunk called Gotti who has a knife and doesn't like you. Two different universes, work and home, separated by as much space as you can possibly cram between them. At least most cops operate that way. Rolf Mueller had a police scanner that he listened to during his off-time.

"Sometimes I yell at it even when I'm home," he told me.

But it doesn't always play out so well, this neat divide. The job has a way of winding itself into your dreams. Police officers have nightmares of shooting people or being shot, often in a scenario where they run out of ammo or their gun malfunctions. I have fallen out of bed on more than one occasion while dreaming I am in a fight with a suspect; one time I smacked my head on a nightstand on the way down. Or you come home from work to a dinner party your wife is throwing. Good friends are already seated. The food hits the spot. The conversation is amiable and engaging. Problem is, you saw a dead baby that morning and are finding it a little hard to unwind. The other couple is chatting about an art exhibit they saw. You're thinking about how gray that baby's skin was. Someone brings up a new Netflix series. You raised the blanket up and there he was. He looked just like a doll.

"How was work?" someone asks.

"It was fine," you say. You think of the sounds coming out of the mother's mouth. A moan that built to a knife-edge wail. Those around you keep talking. About which summer vacation rental makes the most sense and how the back garden is coming along and whether to buy the kids a hamster. And there's no reason why they shouldn't talk about those things. But there you sit, half-listening, a stranger at your own table.

The next day you're out and about and see a police recruiting booth at a street fair. It's run by a couple of uniformed cops you don't know. They have shiny nameplates and warm smiles and glossy pamphlets. Their pitch is that police work is both important and interesting. They ask if you're interested in joining. No, you're already on the department, you tell them. You're trying to get out. Where's the booth for that?

Why the exit strategy? Accumulated wear and tear. A public that doesn't seem to get it. Blow-dried phonies on the nightly news reporting on your department's most recent shooting and trying desperately to manufacture controversy when there isn't enough to suit them. A growing belief that maybe it isn't healthy to do this job for very long. And too many of the kind of days no one should have. Not just the gray baby you were thinking about at the dinner table. It's the four-year-old girl in a pile of soiled laundry who's wasted away to nine pounds from neglect. A drive-by shooting where a random bystander is struck in the head and his brains leak into his baseball cap like soup. A man cut in half by a shotgun blast, still alive for a few more moments, eyes blinking, mouth gaped like a fish. And when your shift is over, you go to your locker and you can't get into it, because although you've been using the same lock for the last two decades, you don't have the slightest idea what the combination is. You stand there looking at it until you remember or you get bolt cutters and snap the damn thing off. Then you go home and turn the television on because TV is about all you can manage. You're still doing far better than the victims and their families. And tomorrow you'll bounce back. But tonight you just want some time to brood and you can't be around people. You're watching an NBA game that doesn't hold your interest, so you change the station and there's a woman in a shampoo commercial shaking her head back and forth, causing her shimmering tresses to flounce about. The commercial shows a computer-ized simulation of the shampoo pouring over the hair, how it protects and volumizes.

"Because you deserve it," the shampoo model says.

Two different worlds. One has brain soup in a ball cap. The other, wavy, shimmering hair. Two worlds that could not be more different.

And at that moment, you know one thing for certain.

You don't want to be in either one of them.

18

Interrogation

You have the right to remain silent; although personally, I don't feel remaining silent is all it's cracked up to be. . . . Smoke?
—Daniel Baldwin as Detective Beau Felton, *Homicide: Life on the Street*

If you want to become adept at interrogation, you have to understand theory, be mindful of case law, and follow people who excel. I've studied approaches like the Reid Method and watched seminars from experts like former FBI agent Dan Craft. I've picked my coworkers' brains about what works and what doesn't. But there's no substitute for putting the miles in yourself. I have sat across the table from many a suspect trying to get them, in some cases, to tell me the worst thing they've ever done. The prize for their candor? Probably state prison, where the food is questionable and the view isn't great.

It isn't always an easy sell. But it's far from impossible. We'll get to that in a minute.

The point of an interrogation isn't to get a confession. The point of an interrogation is to get both sides of the story. To work toward the truth of the matter. Sometimes the suspect(s) didn't do it (see Duke lacrosse or www.innocenceproject.org) or didn't do it in the way the victim claims he did. Maybe this suspect is an awful person who has routinely done awful things but just didn't do this particular awful thing he's currently being accused of. And if he didn't do it, the last thing you want is for him to say that he did, because then not only do you have the wrong man but the right one is still out there and the clock is ticking.

But you don't see a lot of false confessions. Safeguards are in place, like the Miranda warnings as well as the powerful human inclination not to admit to crimes you didn't do. If a false confession comes into play at all, it's typically with juveniles, a few of whom only wish to please you or will say just about anything if they think it will help them go home. You sometimes see it with the developmentally disabled and/or mentally ill. Or one suspect takes the fall for someone else, like when you have three felons in a car plus a loyal fellow from the neighborhood and the cops find a gun in the car. Loyal guy will claim the gun is his, because he knows all he'll get is a misdemeanor summons to appear whereas the felons are looking at serious time.

Before you even step into a room with a suspect you intend to question, you have to do some homework. Is the guy an addict? Homeless? Is this his first arrest or is he a hardened con? Any gang ties? What neighborhood does he frequent and who are his running buddies? Is he on social media flashing a gun and a stack of cash? A brief background check will give you some grist to work with and a general idea as to which approach to use. Facts work better with felons, and emotional appeals work better with folks who haven't been in the system much. The less serious the offense, the less you research, because they aren't all the Black Dahlia. Like the guy who sneaks into a house through an open window and steals two yogurts. It's still a felony, but maybe you don't have to peer quite so hard into this man's soul.

The experts, whoever they are, say interrogations should take place in a windowless room, around ten by ten with a table and two chairs about four feet apart. That's it. You want enough space so no one is cramped, but not so much that you can't get close to your interviewee. The lack of any other furnishings is to minimize distractions. You position yourself between the suspect and the exit door as if to indicate to the suspect that he has to appease you in order to leave the room. It's a nonsupportive environment used by the investigator to create a certain mood, which ranges from understanding to isolation and despair. But isn't this whole business with the spartan décor and the chair and table positioning a bit overwrought? Maybe. But people talk in such rooms and as long as it gets results, you'll keep doing it.

When you first enter, some suspects give you the hard slouch with the crossed arms. You try to loosen them up by telling them they can relax because you don't bite. Other suspects receive you with visible relief or even enthusiasm. Finally, the detective is here. To listen to me. Together, perhaps we can make some sense of these trumped-up allegations. One female auto thief actually told me, "Thank you for coming." "You're quite welcome," I replied cheerfully, like we were old pals, all the while thinking unless you're one of the 3 percent who didn't do it, I ain't exactly here to help you lady. As it turned out, she was not one of those 3 percent and in fact admitted she stole the shit out of the car in question.

When you sit down to interrogate suspects, you extend your hand. It is rare that they don't shake it, although some do so grudgingly. You shake because you're trying to set the tone early that you're open, understanding, even avuncular. You take the handcuffs off all but the most violent. You often bring them a soft drink and a candy bar, and it tells you something when the suspect tears into it like he hasn't eaten all day. I once gave a guy a strawberry scone I was saving for a midafternoon snack. He gobbled it up and then confessed to swinging a metal pipe at a guy's head; I figure the $2.75 I was out was worth it. Hamburgers have helped solve many a violent felony because they make an instant connection between you and the suspect. And because they taste good.

Some investigators prefer to read the suspect the Miranda rights right from the jump and then start in with some rapport-building. Others ask background questions first so the suspect becomes comfortable talking and then hit the suspect with Miranda. But regardless, you have to advise the suspect of his rights before you start asking questions about the crime at hand. I like to tell the suspect, "I gotta read you your rights," as if this represents a mildly irritating obstacle we both have to overcome before we can reach an understanding. Then I'll tell them "and then we'll find a way forward." After all, who doesn't want that? Or I'll say, "We'll figure this thing out together." Like it's a moderately hard science project we've both been assigned.

Investigators will read the Miranda rights directly off a preprinted card even if they've read those same words a thousand times before. It's just one less thing you have to worry about in court, where a defense attorney will pounce on any deviation from the Miranda script, however slight. (You want to avoid Channing Tatum's Miranda oversight in *21 Jump Street* when he claims one of them is the right to be a lawyer.)

You can do all the research in the world and come up with a master game plan for your interrogation, full of challenges, feints, and double-backs, but some guys just ain't having it. Like the drowsy junkie who falls asleep on the bench and whose most comprehensive statement to you, when roused, is something like "Mennnofffrrggg." Or the experienced parolee who is utterly resistant to your wiles and charms. "Man, I been in the *system*," one con announced in disbelief when I tried to get him talking about one of the many felonies he'd committed that morning. "Just tell me what I'm being charged with." A serial burglar who had already been interrogated the previous night on a different B&E wouldn't even sit down when I walked in the room to interview him about my case. "Look," he said, and then paused with a furrowed brow and an expression of intense concentration such that I could almost see the gears working in his brain, "is there . . . any way that talking to you is going to help me?" If I had been more on my game, I would have sold him on the concept of talking to me. I would have told him that maybe he had a good reason to do what he did. Or that it was important for a man to give an accounting of himself. Or that judges looked favorably on truth tellers, because if you were a judge, who would you be lenient on? The guy who asks you to prove it or the guy who steps forward and says, "I made a mistake and I'm sorry." But I wasn't a good salesman that day because after he asked his question, I paused. And the pause was, I think, just long enough for him to sense that whatever I was about to peddle him was gonna be a whole lot of bullshit. He asked to be taken back to his cell. No sale.

And finally there was the armed robber who reportedly hit his victim in the face with a gun the previous night. He proved immune to my tactics. "I really want to punch your bitch ass in the mouth because you don't believe me," he shouted about ten minutes into the interview. Then he kicked the table over and it smacked me in the leg. So I arrested him for battery to a law enforcement officer. I told him all he'd done was catch another case. "Well that's a case I did so I don't give a fuck," he proclaimed.

At least there's a statement I can use.

But a suspect getting physical in an interrogation room is rare and a suspect invoking his right to remain silent or his right to an attorney, while more common, still doesn't happen nearly as often as one might think. I have conducted hundreds of interrogations. I can count on one hand the number of times a suspect has asked for a lawyer at the start of an interview. More often than not, people talk.

So what's going on here? Wouldn't they be far better off keeping their big trap shut? Do defense attorneys instruct their clients, "Go ahead and answer the seasoned detective's many pointed questions about your criminal culpability, Marvin, and when it's all over, we'll see where it leaves us?" Is it ever a good idea to talk to the police after being Mirandized? The answer is a resounding Almost Certainly Not. Only if you're wholly innocent, for instance. Or if you did it but you're a wordsmith who not only can articulate plausible deniability but are a lot smarter than the detective questioning you. A lot of cons are convinced of the latter. Quite a few of them are in state prison right now.

Why do they talk? You just told them they don't have to. You just advised them that everything they say could hurt them in court. But as stated above, some crooks think they can outwit you and talk their way out of trouble. Others want to explore how much of a case you have against them. Some have committed so many crimes that they're honestly curious about which one you happen to have on them today. A few actually didn't do it and want you to know that. Or they did it and they want you to know why. And maybe part of it is that at some level, everyone wants to be heard. To be understood. To be valued. To matter. I've interrogated people who seemed to be talking to me chiefly because they were lonely. Because I was the first person to take a genuine interest in them who wasn't a thief, junkie, or pimp. Because I gave them a strawberry scone.

If you're interrogating a kidnapping suspect and the victim is still missing, you don't have to read Miranda at all. You plunge right in with the questions, even if the suspect asserts his right to remain silent. If he asks for an attorney, you ignore him and press on. Courts have validated this approach, because a life hangs in the balance. It's called the Public Safety exception to Miranda. It exists because someone's loved one is hidden away, restrained, possibly injured. With no food or water and maybe a waning air supply. You don't want the cops to shrug and call it a day when the suspect remains close-lipped or demands counsel.

The rapport-building part of an investigation is a warm-up for the questions you're going to ask about the crime later on. You want the suspect to see you as a confidant. Maybe even a friend, because people tell their deepest secrets to friends. At the very least, you want to be seen as someone who isn't against them but is acting as a fact finder. Someone who wants to give them a fair shake. These last two things are true, or at least they should be. So you ask questions about the suspect like you're on a first date. Where he lives, where he works, what neighborhood he grew up in, which school he went to, if he has siblings, what his hobbies are. Wife? Partner? Kids? Car? Favorite sports teams? You usually don't even touch on the crime at hand until you've gotten him comfortable talking to you. This also helps you set a baseline for how the suspect looks, talks, and gestures when he's speaking about something noncontentious and doesn't need to lie. That way, when you get to the heart of the crime and are asking some tough specifics, you can see how his demeanor changes when he becomes uncomfortable and starts ducking your questions or crafting tall tales. Like a guy who always looks straight at you when asked routine questions but whose eyes wander when pressed about that gas station robbery.

When it comes to getting the nitty-gritty details from the suspect, police styles differ. Some cops begin gruff and get gruffer. Others assume an illusion of intimacy—they straighten the suspect's shirt collar or pick lint off his pant leg. I myself favor the catching more flies with honey philosophy and start out friendly and inviting and get flinty later, if needed. You come at them too hard, they'll shut down, because they think you want to put the screws to them. Act too soft, and they'll walk on you. But bottom line is, you want to ask open-ended questions about their whereabouts and actions during the time frame of the crime in question. Let them tell their side, a story that often makes about as much sense as the Greek tax code. One burglar told me he walked into a stranger's house because their door was open and he wanted to warn them of this danger so as to protect them from, ah, burglars. He didn't knock because he didn't want to scare them. And he started rolling the homeowner's $13,000 customized racing bike out the door because it was creating a dangerous obstruction of the entry way. He proclaimed all of this prima facie baloney earnestly with a straight face. And that's okay. The more preposterous their account, the better. You don't call them out on their lies, not yet. You lock them into a full statement so it gives you more material to play with and shoot holes through when the time comes.

After their story is preserved in time, sometimes you'll ask them to go through it all again. The second version often differs from the first in meaningful ways, because it's hard for them to remember all the lies they just told, some of which they made up on the spot. It's an improbable yarn giving way to fantastic whoppers blending into epic falsehoods.

After the suspect has said his piece, you confront him on any inconsistencies, which often leads to multiple denials. Funny thing about that is, lots of liars preface their denials with what are known in the business as "permission phrases" like "Can I just say something?" This is notable because truth tellers normally don't ask for permission to speak. They just speak.

After the suspect has gone on like this for a while, some investigators like to leave the room first and then return after a spell and say something like "The results of my investigation show me that you're lying." As if they just ran the suspect's statement through some kind of fact-checking super-computer. Then they demand the suspect tell them the truth. I've been taught to tell a guy something like this: "I've been doing this a long time. I know that you are lying. But I understand why you lied. Because it's human nature when someone feels backed in a corner. I'm not mad at you. I get it. Sometimes I lie too when I get accused of something. But I want to wipe the slate clean. I want to start over and have you tell me the way it really happened. Because you can defend the truth, even if it gets a little ugly sometimes. But you can't keep defending a lie."

I like this approach because it involves directly confronting the suspect, followed with a healthy dose of empathy, bolstered by an assurance that your relationship is still on solid ground ("I'm not mad at you. I get it."), imbued with a promise of new beginnings, and closing with just a touch of morality. Sound like some straight-up hokum? If it does, that's because all it really boils down to is "Hey you. Tell me the truth." But I assure you that for a certain type of suspect, this is often all it takes. You ask the suspect for the truth and they provide it, or at least more of it than they had previously, or as much of it as they can stand. It's the power of rhetoric and the badge. On that same note, a retired police detective in Florida swears that when he worked Narcotics, he could sometimes go to suspects' homes, say "Bring me your crack," and they would do it. And be arrested. Just like that.

But the denials of wrongdoing will come, even after all your wizardry. One school of thought is to interrupt the suspect and not let him deny anymore, on the theory that lies embolden more lies and he's just going to dig in deeper unless you cut him off at the pass. This is likely a good time to confront the suspect with your evidence, some real, some imagined. We'll get to that in a minute too.

Toward the start of the interview, you might name the crime you're inter-viewing the suspect about, but you minimize it. Burglary becomes taking something or trespassing or just walking through a door. An aggravated assault is shortened to assault, or a tussle. Not much, really; a lowball offense like when people wear jean shorts to the gym or say "Happy Monday." You imply that whatever they did probably shouldn't even be a crime. Hey, that's just a Friday night on the town. Then you stop naming it altogether. The savage home invasion becomes "this thing." The brutal sodomy becomes "that deal." As if it's some abstract area to improve on, to target for personal growth. Words create pictures so if you keep reminding the suspect he is under arrest for Terrorist Threats or Assault with Intent to Commit Rape, that's going to be in his head and he may be less inclined to give you a full and true accounting. There will be times when you take it a step further just to keep the suspect talking. You tell him that this thing, this deal really isn't anyone's fault. Guns just go off. Knives are just thrust into space, no malice intended, just kinetic energy released. Things just happen to people. It's random swirling forces at play, nothing more.

But what if the suspect is nonresponsive? One way to combat this is to look at the suspect and say nothing. Let silence speak. People are uncomfortable with extended silence. They naturally want to fill that void with words, words that will ultimately trip them up.

Sometimes silence can actually help bolster the case. For instance, when you Mirandize a suspect and the two of you get to talking in a friendly fashion, but when you ask if he committed the crime, he says nothing, that nonresponse is called an adoptive admission and is usable in court as evidence against him.

The stage is set. The recorder is on. The room positioned just the way you like it. You're ready to establish that this man in front of you had method, opportunity, and motive to commit the crime. Then the guy starts talking. And it sounds like he's got a mouth full of cashews. He's speaking English all right, and it's his first language, but this chap in front of you didn't quite attend Advanced Placement at Amherst, and through the mumbling and mangled diction, it sounds like he's speaking some new dialect as yet undiscovered by sociolinguists. And it doesn't help that he goes off on wide tangents, injects frequent personal testimonials, and favors slang, including terms and phrases possibly known only to him. Talk to one such person for a time and you realize you have little or no idea what he just said. He could be discussing the location of an auto chop shop or he could be divulging details on an illegal whaling operation off the coast.

"Hold up. Please speak slowly and distinctly," I told one such man even though it made me sound like a stuffy, impatient ass. But I had to know what he was telling me. I didn't want to raid the wrong whalers.

One suspect I was questioning about a hot prowl burglary described what happened to the phone his accomplice stole from the house. He told me someone else stole the already stolen phone from him. "It got depossessed by me," he explained.

Some of the signposts that point to the suspect's guilt are obvious. You ask them a simple question (Where were you last night?) and they parrot it right back to you (Where was I last night?) because they're trying to buy time to make up a story. Or they dodge your simple yes or no question as if they're subconsciously not quite ready to issue an outright denial:

You: "Did you rob that woman at 20th and Capp last night?"

They: "I don't rob people." (Thinking: *I can say this because I haven't robbed anyone today.*) Or "Why would I rob her? I have my own money."

Another tell? When the suspect shows no interest in the facts of the crime because they are well acquainted with it, having committed it and all. Or when they've denied the charges against them but are sitting there as calm as a Sunday morning. Ever been falsely accused of something? Even something small, like taking a drink that wasn't yours from the work refrigerator? Got you a little hot under the collar, didn't it? Human beings bristle at false allegations. That's what you'll point out to the chillster across from you. Hey, if you didn't do this, why aren't you mad? You're going to jail on six felonies, you're missing your daughter's birthday, and your probation is in serious jeopardy. All for a crime that, according to you, you didn't commit. Why aren't you pound-on-the-walls furious? You'd expect from them, at the very least, a mixture of confusion and disgust like the look I got from one of my groomsmen when he borrowed my iPod during my wedding weekend and saw that my playlist included a song from *Flashdance*.

The answer is, of course, that unless you are an Oscar-caliber actor, it's hard to feign indignation. A lot of these guys aren't mad because they did it and they know jail is exactly where they should be.

The suspect isn't the only one who can be tricky and deceptive. As the investigator, you also have such license. Some investigators favor artificially padding their case file and then dramatically dropping it on the table with a resounding thud so the suspect thinks, Man oh man, look at that mighty tome against me, might as well just give it up. You are also allowed to use lies to get to the truth. Because if you walk into the room and the guy says "I'm innocent" and you shrug and reply "Okay, I'll take you at your word" and leave, it wouldn't be much of an investigation and you wouldn't be much of an investigator.

So even if you don't have much evidence, you can make it up. Your collection of ruses might include the following:

—Video. You'll claim the whole crime was clearly caught on a high-definition surveillance camera, even if the video you have is lousy film shot at night that just shows a couple of gray blurs moving across the screen. And, you'll remind your suspect, people lie but video doesn't. The suspect can call you out on this, but I've found it to be rare that they'll actually ask to see this so-called video. And if they do, either I'll tell them I haven't watched the video yet because the only guy who can download it isn't in until tomorrow (which is sometimes, in fact, the case) or I'll claim that due to county jail restrictions, I'm not allowed to bring a laptop in to play it. If a guy claims that the video might show a guy who looks like him but isn't him, I'll tell him about the department's facial recognition technology that can positively identify him by comparing the video image to his mug shot. The SFPD does actually have a facial recognition program, but as near as I can gather, it's a herky-jerky system that hasn't been updated since 2014.

—Witnesses. You'll let the suspect know you have scads of them. Plus the victim identified the suspect out of a photo lineup. So did a guy who was just getting off the bus and saw the whole thing. My favorite made-up witness is the off-duty cop. No better witness than him. He's going to stand tall on the stand, you inform the suspect, and the jury is going to believe every word he utters.

—The gabby accomplice. He's in the other room and he already confessed, you insist, but claimed it was all your suspect's idea.

—CSI smorgasbord. The suspect's prints/DNA were found at the scene. (You have to be careful with this, because if the guy wore gloves, he's going to know you're full of it.) Or perhaps soil samples or fibers link the suspect to the crime. Most suspects don't know a hell of a lot about the evidentiary potential of soil or fibers, so you can freely exaggerate their properties. I like to take what I learn from watching *Forensic Files* and multiply it by ten.

—The condition of the victim. Even if the victim is on death's doorstep, you insist he's joking around with the nurses in the hospital and is about to be released with a prescription for something no stronger than Aleve and, hey, probably isn't even that mad at the suspect.

While it is lawful for you to bamboozle, trick, manipulate, pressure, cajole, shout, and pound on the table during an interview, you may not use any physical force against a suspect during an interrogation; the days of smacking guys in the face with a phone book have been over for decades. You're also forbidden from using threats or inducements. Threats include telling a defendant you'll arrest his grandmother or make sure he never sees his kids again if he doesn't cooperate. Inducements extend to promises of leniency; while a general "I'll tell the DA you were cooperative, which could help you" is okay, telling a guy that a confession will cut his sentence in half is out of bounds, as is implying that if he just confesses, he can go home. And while the courts have given the police plenty of room to operate, grilling a guy for hours on end with no food or bathroom breaks will be subject to plenty of judicial scrutiny.

There are long streaks of gray in these black-and-white rules. Press too much and the confession could be tossed out of court as not having been obtained freely and voluntarily. Don't press enough and the suspect may not give you anything to work with at all. This is the line you walk and the best investigators toe it like a trapeze artist.

When it comes to street crime, many of your suspects will be homeless or close to it, poorly educated, unemployed, and chemically dependent. They're far from the good life. (I had one auto burglar who drooled so much on the table that I had to towel it down afterward.) Some are more than happy to tell you their hard-luck tale. Forget the actual victim—these suspects see themselves as the wronged party, as the perpetually downtrodden. So you use that in an interrogation. You play up the class divide. Even if the victim is a third-shift cook at a diner who can barely make rent, you might claim he's wealthy and can easily replace the property that was taken or broken. In fact, this guy is so well-off you're surprised he even bothered to file a police report. And, I gotta say, he's a rich prick, the kind of fat cat who's had the world handed to him all his life. You let the suspects play the victim role while at the same time showing them that you understand them. Then you give them an out. So you say something like: "You're in a rough spot. You're living on the streets. No one will hire you. Meth has its hooks in you. You've got an abscess on your arm, man, and you haven't eaten since yesterday. Did you break into that house just to look for something to eat? To rest for a while?" You'll get confessions with this approach because you've learned never to underestimate people's capacity to feel sorry for themselves. All you're doing is leading them by the hand to the place they already want to go.

When you interrogate multiple suspects, they distance themselves from the crime. For instance, you'll have an armed robbery with four people in a suspect vehicle and every person will claim to have been the driver, which is odd because you didn't see four steering wheels in that Buick, you just saw the one.

Multiple interrogations are labor intensive, because you go at Suspect A and then you talk to Suspect B, but B says something that compels you to talk to A again. Then Suspect C gives you information that makes you want to revisit both A and B. Then some evidence comes in from the field that makes both A and C liars and leaves you wondering if B, although arguably a birdbrain, really did anything criminal at all. You need flashcards to keep track of it all. A flowchart. And a handcart to hold all the flowcharts.

But one of the very best questions you can ask A, B, or C is this: Do you want to be a witness or a suspect? You ask this question even if the person in front of you clearly is a suspect and there's no way they are going to cross into the blameless column of witness. It's a question that gets results. Because people are comfortable with the witness label, which implies they were just along for the ride, a seer, not a doer. And if you get A, B, and C all pointing the finger at each other, you can use that in subsequent interviews to augment your case.

A few suspects will readily admit to their culpability, not because of anything clever you said or did but because they want to unburden themselves; you get the sense these guys would have confessed to a bowl of almonds. But that's the exception to the rule. With everyone else, you have to put the work in. So in addition to the various lies you may tell a suspect that I listed on the previous pages, here are other approaches investigators use to try and get the whole story:

—The sentimental appeal. If suspects seem tight with their family, you ask them something like "Do you think your father will love you any less if he found out you made this mistake?" You tell suspects that the crime they committed will stay with them. Haunt them. The only way to get out from under that weight, to know relief from that secret burden, is to tell you the truth. Or you ask them how they want to be remembered. As a thief and a liar? Or as someone who made a mistake and wants to do better?

You let them know that no matter what they admit to, it's okay, because you'll understand. Because you've heard far worse. Experienced cons often snicker at this approach, but it can work on the criminal novice.

—The other guy. No one is perfect, you tell them. You've never met a perfect person. Maybe they committed this crime because they were drunk. Or they just broke up with their girlfriend and were in a bad place in their own head and that's why when some stranger accidentally brushed into them, they nearly beat him to death. Or was it drugs? Drugs have made good people do things they later regret, you tell them. Point is, the person who did this thing wasn't them. Something, be it rage, narcotics, or alcohol, turned them, just for a moment, into The Other Guy. And we all have that Other Guy in us. We all lose it sometimes. So just tell me what the Other Guy did tonight.

—Invasion of personal space. You start out a distance away from the suspect in a rolling chair and, as the interrogation proceeds, you wheel yourself in until you're close enough to knock knees. Or you touch their shoulder with a reassuring hand. They can't ignore you, you see, because you're practically in their lap.

—The written apology. There are suspects who can't quite bring themselves to verbally confess, but when you float the prospect of writing an apology letter, they leap at it. The mentality at work is Hey, if I say I'm sorry, maybe the consequences won't be so bad. Some of these apology letters are as incriminating as anything the suspect could possibly have said. Some of them, in all their rambling and self-serving glory, are as fun to read as Yelp reviews of the county jail.

Suspects flail about for something, anything, to mitigate their criminal conduct or give themselves a leg up, however dubious. A serial burglar will tell you "Hey, I'm not out here murdering people. Raping people." Okay. Your hot streak of no rapes or murders is certainly appreciated, but it's not much in terms of bragging rights. It's akin to when one of my daughters tells the other, "I'm older than you and I always will be." A career crook once informed me "My friend Miguel will vouch for me." Ah yes, the voucher from ol' Miguel. That will break this case wide open. Maybe Miguel can be a character witness at your sentencing, but for now, unless he was an eyewitness or can commute a prison sentence, his voucher is about as helpful as a frozen turd.

During an interrogation, you gotta roll with it, to switch to Plan B when Plan A shows every sign of not working out at all. You tailor your approach to the person sitting across from you and become who you need to be to get the job done. You may start out as the doctor (if a suspect is sick or hurt, you express concern and give some tips on treating the injury). Then you become the priest offering absolution and in your homily you tell them that God sees everything and they need to get right with the Lord by confessing what they did. You're the understanding barkeep, who knows, with near certainty, that they robbed that liquor store because they have a baby at home and Pampers are $38 a box and they're just trying to do right by their family. You're their life coach, building their self-esteem with a "You're better than that" and a "Don't be so hard on yourself." You play to their ego, telling them, "I hear you're the guy to talk to." (One detective I know openly doubted a criminal's ability to have committed all the burglaries he was accused of in such a short time. The crook took issue with this and felt the need to convince the detective he sure could have and then laid out the details of a dozen B&Es.) Or you inform the accused across from you that just from the short conversation you've had, you can tell they're an intelligent person because in just a minute, you're going to tell them that only an idiot would stick to their raggedy-ass story and you've already established, of course, that they aren't an idiot, so now it's time for them to tell you the truth, the whole truth, and nothing but. Ally, bully, storyteller, skeptic— you cycle through them all if you have to.

Sometimes the persona you create is not so different from their own. You're looking for common ground, and if you can't find it, you invent it. They tell you they have three brothers, suddenly you have three brothers as well. They went to Lancaster High, well how about that, you too, class of '93. If you are interrogating a domestic violence suspect, you'll tell them you hit your old lady too, especially if you've been drinking, because sometimes the bitch just has it coming. In fact if the department knew half the things you've done, you insist, you'd be out of a job and inside a jail cell. SVU detectives will tell a suspect they've had fantasies about doing the exact same thing the suspect is accused of doing to the victim. They'll say something in the order of "Hey, I don't blame you for what you did. You see how she was dressed? She's a tease. She practically came on to me when I was talking to her outside. Besides, you're just giving her the love she isn't getting from her parents." And the detectives are referring to a victim who is six years old. They do this because a pedophile isn't likely to confess to you if it's etched all over your face how utterly revolting you find him.

But while you strive to connect with a suspect, you take care not to stretch your act too thin. Suspects can sniff out artificiality, and if you didn't grow up in their neighborhood, you shouldn't try to sound like you did. I can engage a guy in a conversation about God's anger and mercy because I grew up in the church, but I can't quite pull off the greeting of "What up, blood?" that some of my coworkers can. I'll slip in some slang here and there, like telling a guy "Let's keep it one hundred," as in let's be one hundred percent honest with each other. But I know that I come across as a somewhat folksy white guy from the Midwest with a bit of education under my belt. I try not to stray too far from that. For instance, I'm unable to mask my disgust with child molesters and their ilk and would be utterly ineffective in an interrogation with one. I couldn't form the right words. I don't want to talk to them, I want to shake them until their teeth rattle. But that's why I don't work these cases and greatly respect those who do. As a fabled SF inspector once said, a man has to know his limitations.

At some point, you know you've got them against the ropes. Their protests are getting less and less vigorous. Maybe they're hanging their head a little or there's the start of a sag to their shoulders. They're nodding at what you're saying. You've gotten them to listen to you and now they're just about to agree with you. Their face has softened from defiance to something more like resignation. Some pause and you can see them recalibrate: Boy, that's a lot of evidence against me. Others audibly sigh. They're about to give it up, maybe not all of it, but enough. The spell they're under is fragile and easily broken by a knock on the interrogation room door or a call from a cell phone you forgot to silence. Or by you using just the wrong word at just the wrong time. I once talked to a robbery suspect about mitigating factors on his case. "What does mitigating mean?" he asked, and I had to remind myself, Easy on the fancy talk, college boy.

But if you can maintain, you're nearly where you want to be. Sometimes you let them get there at their own pace. Or you give them a little nudge by asking a question like "If you had to do this all over again, what would you do differently?" Their answer to this question often gives you, as the investigator, a solid foothold. But one of the most time-honored investigative tactics to use right around now is to offer up the Choice. Were you trying to kill him, Lamar? Or just scare him? Did you intend to keep the money, Rebecca? Or were you thinking about returning it? Was any of this your idea, Jaime? Or was it your friend's? Did you plan this, Ethan? Or did it just happen spur of the moment? I'm sure it was spur of the moment, right? The thing about the Choice is that either way they answer, they've sunk themselves.

During an interrogation, you can almost see a suspect dissolve in front of you. You walk through the rooms of their lives and those rooms are in shambles. One man who had beaten another man half to death with a piece of rebar told me, "I'm just a junkie piece of shit. Can we just get straight to the point? I have no control over my life. I can't even support the kid I'm going to be having." I've seen more people than I can count cry during an interrogation. A few have put their heads in their hands and openly wept in front of me. As if they were looking back and could see precisely when it all came unglued. I get the sense on occasion that it's part of an act meant to garner sympathy, but not often. It's not easy to pretend you're looking into the abyss.

You observe this show of emotion clinically. You might enter into the suspect's grief for about half a second. Then you're over it, because you want to avoid what the Buddhists call Idiot Compassion—trying to give people what they want for no other reason than they appear to be in pain. It's also not lost on you that some of the hardest criers will never once ask about the condition of the victim they brutalized. How the victim is doing doesn't matter, unless they're trying to gauge how much trouble they're in. This is because they have, in the words of comedian John Mulaney, the moral backbone of a chocolate éclair. As for you, you figure you have a finite amount of empathy for their woes.

Because it is important to record the suspect's demeanor during the interrogation, you write "He wept frequently" in your police report. For one man, I noted that at the end of the interview he fell to his knees and raised his arms toward me as if in supplication. Made me wonder if I had taken the priest thing a little far.

Even when you've had a decent track record of obtaining them, you still find confessions remarkable. "I'm gonna tell you the real deal, Holyfield," a two-striker named Charles said just before telling me he'd stabbed my victim twice in the chest. I felt a jolt in my sternum of equal parts elation and wonder. This man just admitted to attempted murder. There wasn't much of a case before we walked into this room. Now, if things go the way they're supposed to, he'll be spending the remainder of his criminally productive years in a place like Folsom. Charles had dozens of prior felony arrests. He'd been in rooms with guys like me time and time again. Didn't the last detective try these same tricks with him? Didn't his last public defender warn him about the games cops play? How is this well not completely dried up? How are experienced cons still falling for this happy horseshit?

At times, the confessor finds his confession as remarkable as you. One of my suspects admitted to a damning crime and then shook his head, as if emerging from a trance, and said, "I can't believe I just sat here and fucking . . ." He couldn't even bring himself to say the word *confessed*. Another defendant, during the midst of his aggravated assault confession, had just a blip of self-awareness. "I'm incriminating myself," he said, "and you know it." I told him all he was doing was squaring up to this thing. Like men do. He nodded, as if I had said something meaningful, and kept right on incriminating himself. An eleven-time convicted burglar who had just confessed to six more burglaries and misheard my last name told me, "I've already given you too much, Sgt. Flannigan." Sgt. Flannigan agreed whole-heartedly.

When your interrogation is over, a suspect who has confessed might ask what happens next. An investigator, still riding a high for playing him and playing him hard, might feel the urge to answer, "What happens next is you're gonna go to jail for a long time, dumbass, because you just confessed to a Class A felony." This might feel good but isn't the way to go. For one, it may not be true. Victims recant, cases fall apart at trial, and defendants get acquitted. Even if he's convicted, he might serve only half his sentence due to good behavior and jail overcrowding. Odds are he'll be committing crimes upon his release so you'll probably be seeing him again. He'll be sitting right back where he was, across the table from you as you try to portray yourself as the understanding cop he should confide in about his most recent offense. And maybe he recalls that you were the asshole who talked down to him. It's the kind of thing people remember.

But even if you will never see this fellow again, you don't lord it over him because you are a professional. No need to gloat. You've done your job. The rest is up to the courts. In fact, you try to leave people on an uptick when-ever possible. I always thank suspects for their time. I tell them to keep their head up. The Don't Be a Dick rule applies even here. And it yields some interesting results. "Sorry, Oficial," one Spanish-speaking burglar told me in what seemed like all sincerity after he admitted to his crime. As if he had personally let me down. "Nice talking to you," a suspect told me earnestly after confessing to aggravated assault for smashing a security guard in the face with a bottle. Another guy, who had told me many things that would hurt him in court, turned to me before I left the room and said, softly, "Thanks for listening to me."

You're welcome, man.

Some departments use video and others just employ audio to record interrogations. Most investigators hide their recorders in their shirt pocket or inside a folder. Any thinking criminal knows you're recording, but they often seem to forget it, just like they forget it is largely against their best interests to speak to you at all.

Now and again, a confession will be informed by the suspect's failure to grasp the role of the recorder. I interviewed one man who was under arrest for attempt homicide. "Can I talk to you off the record?" he asked me earnestly, like I was a beat reporter. I told him I was there to listen to him. He then promptly confessed to the assault, which fractured the victim's skull, sent a section of bone pressing up against his brain, and caused temporary paralysis. The tape kept rolling. There is no off the record.

When you listen to the recording later back at your desk, you always think of the question you should have asked. You are struck by how many times your suspect said "You feel me?" and how many times you started off a sentence with "Umm." Or you hear him say something important, like the street name of a possible codefendant, but you glossed over it because you were too busy prepping your next verbal sleight of hand. That's why, although some investigators prefer to interrogate alone to avoid clashing styles, it's helpful to have a partner in the room to pick up on what you miss.

I can understand how the general public might find some of the tactics that the police use in an interrogation room to be cold, manipulative, even morally questionable. I won't argue with that. (I have also not revealed nearly all the tactics we employ because you gotta keep some stuff close to the vest.) But I hold that these measures are necessary. They don't give you a truth lasso like Wonder Woman. You can't compel suspects to undergo a polygraph exam, although you might ask them to take one just to gauge their reaction. The suspects seated across from you are often warped by drugs, abuse, and hard living. You may not be able to appeal to their nobility or sense of fair play or the need to make the victim of their crime whole. So you use the tools at your disposal. You are fair but relentless, bordering on ruthless. You treat your suspect with some measure of dignity even as you look for weaknesses to exploit. You fight fire with fire and then some. Because your cause is just. It is your sworn obligation as a law enforcement officer to protect society from these kinds of people, and if that means you have to edge into darkness yourself, so be it. You owe victims that. The victims who have been raped or bludgeoned or shot. That's how you recognize the victims' personhood. That is how you honor them.

So how long do you go at a guy before you give up? If the crime in front of you is a legitimate violent felony and you are dedicated to your craft, the answer is as long as it takes. It is your duty to stay in that room until they ask for a lawyer, tell you they're done talking, or until you've exhausted everything in your bag of tricks. I know a cop who spent three hours in a room with a suspect just to get him to admit to his gang affiliation, which can be a crime enhancement. He didn't get a confession, but it was still three hours well spent. Homicide investigators will grill a suspect for hours, even into the double digits.

As for the rest of the cases, you have to triage, because there's a stack of files on your desk and they can't all get the royal treatment. And maybe your partner is out with shoulder surgery or on maternity leave. If a suspect isn't giving it up after, say, an hour, you may just let it be. You don't have unlimited time for interrogations.

Family matters also come into play. I remember gearing up for an interrogation while also thinking how nice it would be to get home for my kids' soccer game. Or at least in time to tuck them in. After yet another grim week of fourteen-hour days, my wife told me she felt like a single parent. I missed her and my kids keenly. My older daughter's bouncy good cheer and frequent offbeat questions like "Daddy, were you alive in ancient times?" My younger daughter's self-administered, magnificently uneven haircut and wide, goofy grin. So I'd fast-track the occasional nonviolent case, especially if it was already pretty solid. Maybe the burglary suspect got caught red-handed. In his backpack is the book *Practical Lock Picking: Second Edition*. In his pants pocket—the victim's wedding ring. I recall a scenario with one such suspect.

"So did you do this or what?" I asked after I read him his rights.

"Nope," he said.

"Okay, sounds good," I replied. And left the room and headed home to see my girls.

19

OGs

When Wilson and I were chasing that kid. . . . Do you know what it feels like to be running down 43rd Street, and your partner is cornering a guy on 52nd? Do you how I found out what happened? I asked a reporter! Four radio stations beat me to the scene of the crime!
—Abe Vigoda as Detective Phil Fish, *Barney Miller*

You've been on the job for a time. You don't know it all, but you know just enough to be wrong less often. One day you look in the mirror and wonder why you appear so cranky. What's there to frown about? You have stable employment. The game is on. Your wife just made you a bacon omelet. Then you realize that's no mere frown, that's a permanent forehead crease. And you look further and you see flecks of white on your chin. Truth be told, you initially think they're pleasant reminders of that powdered donut you just wolfed down. But they don't seem to go anywhere when you try to rub them off. Hang on. That's not powdered sugar. Those are white hairs.

Then you think on it some more. No one would describe you as dynamic; you need a brace on each knee just to use the elliptical at the gym. You've lost a belt loop of late—used to be you could cinch it four notches and now it's down to three. At work, you still say the proper things to members of the community, but you say them more tonelessly now, like how a tired waitress sounds when she tells you that'll be right up. Your station just hoisted a giant banner above the exit door that says "Remember, *You* Are SFPD's Finest!" and when you see it, you kind of want to give it the finger. Some days you wonder what's going on in the command van and how nice it would be to sit in there and take your shoes off. You've found yourself incessantly grumbling about your department, noting, for instance, that you all recently received new uniform patches, fancy dark blue ones with the embroidered city seal. The same emblem is now emblazoned on all the police cars, which caused hundreds of them to have to be repainted. New patches and emblems, hooray. That will really put a dent in the crime rate. Thank goodness all of that money wasn't foolishly squandered on technology or infrastructure or elevators that don't break every other week.

All of this means you're getting old. Not old-old but cop-old. You are becoming someone and that someone is known in police circles as the OG (Old Guy). The OG, loosely defined as a cop with more than twenty years on, is the backbone of the police department. And, at times, the bane.

OGs are aging, sure, but they aren't washed up yet; they can do everything the job requires, just more slowly and with joint pain. OGs wear an unhurried air. They still think it's fun to outfox the bad guys, although not as fun as it used to be. OGs lament how times have changed. Used to be that if they screwed up, a supervisor would call them into the office and tell them to straighten their shit out. Now every complaint is put on paper. Probably a van parked by their house filled with Internal Affairs watching them with a damn periscope.

The OG will pass on to other officers what their mentors passed on to them. Much of what they have to say is clear, wise, and vulgar: "Kid, stay clear of the money and screw at home."

OGs will describe the Ghetto Retirement Plan to anyone who will listen. Step One is to do a crappy job parenting and raise a criminal moron. Step Two is to wait for him to be killed by the police. Step Three is to sue the city for millions and hope for a settlement. That's the plan in a nutshell, with the overriding theme being that no one gave this man a second thought until he died.

OGs were on the job at a time when they carried revolvers, the old wheel gun. Tennis shoes were forbidden and the standard issue pants were wool with white stripes down the side, the stripes preventing cops from wearing them to church. In the summer, officers were required to wear blazers similar to suit jackets, which looked better than the regular garb but were roasting in the heat.

OGs remember when there was a height requirement on police departments. For SFPD, in 1966, it was 5'8". A police commander told me that one fellow who applied that year was only 5'7", but he really wanted to be a cop so when he was in the doctor's office just prior to being measured, he got hold of a two by four and whacked himself in the head. When his height was officially taken, the knot on his skull put him at 5'9". He got the job.

The OG knows to check under parked vehicles for discarded handguns at shooting scenes. When his winter turtleneck gets worn at the edges, he doesn't buy a new one, he just uses a black permanent marker to fill in the gaps. He has mastered the "As long as they keep paying me every other Tuesday" head shake. Has struggled mightily with the transition from handwritten reports to typed, because the only people he knew who typed were secretaries. Old-timers like to grumble but don't have much patience for other grumblers. Because no one forced you to join the department. How did you think it would be like? What did you think you would see?

CompStat, short for "computer statistics," is a data-driven police system thought up by NYPD cop Jack Maple that targets chronic offenders and floods crime-ridden areas with the most resources. But OGs don't need any fancy crime-mapping software to pinpoint hot spots. Ask an old-timer where the crime is and he'll point north. Then east and west. So to the south, is that okay then? Nope, it's bad down there too.

OGs have archenemies who fall in the following order:

1. The career criminal.

2. The unreasonable citizen who knows nothing about the job but sees fit to tell you how to do it. The proper response for these people? *Work these streets just for a week and come back and see me. Until then, shut your piehole.*

3. Supervisors. OGs feel they've been wronged by so many bosses—passed up for promotions, unfairly disciplined, transferred out of a coveted specialty unit because they had the audacity to arrest the assistant chief's crackhead brother—that they'll say the greatest threat to a working cop is from the inside, not the outside. And they'll believe it with all their heart. In fact, as far as the OG is concerned, the entire police command staff should be fired and replaced by pill bugs. The bugs would just crawl around in the dirt and curl up into a ball when approached, which would be far more productive than what these idiots are doing.

4. Rookie cops. They don't know jack shit. Bunch of college kids with their sensitivity training, more social workers than anything, want to connect with the community as they learned in the academy. Hey, look

at this community. There's Ray-Ray sleeping in his van. He always has lice and likes to carry a straight razor in his shoe. Just got paroled for lighting his girlfriend on fire. And Martha, the toothless hooker whose children were taken away from her because she tried to sell them for cocaine. There's your community, kid. Go bring them hope or some shit.

The OG ranks are populated by tough guys who have uncompromising rules about calling in sick, because when you take an unscheduled day off, it leaves your fellow officers short on manpower and backup. My FTO, Gilbert Gwinn, cut his hand open with a saw while off duty. He swathed it up and came in the next day, adding that he enjoyed a certain level of pain. "It says God is paying attention to me and knows who I am," Gil mused. Rolf Mueller worked his last twenty-three years of street patrol without calling in sick. Take that, Cal Ripken Jr.

OGs scoff at the new breed of officer who not only has the temerity to take a sick day but then tries to inform the shift supervisor of their absence via text instead of a phone call. The OG will imitate the rookie softie by mock-whining "I can't make it in, lieutenant. I got a doctor's appointment. There's a rock in my shoe. The sun's in my eyes."

Just as deplorable to the OG is the cop who calls in sick every time his partner calls in sick, because neither feels like working with anyone else on the shift. Words like dependability and trust still mean something to the OG, who knows that these kinds of sicky-sick duos are cementing a certain reputation; their fellow officers won't remember the great felony arrest they made but will remember that they couldn't be counted on. That they didn't show when it mattered.

My wife and I dated long-distance for several years while I was in Milwaukee and she was in San Francisco. One weekend, she flew in for a surprise visit. I was delighted to see her, but I had to work Saturday. She told me to call in sick. "I can't," I said, channeling the OG. "I'm not sick."

This did not go over well.

So what do OGs want from their supervisors? To have their backs and maybe go light on the speeches. Competence is a nice bonus but is in no way required. The old guard really wants supervisors to do three things:

1. Stay out of their way.
2. Give them the off-days they want.
3. Sign their overtime cards.

If an OG is close enough to retirement that he can leave whenever he'd like, he'll acquire a KMA pin for his uniform. KMA stands for Kiss My Ass. Way it works is, if an OG is given an order he doesn't care for, he'll say he won't do it, and if he is told he'll be written up for insubordination, he'll say go right ahead. Look at the pin. He's on his way out, there's gonna be a vacancy, and the bosses should just go ahead and post the sign that says Help Wanted, Inquire Within. KMA, suckers.

OGs have the best go-to lines at work. One of their favorites, said with cheerful cynicism, is "I'm from the government and I'm here to help." I once heard an old head proclaim, "In the '70s, we were allowed to do terrible things. Ask an OG 'How are you?' and some will reply 'Fat and white.'" Rolf Mueller liked to say, "It's a dirty job. And you win some and you lose some. And the wins never quite add up to the losses. But that's all you got." I'm not sure if he picked that up from a movie or a book or if it was born in some organic pool of toughness. But I haven't forgotten it.

OGs also have all the best hypotheticals. If you're in the station parking lot and back into your personal car with your patrol vehicle while on the clock, does the department have to pay for it? If you total your car, will the department have to buy you a new one?

OGs watch rookies with a mixture of amusement and thinly disguised contempt. After a heart-pounding foot pursuit or car chase that ends in an arrest, they'll hear some giddy new cop exclaim, "I'd do this job for free!" The OG had that kind of enthusiasm once, a decade and a half ago. Give it time, rook. Soon you'll be disaffected just like the rest of us, absorbed into the Collective. An OG will come across a parked patrol car with two young cops in it, both of their heads buried in their phone texting or playing games. "If I'd been a bad guy, I could have capped them both," the OG will announce back at the station. Look up, youngsters. There's a big world out there, outside of Candy Crush.

What's even worse, to the OG, is the new cop's tendency to ask a street sergeant about every single thing. Used to be calling a boss for advice or to come to your scene was considered a sign of weakness. Now guys with four, five, six years on are still calling to "run something by" a supervisor. The OG's position is this; you get paid a decent amount of money as a patrol cop to make your own decisions. So make one.

But while the rookie freeze-out is commonplace, a notable exception is made for soldiers. Veteran cops have great respect for those who have served our country in the armed forces. Soldiers, especially those who have seen combat, know more about brotherhood, danger, and loss than many cops ever will.

As a new recruit, you are often assigned an OG as a field training officer. This could be a mixed bag. When you check in with the desk sergeant, he might gesture to a sour-looking old-timer in back chewing on a toothpick with a yellowish cast to his face from thirty years of smoking cigarettes, sigh, and say, "Okay, kid. You've got Screwy Louie." The Louies of the department are FTOs solely for the modest spike in pay and will make their recruits write parking tickets in a downpour because it's both funny and pointless. But most OGs train out of a sense of duty. They'll be tough on their charges because twenty-five years ago, their FTO, who was light infantry in the Korean War, was tough on them. The OG's FTO had them halfway convinced that they policed at a time when there were no cars or handcuffs, so if you made an arrest and couldn't find a wheelbarrow, you'd have to beat your prisoner into submission, throw him over your shoulder, and carry him to the precinct like a sack of wheat. OGs will make it a point to respond to all the worst calls, even if it's far from their car sector. They'll yell to inoculate recruits against stress (or just because they're annoyed). One of my coworkers lost twenty pounds on field training under the supervision of a righteous OG who refused to stop for meals and rode him every step of the way.

When I was a new recruit in Milwaukee, a prisoner slipped his handcuffs, jumped out of my patrol car, and disappeared into the woods. He completely outclassed me and the day was his. The next morning I had in-service training. Two OGs behind me were talking about the incident in disgust.

"That had to be a fucking rookie," one of them said.

The fucking rookie looked at his shoes and said nothing.

I was subsequently suspended from the police department for four days on a negligence charge. I didn't bother appealing the decision. I had seemed pretty negligent to me too. I ended up taking the red-eye to Vegas for a long weekend. It seemed like the right place for a suspended cop to go. OGs call getting suspended "days on the beach." Some of them don't seem to mind suspensions that much. The attitude is, you know, I could use the break.

OGs have more than one locker in the locker room. Some OGs have four, this in a station where lockers come at a premium, where recruits are actually changing clothes in the hallway because there is nowhere else for them to go. Multiple lockers equal status. And the sign on your locker that the hapless facilities manager posts saying Please Identify Yourself or This Lock Will Be Cut Off and the Contents Removed—that sign represents an empty threat, because nobody messes with an OG's locker. KMA, everyone. KMA.

Some OGs will go to court in uniform without bothering to strap on their holster, opting instead to tuck their gun in their often generous beltline. You want to tell them, "You, my friend, have just significantly increased the odds of shooting yourself in the scrotum." But they are who they are and will do what they do.

OG cops tend to leave OG criminals alone. Not because they don't believe old people do wrong but because OG criminals aren't usually the ones committing violent crimes; last night's drive-by probably wasn't planned and carried out by the sixty-five-year-old on the corner with a porkpie hat and diabetic socks. OGs know they aren't going to change their criminal namesakes and vice versa.

Conversely, older cops look out for and engage with older citizens who require the kind of light touch that a younger cop might not have the patience for. Like the elderly woman who calls the police to report a prowler, but when the officers show up, doesn't seem interested in what they've found or not found. The real reason for her call is she wants company and knows that if you dial up the police, they have to come. She has coffee and cake already set up. Please sit down, she says. She wants to chat. About her childhood. About how her sons don't visit her anymore. She talks like she's used to no one paying attention to her and answers questions about herself that no one has asked. When the OG rises to leave, she wonders if he could stay a little longer? And he will sit politely with her for as long as he's able, because he understands something about human nature and human kindness. Understands something about how painful and crippling loneliness can be. She'll probably call again next week. And he'll come back. "Old age is a shipwreck," Charles de Gaulle observed. Maybe he was talking about the old woman at the table with coffee and cake. He might as well have been talking about cops.

"Back in the day" is the OG's preferred way of starting sentences. Got a lippy prisoner? "Back in the day, into the dark corner we went," the OG muses. "For some behavior modification." (With the prevalence of surveillance cameras and cell phone videos, there aren't as many dark corners as there used to be now, which is good for citizens, criminals, and cops alike.)

Back in the day, the crooks were still afraid of the police. An OG would battle some guy on PCP and kick him down a stairwell. A few weeks later, he'd see the guy and would actually get an apology. There should be an "oh damn" moment when thugs see the law coming, the OG will postulate. When you come out of your car, they should want to go inside. They aren't scared enough. They need to be scared.

Back in the day, some OGs would bust up a teen party and put all the confiscated alcohol in their car trunks. Funny thing though, this booze never made it into evidence, but swing shift sure had a blowout after-party that night.

In this enlightened era, if you get in a job-related shooting, you attend department-mandated counseling with a shrink. But a few decades ago, the after-action shoot team was a couple of tough pieces of meat with some notches on their belt who would slap you on the back and then you'd get drunk for three days. No one had heard of posttraumatic stress. Back in the day.

"Back in the day" is exclusive territory; if anyone with fewer than ten years on ever says it, his fellow officers will roll their eyes. Because he hasn't earned the right yet, and it makes him sound like kind of a dork.

Old-timers can still throw down if called on but get by more on wit and guile than brute force. Plus pepper spray. A boatload of pepper spray. At this stage in their career, OGs just want the suspect to get in the car. Just get in the car, man. Who needs the drama. They've gotten in enough fights over their police career. They don't need any more. Just get in the car.

Except when the guy doesn't get in the car, the OG has to show he hasn't lost it, not yet. He has to show he's still relevant. That it is proper and fitting that he wears a police uniform. So the struggle is on. And if he tries his favorite take-down move, the one that has worked so faithfully over the years, and it fails, then out will come the pepper spray, and the whole room's getting lit up.

Veteran cops approach retirement in vastly different ways. Some guys stagger toward the finish line, their life made up of Used Tos. They used to bike. Used to be in a softball league. Used to get together with friends. The constant adrenaline spikes and crashes from street duty have taken a toll. They treat their families like suspects. They brood. You worry about them when they're on the job and maybe even more after they've left. As any good police psychologist will tell you, now that he's retired, a cop has unstructured time and money. And maybe the shield was the only thing that kept him off the bottle.

But others reach the final lap with a bit more in the tank, or seemingly unscathed. A few, hale and hearty. Marrying well helps, tethering yourself to someone healthy and true.

But regardless of what kind of shape they're in when they get there, every cop has a plan for their last day on the job. Who they're gonna tell off. Where they're going to eat lunch. What sincere or snarky comment they're going to make on the radio. And then that beautiful day arrives when the department calls with a question about a case, or to try to serve you with a subpoena. But you don't answer. Because you just turned in your gun and shield. Here it is, lieutenant, one police career, gently used. We're closing down shop over here. Thank you for your patronage. Thank you forever. You're doing other things now. You've got hobbies. Doubles tennis. Abalone diving. Rebuilding the engine on your Mustang. Planting corn in the back forty. Your summer place has a sign above the door that says Better Times. Whatever the case, you're busy. You are, in fact, busy for the rest of your natural life.

This high doesn't last forever. Some OGs miss the job even knowing it left scars. They'll still use the station house gym with the fellas or sign up to be a police auxiliary. It's not unusual for an OG to join another police department to supplement their pension and fill their day. Being a cop is a significant portion of your identity. Some veterans struggle with that. If I am no longer this, who am I?

You're an OG an hour into your shift and you're already tired. Your lower back sports a bulging disk that feels like the size of a cantaloupe, which isn't helped by twenty-five years of carrying an extra twenty-five pounds on your duty belt. You're pretty sure the time it took you to run a mile and a half in the academy is now the time it takes you to lace on your running shoes. Your to-do list for the weekend has two things on it, "Get bread" and

"Colonoscopy." The shifts when you go to work but aren't wholly there are more frequent now. You wonder if the drug dealers on the corner still see you as a threat. Your disenchantment is such you transfer to a new station for a fresh start because someone once told you change is good but you find it to be the same circus, just different clowns.

You have been anesthetized against people's pain because you've seen too many deaths, some of them children. You have adopted a kind of surly stasis. Have started to doubt the worthiness of your cause. Harry Bosch says, "Everybody counts or nobody counts," and there was a time when you believed that, but on your bad days you're leaning toward the latter. Certain members of the public hate you and you hate them right back. When you took this job, you actually thought you'd make a difference. And once in a while you did. But not often enough.

Then you see some jittery new recruit struggling to perform basic hand-cuffing, or going to court and checking in at the Public Defender's table instead of the DA's because he can't tell the difference between them. He's doing his best, but his best ain't much. The fact that his shoes are extra shiny and his stomach has not yet begun to creep over his duty belt are about all he's got going in the plus column right now. He doesn't belong here, not yet. Like some flatlander trying to acclimate to the altitude. He'll probably be fine—he's not who he's going to be. The department will survive his incompetence. After all, you were him once, and it survived yours. But you don't want to be him anymore. He's got thirty years of this left. You can count your remaining years on one hand.

So you watch him. And you are glad you are no longer young.

20

Evidence

(Academy recruits are brought in to help Homicide Detective Rich Garvey search a large outdoor area for homicide evidence.) One enterprising recruit produces, from the rear yard of 704 Newington, a clear plastic bag half filled with a dull yellow liquid. "Sir," he asks, holding the bag up to eye level, "is this important?"
"That appears to be a bag of piss," says Garvey. "You can put it down anytime you like."
—David Simon, *Homicide: A Year on the Killing Streets*

The hard sciences have never been my strong suit. If memory serves, I scraped out a D on my senior physics final. So when I became a cop, I made a point to pepper the CSI techs with questions to make sure I was on the right track in terms of gathering evidence at crime scenes. And when I heard a lieutenant from Bayview Station say, "If I ever commit a crime and Ronan Shouldice is assigned to the case, I may as well just turn myself in because he'll find the evidence that will put me away." I thought, Ronan Shouldice, I gotta have lunch with this guy. I had heard of Inspector Shouldice before, a native of Dublin with nearly thirty years on the job and over twenty in CSI, who used to carry a tool kit with him to help burglary victims shore up their broken doors and windows until the repairman could come in the morning and who once sealed the fate of a murder suspect by finding his partial prints on the underside of a toilet lid at a brutal slaying scene. Shouldice was kind enough to meet me for that lunch and helped confirm and fine-tune the facts that follow here about prints and DNA.

Baseball bats are notoriously hard to get prints off, unless they have a fresh lacquered finish, not only because wood isn't the best surface for prints, but because the wielder of the bat tends to grip the instrument so hard that any prints left become pressure distorted and opaque. Handguns aren't much better—Shouldice told me his team gets usable prints off about 5 to 8 percent of firearms. This percentage is low because guns have checkered handgrips and serrated edges where the shooter handles them, and when you're looking for prints, smooth is good and textured isn't. The best chance for gun prints is off the magazine, which has no rough edges. But all those grooves and crevices are a good bet for DNA because they scrape the skin cells off the shooter's hand. Even if the shooter wore gloves during the crime, that doesn't mean he was wearing them the day before when he was doing his Tom Mix quick-draw moves in the mirror. So when processing a gun, the seasoned ID tech will print the smooth parts and swab the serrated parts for DNA.

DNA can be found in blood, saliva, mucous, semen, hair roots, and sometimes in vomit and urine. Conventional wisdom used to be there was no DNA in feces unless blood was found in it, so if you sent bloodless poop to the lab, all they'd be able to tell you is that maybe the guy had pizza for lunch. Then they'd tell you, please stop sending us poop. But on July 28, 2017, the Ventura County Sheriff's Office in California arrested a suspect named Andrew Jensen for burglary based on DNA evidence yielded from the dump Jensen had taken in the burglary victim's toilet and neglected to flush. I called the detective on the case, and he confirmed the DNA came from a swab of blood-free poop. I checked with our Crime Lab and was told that if you have a "solid poop coil," CSI can swab the outside of it to collect epithelial cells that get sloughed off during the process of elimination. I bet CSI techs everywhere are rejoicing at this news because, folks, work just became a lot more fun.

With every serious crime scene, you have to consider contact DNA, which can found on a suspect's clothing or on things that he touches. It's more difficult to get than DNA from bodily fluids, but still viable. Basically, if the suspect wore it, held it, or drank from it, it might have his DNA on it. If a criminal abandons his jacket at the scene, an astute investigator will submit it to the lab to swab the inner collar and hood, the insides of the sleeves, and the zipper for DNA. The inside of ski masks is pretty good for contact DNA as is the inside of hat bands. Fake fingernails broken off and left at a crime scene might result in a DNA profile. DNA from the hands of suspects has been found on the necks of strangling victims. Our SF lab has recovered DNA from a crowbar and from the noseguard of sunglasses that have helped me solve cold burglaries. But just because a suspect's DNA is on an item doesn't mean he was the last one to hold that item. Maybe he sneezed on it or shook hands with someone who then handled it. And there's no way to tell when DNA was left—it could be from six months ago or from today.

If a DNA profile is generated from evidence, it's entered into CODIS (Combined DNA Index System), the FBI's computer warehouse. Then you sit back and wait. Bring your copy of *The Silmarillion* because it's gonna be awhile. I had a burglary that happened in November and I got DNA results from the scene the following July, which was actually pretty quick for San Francisco. Even for homicides, which are fast-tracked, the quickest turn-around for DNA results is probably going to be one to three weeks.

If the computer makes a match, you'll receive some gobbledygook paper-work from the state that says the chances of your profile not being from your suspect are something like one in forty nonillion. In my jurisdiction, you still have to get a confirmatory sample from the suspect to seal the deal. This is a royal pain in the ass, especially if your suspect is a transient who likes to play hide-and-seek with the cops. Last you heard, he had no fixed address but could possibly be found underneath the 101 overpass, through the hole in the chain link fence, and in the seventh tent on the left as you count forward from the shopping cart filled with bicycle parts.

Need DNA from your suspect but lack the probable cause for a warrant? If you're in a public place shadowing your target, you can retrieve his discarded cigarette butt or soft-drink straw and submit it for DNA testing and the results will be admissible in court.

Advances in DNA come at a rapid clip and labs are increasingly able to do a lot more with a lot less, such that some of the information I have relayed here could be out of date in the next few years. It used to be that a single DNA test from Crime Labs in some jurisdictions would run upward of $2,000, especially if the sample had to be outsourced. When I last checked with our lab, now it's more like two hundred, which means we can afford to fight crime again.

One of the more delightful moments in evidence collection is when a crook, under the mistaken belief that getting rid of the security camera means getting rid of the video footage, climbs up to disable the camera, thus affording the surveillance system a close-up look at his face. My colleague Sgt. Nick Pena once said of such a fellow, "He does everything short of fogging the lens and wiping it clean." The delicious irony, of course, is that this man, in trying to avoid detection, is putting himself on full display. But some thieves just don't get it. Some, in fact, stare down that camera so intently, it's as if they think there's money inside it.

Not all views of the suspect are so crystalline. I've watched many a surveillance tape where the main action takes place just around the periphery of the camera view. All you see is a flurry of knees and feet. Could be some guys fighting or they could be doing the lambada. And you know who has surprisingly lousy surveillance cameras? Banks. You see still photos from bank robbery Crime Alerts all the time that are consistently grainy. I asked one robbery investigator why this was, and he mused that banks have no incentive to invest in a high-end system. All their money is FDIC insured. If a robber steals their cash, the federal government replaces it. I'm waiting on someone in Washington to institute quality standards for bank video surveillance to help catch more of these folks who are ripping us all off. I don't know. The feds should consult me on more things. I have good ideas.

They don't quite have the technology to get workable prints off spent shell casings, and Ronan Shouldice was unimpressed with the machine that purportedly does. Most people know you can match both a bullet and a shell casing to the weapon of origin by the distinct markings left on the round as it travels through the gun barrel. But you can also, at times, match the cartridges to the magazine they came from. This doesn't normally work with the first several rounds you load, because they go in easy, but as anyone who has ever thumbed bullets into a spring-loaded magazine will tell you, the last few cartridges carry a lot of tension. That tension leaves unique patterns on the cartridge. This is helpful when you find some shell casings at a crime scene and then find a nearby thug with an empty magazine in his pocket. You can use the sweet science of ballistics to pulverize his dreams of getting away scot-free.

Another ballistics staple is the collection of gunshot residue (GSR), which is made up of tiny particles formed from the burn of a fired bullet. It's a tool law enforcement uses to see if a suspect recently pulled the trigger. You want to get it within four hours if possible, and if you can't obtain it at the scene, you bag the suspect's hands until you can swab them later. You want to ask the suspect if he's right- or left-handed and if there would be any reason why he'd have GSR on him.

GSR has considerable limitations. A suspect in the know might claim he works in an auto shop and got the equivalent of GSR from a car's brake pads. Or he might protest that he was near the gun being fired but didn't fire it himself. Or his lawyer will surmise that his client picked up transfer GSR from one of the cops who arrested him, probably the officer who qualified at the range earlier that day. A specially trained forensic analyst at a lab with the right equipment may be able to break down the test results by number of particles—this fellow had ten particles of GSR on him and this woman had two hundred. But odds are your department doesn't have the funds to send hundreds of shooting cases a year to this specialist. So you opt for standardized testing, which simply tells you if GSR is present, not how much of it there is.

Given these shortcomings, some jurisdictions don't even bother with GSR. But it can serve as a good interrogation tool with a rookie criminal. You can try to convince him GSR is better than DNA and tells you all you need to know about him and the gun he fired and the ammunition he used. After all, GSR and DNA are both three-letter acronyms that sound kind of science-y.

Bullet trajectory analysis is another vital area of ballistics science. A trained CSI officer will use long lines of colored string to show the jury the path of the bullet to debunk a defense attorney's claim that his client was on his knees in the process of surrendering when the police shot him. On a homicide case, trajectory analysis can mathematically prove, for instance, that the driver fired the fatal shot, not the passenger, unless the passenger happened to be thirty feet tall.

Police work is a job where you delve deeply into other people's cell phones and call records looking for evidence to shore up your case. Their phone configurations are often different from yours. Take Contacts, for instance. On your own cell, you might have an old pal saved on your scroll-down list with his college handle of Squid. But the majority of your list tends to be birth names, either first or last. Antonio. Natasha. McMilton. Not so with many of the street criminals' phones you encounter. Contacts are listed by their nicknames. Like Kupcake, Lil' Blue, and D-Boy. Some are just classified by their customary garb, like White Tee. Others by produce, like Melon. There's Dirtball and the enigmatic Dug Freeze. One poor soul is just called Ugly. One of my favorites contacts of all times is Skeeznutz. I almost called him just to get the backstory.

Colorful nicknames aside, looking through someone's phone records is excruciating. The resulting report from your search warrant can total thousands of pages of texts, emails, calls, videos, and photos. This glob of information traditionally includes commercial and homemade porn. Selfies of the suspect smoking weed. Multiple photos of orange soda and orders of fried fish in Styrofoam cartons. Money is a recurring theme. You'll see the suspect holding a wad of cash, biting down on the bills like it's a stack of flapjacks, and spreading money out on his bed. Group photos follow a common theme—a dozen or so scowling males on some project stairwell holding their arms out simulating handguns or rifles that they point at the cameras. A few will be wearing ski masks despite sunny conditions.

As far as what they're looking for in a woman, jean skirts and leopard tattoos on upper breasts seem to be in fashion. And then there's this text I came across from the girlfriend of a gang member:

"Listen, any bitch can spend time with you, blow a dime with you, cuff online with you, fuck & 69 with you, but me? Ima ride with you, hold a 9 for you, if you need it, I got it, ima grind with you, if the cops come & snatch you up, I'm doing time with you & putting my right hand on the book and I'm straight lying for you."

The loyalty is admirable. You gotta give her that.

Photos are among the most basic and powerful evidence available to an investigator. A good FTO will instruct his recruit to take them in logical progression and describe them in the police report, so that a year from now, when the cop is on the stand, he can remember what he took a picture of and why.

I especially like taking pictures of drunk people. Say some plastered Chad takes a swing at you and you arrest him. Months from now, he's going to be in court, all polite and with a snazzy haircut saying, No, your honor, I did no such thing. But your photos at the scene show him with bloodshot eyes and crusted vomit on his shirt and he's grabbing his own crotch in defiance. You have crystallized this special moment for all of time.

I wrote about jail calls briefly in *400 Things Cops Know* and have touched on them earlier in these pages, but I'm returning to the topic because I find it fascinating, chiefly, how a suspect will incriminate himself despite the clear, audible warning that jail calls are recorded and subject to monitoring. The way it usually goes down is like this: A suspect will call a friend or family member from lockup and that person will ask what happened. And having just heard the warning, the suspect will respond with something like "I can't get into it too much on this phone." Or he'll say the obligatory "I didn't do shit." But then he keeps talking. And talking. And he forgets about the warning, sometimes just a few minutes later. He might describe precisely where he discarded the handgun he used in his crime, using only flimsy code—calling the gun "the bitch," for instance—to try to cover his tracks. When a concerned relative asks why he's in jail again for robbery, he'll admit he "got greedy." One of my colleagues told me of a jail call he listened to where his shooting suspect expressed indignation about the purported facts of the case, saying hell yeah, he shot the guy but he for damn sure didn't rob him. In short, the suspect inadvertently tells on himself. Perhaps he can't help it. There is far too much in his life that is lawless. It's bound to surface.

Beyond their evidentiary value, jail calls give you a window into the suspect's world and that world is frequently bleak. Suspects alternate between bluster ("I been locked up my whole fucking life, this ain't nothing") and outright despair ("Can't do no more time, I'm going crazy up in here"). You get a sense of the tremendous pressure they're under. The phone call itself is stressful. The first few are free, but then it's ten bucks for fifteen minutes, like long distance used to cost in the '80s. And the girl-friend is irate because she's got a baby on the way and now her man is in county again and just who's gonna pay rent? You'll hear relationships rise and fall in the span of a few phone conversations as two people try to pick up the shards of their lives while a robotic voice interrupts them to report "You have one minute remaining." And then the suspect will hang up and invariably call his second and sometimes third girlfriend and profess his love and devotion to them too. (Although judging from the fallout of the Ashley Madison scandal, this unfaithfulness is perhaps no more than the national average.)

Students of linguistics will note how jail call conversations are peppered with urban vernacular. The possessive "mine" is pronounced "mines." "For sure" is pronounced "Fo sho." The n-word is tossed around liberally, regardless of race. The white or Hispanic suspect calls his white or Hispanic friend nigger. Cops are referred to as niggers ("These niggas hit me with some bullshit, blud"). Attorneys are niggers. Probation officers. Judges.

One of the problems in making a jail call is that the sheriff's deputies have the suspect's cell phone stored in property so he has to dial from memory. If he does recall a number and gets through to someone, he has to ask that person for other people's numbers, which he then has to remember too, because they don't let you have a pen and paper in your cell. One enterprising prostitute whose jail calls I listened to took her sandwich apart and used her fingernail to scratch a needed phone number in a piece of processed cheese.

Talk of bail dominates jail calls. How much it is, who can raise it, and what bail bondsman will be willing to work with them. These discussions frequently lead to gangster math, as found in this exchange from one of my assault cases:

Suspect: "My bail be a quarter million."

Friend: "How much is that?"

Suspect: "125,000."

Friend: "Damn . . ."

But despite the grim picture jail calls paint, there are people in the suspect's life who are trying to stand by him and steer him right. An uncle will implore the suspect to speak properly to the judge. A cousin will tell him he can crash on his couch if he gets evicted. There's a fair amount of Bible talk. *God's got his hand on you. The Lord has not left you. Let's pray together.*

But even if the suspect has some family support and a shot at beating the case, his prospects for the future are often dubious at best. I was struck by this when I listened to the jail calls of a twenty-three-year-old gangbanger who had never worked a day in his life. His girlfriend demanded to know what kind of job he was going to get upon release. The suspect paused for an uncomfortably long time. It became clear he couldn't think of one job he would like or could do or know how to get. He ended up saying, "I dunno. Something that's good. I just wanna make hella dough." I tried to think of a lucrative and appropriate work field for him, a man with no education, skills, or interests and a violent felony record. Roller derby?

When you listen to jail calls, you're on high alert for threats to any witness. Nobody but nobody messes with your witnesses. But once in a while, the threatened witness is you. The threats won't be formal or clearly spoken. No one is going to say, "I have sinister intent toward Officer Marvin Johnson and his partner and I seek to quell them." It will be a general comment that someone needs to "take care" of a problem. And who might this problem be? Well if Officer Johnson is a plainclothes cop who always wears a baseball cap, he will be described as "Ballcap." Johnson's partner? He doesn't even merit a nickname. He's "the nigga that be with Ballcap." I myself have not yet been threatened on jail calls, but my name's come up. My moniker has been "That Marine-looking motherfucker," which, having known some Marines, I take as high praise.

These threats don't always materialize. Even the most stone-cold thug knows the risk/reward formula in going after a cop is skewed against them. If you are the named party on one of these calls, best-case scenario is you get an uneventful two weeks off with a cop stationed at your door and you catch up on every episode of *Stranger Things*.

You don't deal with hairs or fibers much as an investigator unless you're working a serious violent felony. Your department doesn't have the time, resources, or manpower to trot out the evidence vacuum for every auto burglary. But you know that a single strand of hair can give you the sex, age, and race of a suspect. It can tell you if that hair was ever bleached or permed, and if it was cut, fell out, or was yanked out. If there's no hair at a crime scene, it means the suspect was probably bald or was wearing a skull cap. Because people leave hair around all the time. We're like shedding cats.

Another somewhat uncommon but still viable evidentiary tool is to use a mold of a suspect's teeth to compare to the bite marks left on a victim. During trial, both the prosecution and the defense might call in forensic odonatologists who will debate over the strength of the ID in court, which is why you're hoping the bad guy has something distinctive in his mouth, like a broken molar.

As a cop, you sometimes just plain blow it when handling evidence. Part of this is the tendency of line cops to act like mini-detectives at major crime scenes. To think they're going to come up with the big breakthrough. So they open drawers they have no business opening. Pick up evidence and examine it before it's been photographed or processed. Move things around for no objectively good reason. This is called "finger-fucking" a scene and everyone has been guilty of it, even seasoned investigators. And most cops have heard a story about a colleague who has returned to a crime scene to retrieve something he forgot, like his flashlight or a bottle of soda, only to see an ID tech already bagging it as evidence. The resulting conversation is super awkward.

It's sobering how much evidence gets overlooked on the first pass. Like the narcotics squad that executes a search warrant on a house and somehow misses the stack of dope packaged for sale in plain view on the kitchen table. I have found items of evidence that other officers have missed and have missed items myself that other officers have found. As a newer cop in Milwaukee, I was sure I had thoroughly combed a shooting scene up until the point when the detective on point went outside and found an additional shell casing on the walkway leading to the garage.

"And that's why we double-check," he said, casting a dubious eye at me.

21

Going Forward

You risk your skin catching killers and the juries turn them loose so they can come back and shoot at you again. If you're honest, you're poor your whole life and in the end you wind up dying all alone on some dirty street.
For what?
For nothing.
For a tin star.
—Martin, *High Noon*

Political commentators often don't get it when they talk about police-related issues. The curiously well-preserved television anchors on the right border on blind adoration for law enforcement and equate questioning of police methods with being antipolice. You certainly appreciate the support, but it doesn't need to be unconditional; the public can back law enforcement while at the same time bemoaning instances of corruption and abuse of power. Commentators on the left decry all stop-and-frisks as inherently unconstitutional despite the existence of a seminal court case called *Terry v. Ohio*, which has been green-lighting such stops since 1968. MSNBC's Rachel Maddow claims on air that it's irrelevant that Michael Brown was shown committing what appears to be strong-armed robbery prior to his deadly encounter with Officer Wilson. I assert it's wholly relevant. It speaks to Brown's level of criminality and his probable belief that Ofc. Wilson was going to arrest him for that robbery, which could easily make Brown more prone to use violence against Wilson. Maddow should know better because I figured that out and I'm reasonably certain she's a lot smarter than me.

When the news media run controversial police incidents—whether they be questionable uses of force or cops violating the previously mentioned Don't Be a Dick rule—in a continual loop on air, it's all fair game. When you're in uniform, you subject yourself to intense scrutiny and you are responsible for everything you do and everything you say. But it would be much appreciated if they also presented more counterbalance to the general public. Perhaps the station could run the clip of the cop saving a kid from choking in a restaurant or the state trooper pulling a man out of a burning car or any of the hundreds of meaningful, high-profile acts that police officers do every day. How about putting those in the regular rotation too? Otherwise, it's like ESPN's highlight reel only showing the fifty shots the Celtics missed that game.

When cops are being pilloried on every channel, you tend to hunker down in full defensive mode. You think the public doesn't get it and they never will. But that can't be the end of the conversation. Both of us have much room for improvement. We both need to explain ourselves. Apologize if we have done wrong. Work on ways to reduce tension instead of amping it up. Because it's a partnership between the police and the community and if one of us goes down hard, so does the other.

But with all that being said about constructive dialogue and understanding and the like, you know that police work is a contact sport. It is and will continue to be a volatile business. There is always going to be a Ferguson.

It will just be called something else.

One of the many lessons of Ferguson was that if there's a high-profile incident like an officer-involved shooting (OIS), police departments need to frontload information as soon as they can without compromising the case. An OIS is a complex, multifaceted investigation where everyone from the DA's office to civilian watchdog agencies to Internal Affairs gets involved. The officers who fired their weapons will go through multiple interviews and are entitled to due process. But when it's appropriate to release the facts, they should be released. Because if you are too slow to do so, the public will invent their own narrative. Damaging speculation and misinformation will weave its way into the conversation. If you weren't there, of course, you don't know what happened. Even if you were there, you may not have seen everything the officer saw. That officer's testimony is the most critical piece of information to the case.

For some people, it won't matter—all the videos and graphs and hard evidence in the world won't change their predetermined beliefs. But you have to try. That's why you're seeing departments nationwide releasing police body camera footage far earlier than they did in the past. It doesn't always answer all of the public's questions, because people want the simple story and it isn't always simple out there. But it can go a long way toward keeping the peace.

Those who claim there's an epidemic of police shootings would be wise to look at the actual statistics. For instance, a five-year study of SF officer-involved shootings culminating in 2010 found that about one in ten thousand arrests resulted in a police-related shooting. One in ten thousand. It's important to emphasize that we're talking actual arrests here, not mere citizen contacts or even detentions that don't lead to arrest. When you arrest someone, you're taking their liberty away, which always brings with it the prospect of violence. And ask any street cop with some time in and he'll tell you about a host of times he could have justifiably used deadly force but elected not to. That's why cops bristle when they see some protestor screaming that the cops are indiscriminately shooting people as he holds up a sign that says It Could Be My Son Next. Sir, if your son comes at the police with a knife or a gun, then yes, God help him, he could be next. Otherwise, the one in ten thousand chance he has of being shot by the police is the roughly the same risk he runs, according to the National Weather Service website, of being struck by lightning in his lifetime. The police are to uphold the sanctity of life whenever possible and must justify every bullet we fire. But when the public grossly overstates the problem, we all lose.

In some people's minds, every time a white police officer has a negative encounter with a black suspect, racism is clearly afoot. It's a simple mathematical equation. White cop + black suspect = racism. What else could it possibly be? In this worldview, if Ferguson's Michael Brown had been white, Ofc. Wilson wouldn't have stopped him in the first place. Or, if a white Michael Brown punched Ofc. Wilson in the face and went for his gun, Ofc. Wilson surely wouldn't have shot him, not over the misguided antics of a fellow Caucasian.

To be sure, racism is threaded through every institution in our country, from mortgage lending to how kids are disciplined in school. Think tanks have put on several studies that feature a variation on this theme: two candidates, equally qualified on paper, are up for the same job. One has a traditionally white name, like Trevor. The other has a traditionally black name, like Darnell. It may not surprise you to learn that in these studies, Darnell doesn't get a lot of call-backs. And go into any courtroom in America and you'll hear about the time a black defense attorney was confused with a defendant. That just doesn't happens with whites.

What complicates such discussions is the documentation on how blacks commit a disproportionate amount of violent crime in this country. The DOJ reported that between 1980 and 2008, blacks committed more than half of all murders in the United States while making up only 13 percent of the population. Alternatively, Uniform Crime Report (UCR) statistics show that when adjusted for population, blacks are roughly four times more likely than whites to be killed by the police. That's a deeply troubling figure. Also troubling are recent FBI crime stats, again adjusted for population, that show black men are five times more likely than white men to kill police officers. (I'm no statistician—I got this data from Dr. Peter Moskos's 12/14/14 entry to his thought-provoking blog *Cop in the Hood*.) Books and dissertations have been devoted to the study of this racial disparity, with socioeconomic factors no doubt playing a weighty role, but the disparity remains an uncomfortable one.

It is also the case that somewhere right now in our United States, some variation on this scenario is occurring: a black person is sitting at a table across from his white neighbor and musing on the fact that he's been stopped by the police seven times in the last two years. The white counterpart? Zero. Both are good drivers who operate perfectly functional vehicles. Now maybe the tendency for the white neighbor is to think the black neighbor is exaggerating. After all, it's pretty safe to say nonminorities tend to greatly underestimate the level of prejudice minorities experience. I'm no different; I heard a piece on NPR some time ago where a law-abiding African-American said he gets stressed when the police are behind him because he thinks they're going to kill him. As a cop, I heard this and my gut said what alarmist nonsense. But is my reaction fair? Whether his fear is reasonable is almost beside the point—if he feels that way, the police have a serious image problem. It's our issue as much as his.

Moreover, you talk to black police officers who muse about being profiled by law enforcement both before and after becoming cops. If you don't listen to them, who are you going to listen to? All of that means something. It means that racial profiling is real and damaging. All of these perspectives need to be acknowledged in a serious conversation about law enforcement and race.

But it seems to me that it's irresponsible to automatically assume a police encounter between a white cop and a black suspect is about race and also to assume that it isn't. Like any important issue worth exploring, it's best to have some facts or at least informed theories before rushing to judgment. Did this particular officer let loose with a racial slur? Does he have a history of race-based complaints? Did he see both a white suspect and a black suspect commit precisely the same offense and ignore the white guy and throw the black guy in cuffs? In the absence of something tangible like this, the community may wish to entertain the possibility that this cop is doing nothing more than going about his workday and the race of the suspect doesn't play into it in the ways some people might expect.

I come to this discussion with all my own biases. My natural allegiance is to the men and women in uniform whom I serve with and who inform my outlook in ways I am aware of and probably in some ways that I'm not. I know that I am inherently resistant to the prospect of significant swathes of police departments being racist. I've heard another officer use the word *nigger* once in my police career, over a decade ago in Milwaukee. But the belief that police departments are racially prejudiced isn't some anachronistic notion that materialized out of thin air. History takes us from Bull Connor and his dogs and hoses in Birmingham in '64 to a deputy police chief in Florida named David Borst found to be a member of the Ku Klux Klan as recently as 2014. SFPD's 2015 racially charged texting scandal, where multiple officers referred to blacks as monkeys and niggers and made white power references, left me both disgusted and reflective of whether I knew cops as well as I thought I did. Police can be tone-deaf to the effect their words and actions have in communities of color. We have a tendency to blunder down the block when we need to tread lightly. A tendency to predesignate an entire community as "bad." As criminologist David Kennedy rightly points out in his book *Don't Shoot*, when there is a controversial incident in a black neighborhood, the police focus only on the incident. But the neighborhood focuses on the whole *history* of the police in that neighborhood. We need to recognize that and do better.

But none of that makes it justifiable to cry police racism without any evidence to support that claim. Because you're talking about what is in an officer's heart. Hard to know such things.

I'm not trying to speak for the black community, and if it sounds like I am, I'm not as good of a writer as I hope to be. What I do know is that when accusations of police racism are well founded, those offenders need to be aggressively rooted out in the same way you'd go after a particularly toxic virus. But if a police controversy is about race only because some people decided to arbitrarily make it about race, the damage that can be done is about much more than the Boy Who Cried Wolf syndrome. Accusations of racism are incendiary. And when the community makes such claims absent logic, discernment, and constructive dialogue, it can quickly lead to bedlam.

And yet another city will burn.

The perception that the police actively use racial profiling has the community up in arms and rightly so, because as a cop, you are to focus on the behavior of people, not the color of their skin, in determining whom to stop and arrest. Equal enforcement of the law is a cornerstone of democracy. But this isn't quite as simple as it may appear. I'll use the racial demographics of my own city as an example. As it stands now, the majority of street-level drug dealers along the 6th Street corridor are black. The majority of the suspects selling stolen property at 7th and Market are Hispanic. The majority of the auto burglars in the area of 9th and Howard are white. Although there are some prickly types out there who will claim even a statement like this is racist, I know what criminal behavior looks like and I have eyes that work. My partners and I have spent years in these areas, conducted surveillance operations there, made numerous arrests, and spoken with our coworkers who have had equivalent experiences. So we know how the demographics shake out.

Now, if you have been tasked by your captain with putting a stop to the fencing operation at 7th and Market and the last ten guys you've arrested there for receiving stolen property are Hispanic males between the ages of 18–40 and here comes Hispanic guy #11, 18–40, hanging out on the corner, can you automatically assume he's in the stolen goods game too? After all, the last ten fellows who looked like him were. The answer is, of course, that you may not. The eleventh guy shouldn't have to pay for the sins of the ten guys prior who just happen to share the same skin tone. Could be he's as criminally culpable as the others, but you can't start with that. You have to give him a fresh slate. This is what fairness demands. But this is easy to say and harder to do. We see patterns and become used to them and must closely guard against them becoming self-fulfilling prophecies. Now if the eleventh guy is approached on that corner by someone who appears to be a stranger and starts closely examining this stranger's iPhone, and then currency covertly exchanges hands in an area notorious for fencing, now you're onto something. If your own mother did that, you'd jack her up and ask her some hard questions. Come to think of it, maybe we've gotten to the point in our society where this should be the new litmus test for police to avoid racial profiling. If you saw your mom do it, would you stop her too?

The Eric Garner case on Staten Island is profoundly unsettling, but perhaps not for the reasons that have gotten the most media attention. Garner was committing a minor offense (selling loose, untaxed cigarettes) and he resisted arrest. Although it didn't look like much by way of resistance, it certainly justified police use of force against him, especially given his 6'2", 400-pound frame and the fact that the officers on scene didn't know if he was armed or had any arrest warrants. The type and intensity of the force required to take him into custody is its own debate, as is the exact cause of his death (the autopsy report listed several contributing factors beyond any type of choke hold, including Garner's obesity, congestive heart failure, and asthma). What isn't up for debate is the woeful lack of medical care he received on scene.

"I can't breathe," Garner reportedly said. Eleven times. Then he stopped breathing. And no one, not the cops and not the responding medics, took appropriate action. The hospital center that dispatched the treating ambulance later paid a $1 million settlement to Garner's family.

The problem, historically, with suspects saying they can't breathe is that if they actually couldn't breathe, they wouldn't be able to utter the words "I can't breathe." You tell suspects this all the time. And you're not alone—you'll hear firefighters and paramedics tell patients the same thing in the field. It reaches the point where you can get tone-deaf to such claims because you've arrested scores of people who assert any and all forms of health trouble, including shortness of breath, in hopes that the cops won't want to deal with their various maladies and they'll be able to wriggle out of an arrest. But Eric Garner's death as well as other deaths (in July of 2011, a man named Derek Williams died in the back of a Milwaukee patrol car after complaining of shortness of breath for fifteen minutes) remind us that as police officers and first responders, you have to take such claims seriously. You have to listen. You must call for an ambulance and closely monitor the person who's in your custody. Even if 98 percent of the time everything's fine, that 2 percent is what it's all about.

You will make mistakes on this job. I once wrote in a police report that a Milwaukee Fire Department ambulance responded to the scene to assist the victim, which would have been all well and good, but I was working for the San Francisco Police Department at the time. Would have been a bear of a commute for that med rig.

But do this kind of work long enough and the errors you make on the job could be critical ones. Maybe you'll broadcast the wrong direction of travel for an armed robber, sending all responding units west when the suspect went east. You might lose control of your squad car during a pursuit of a murder suspect and barrel into a pedestrian—the doctors think she'll live but doubt she'll ever walk again. A felon pulls the trigger on you and you return fire, hitting the suspect once and a bystander twice. You will make these mistakes because you are part of a dedicated but flawed profession doing a job where you need to be a psychologist, centurion, street lawyer, pilot, coach, marksman, and soothsayer. The public looks to you and there are times when you let them down. Let yourself down. The mistakes come with a heavy price.

So what now? Let your failures leach into your system? Let them define you? Maybe not. "You've got to learn to forgive yourself on this job," Rolf Mueller used to say. So you take what happened and teach it to others, to help them avoid the same pitfalls. The goal is progress, not perfection, someone said once. You can't sit there and wring your hands forever. You move forward. It's always got to be forward.

In 2007, Richmond, California, was America's ninth most dangerous city. City Hall started an experimental program that supplied targeted chronic offenders with both a mentor and a monthly stipend ranging from $300 to $1,000. By 2015, Richmond's homicide rate dropped to the lowest in thirty-three years and officer-involved shootings declined to less than one a year. Hard to say if there is cause and effect here (the police department was hard at work too, not just City Hall) and you gotta play the long game to know for sure. But it's hard to ignore those numbers. Richmond was trying to make things better, which is what we all want. We want reform. And police departments across the nation are working on those very reforms. Here are some of the most common ones.

—Body cameras. SFPD got them in 2016. When you know you're on camera, you're on your best behavior. And isn't that what everyone wants? Cops on our best behavior? Body cameras aren't an all-encompassing solution. You may be wearing a camera, but your mind is far from a video recorder. Body cameras can't pick up on the auditory exclusion and tunnel vision that comes with, for instance, an officer-involved shooting, as I have previously mentioned. They won't capture your prior knowledge of a suspect's penchant for violence as you grab him to stop the fight before it starts, or the closeness of the pissed-off crowd you know is forming behind you. But they're a good tool and a good start.

—Better training. Some of the most effective training involves scenario-based exercises where you learn to slow things down and make a plan before you rush into a hot scene, so you don't create your own exigency. For instance, it's police instinct to immediately go hands on to control someone's movements, but letting someone in a mental health crisis pace around can greatly de-escalate them and aid in the intervention. In these encounters, the Ask/Tell/Order/Make spectrum is greatly elongated; time and distance are your friends here and you might stay on Ask for as long as the situation allows. Also, courses that emphasize medical and first-aid skills can help officers recognize the difference between a chemically altered lawbreaker who wants to fight you and a guy who's in desperate need of an epinephrine injection to stave off an allergic reaction.

—More refined screening procedures to keep problem recruits out of the academy.

—Better tracking of officer activity, including keeping records on the demographics of all subject stops in order to guard against racial bias.

—A renewed emphasis on peer leadership. FTOs, veteran cops, and street supervisors need to be the ones who step up and call each other out when needed. It means more when it comes from someone you know and respect as opposed to a bunch of high-minded department goals and objectives on a glossy pamphlet no one will ever read.

Something else I would toss onto the pile here is the fact that after the salary and benefits are added up, a single officer can cost the taxpayers anywhere between sixty and well over $100,000 a year. Is that officer providing the community enough safety, security, and competent police service to warrant that sizable cost? Some cops never ask themselves that question. Every one of us should.

Bottom line, if there's any profession that should hold itself to high standards and constantly strive for excellence, it's law enforcement. But the department and media buzz around police reform can end up grating on the average cop, especially the aforementioned OGs. It's as if you've been screwing up royally all this time and are in desperate need of your city to bring in some think-tank doofus to put a bunch of flowery hug-a-thug crap on a pie chart so you know how to do your job. What the fresh hell is this? Hey, I've been doing de-escalation techniques on violent suspects since 1987, pal, but sometimes you gotta get in there and mix it up because the bad guys don't handcuff themselves.

The unfortunate underbelly of police reform is that some cops will overthink their response and use lousy officer safety techniques with dangerous suspects just to appease a squeamish public. I've seen that more than once on the SFPD. What you don't want is cops second-guessing themselves and getting hurt over politics. We need to listen to the public, but they need to listen to us too. Our lived experience should count for something. Maybe you take exception to the aggressive way those officers just took a suspect into custody, but that right there is the Make in Ask/Tell/Order/Make. Just because something's hard to watch doesn't mean it's unjustified.

You open the paper and there it is. Another cop convicted of a destructive felony. There are certain expectations the public rightly has of law enforcement, and one of those expectations is that police themselves won't commit crimes. That they won't take bribes, tip off drug dealers to police activity, and sell meth, like Bakersfield police detective Damacio Diaz. Won't grope, rape, and sodomize women like Oklahoma City officer Daniel Holtzclaw, whose thirteen victims reported he assaulted them while on duty. Won't steal the life savings of their own father, like Irwindale police officer Dennis Alva. The honest cops have a message for the Diazes and Holtzclaws and Alvas of the world. You disguised yourself for a while as one of us. You fooled us and gained our trust. But you have been revealed for what you are. You hurt people. You tarnished the badge. You have been sentenced to prison, and it is right that you are going there. You have been cast out of the brotherhood. We don't know you anymore.

The cops I do know are different. They took the job for the right reasons and do it the way it's supposed to be done. They believe in a cause greater than themselves. They pursue and arrest dangerous criminals and take their guns away. They read to kids in schools, give away pumpkins on Halloween and turkeys on Thanksgiving, and run youth sports and wilderness programs. They replace a family's stolen Christmas presents out of their own pockets. Give generously at fundraisers for fellow officers who have been hurt in off-duty accidents or lost a loved one. And speaking of giving generously, the SFPD police union annually gives thousands of dollars to charitable causes and is, I would hazard a guess, far more active in the community than many of the activists who disparage it.

Let's get down to specifics. I'd like to name some cops on the departments I've worked for. Like Sgt. Tracy McCray, who was raised by a single mother in the very type of housing projects she now patrols as a twenty-six-year veteran assigned to Bayview Station. Tough, affable, and soft-spoken, she still goes hard at a stage in her career when a lot of officers are dialing it back. If you happen to meet her, congratulations are in order because the San Francisco Police-Fire Post named her 2016 Sergeant of the Year.

Or how about Officer Stephen Pinchard, my former partner in Milwaukee, who just called it quits after two and a half decades of police service, all on the street. A plain-talking Wisconsin native with a long fuse and unblinking resolve in the face of crisis, he worked gang crimes, hunted parole violators, and good-naturedly but persistently questioned why the Packers drafted Tony Mandarich ahead of Barry Sanders in the '89 NFL draft. During the years I worked with him in our station's toughest patrol sector, I never once saw him belittle anyone, use excessive force, or, in short, act anything other than honorably. In March of 2016, he was first on scene to a report of gunshots inside an apartment complex near 92nd and Beloit where he encountered a man named Dan J. Popp who had just methodically murdered three of his neighbors and tried to murder a fourth. Pinchard caught Popp coming out of the building with a rifle slung over his shoulder, forced him down at gunpoint, and arrested him. Pinchard is a hero of the first order, although he would never say so. But I sure can. I hope he's enjoying his retirement. No one has earned it more. The district where he finished up his career feels the same way; they just retired his locker.

Or take San Francisco officer Kevin Downs. He's a sturdy guy, but forgive him if it takes him awhile to get up. He's still working through some mobility issues after taking a bullet to the skull while responding to a report of an armed suspect in a shopping mall; the round missed his cerebral artery by less than a centimeter. That hasn't stopped him from continuing to work with the charity he and his wife Corey cofounded, Ranchin' Vets, which assists war veterans coming back from Iraq and Afghanistan readjust to civilian life and get jobs in ranching and agriculture. In fact, as soon as he could stand up straight again, his first public appearance was at a fund-raiser for his organization. "I guess I had to get shot in the head for this many people to come out," he said during his opening remarks. He's got that dry cop humor too.

McCray, Pinchard, Downs, and so many more.

Those are the cops I know.

You crest a hill in your patrol car and there's the city spread out before you, that whole skyline your office. You're feeling pretty good. You just won a fight with a parolee whose considerable mass earned him the street name of The 300; he went for the gun in his waistband, but he never got there because together, you and your partner were stronger than he was and got the cuffs on without a shot fired. Or you just identified a rapist off a Crime Alert—doesn't matter that he was wearing shades and a ball cap, you've arrested him half a dozen times and can recognize him by his brow and jawline. The radio crackles with a report of an armed robbery vehicle and lists the driver's name—you already know his street handle is Cheddar, he hangs out in the 400 block of Minna and keeps his dope in the end of a drain pipe in the alley. You feel like you're at the center of all things and have the overwhelming sensation that this is the right job for you. You like putting bullies in their place. You enjoy solving puzzles. You are comfort-able around death, violence, and chaos.

You took this work because you believe in right and wrong and do your best to act accordingly. But you've been around the block a time or two and you're no idealist—you know now that such neat divisions do not always exist in law enforcement. You must get good and comfortable in the gray because you'll be spending a fair amount of time there. And your moral compass, which used to point due north, now, with the passage of the years, shows a tremolo here and again. The job has hardened you. Has stretched you out. And in the end, you may not even wish you had taken it. They do these surveys with city workers after they retire. They ask them if they had to do it all over again, would they still have picked their chosen profession? The last nationwide figures you heard, 80 percent of firefighters said they'd still be firefighters. For cops? It was around 30 percent. Part of the job that wears on you is that police missteps and excesses become frontpage news, ripe for second-guessing in papers and round-table discussions. People outside the police sphere want cops to do a whole lot better; cops inside that insular world know that the public is lucky it works out as well as it does. It gets complicated, if you dwell on it much. For you have a profession inherent with paradox. You need your city while at the same time you're desperate to get away from her. You love the job even as it corrodes you. But you still wake in the morning knowing there is honor in this work, if not always satisfaction. You wake in the morning knowing your cause is righteous. Applications to the Dallas Police Department surged after the assassination of five officers and the wounding of nine others. In 2016 in Evesham, New Jersey, Police Officer Brian Strockbine saved three lives in ten days. He first revived a sixty-nine-year-old assault victim with CPR. Four days later, he pulled an unconscious man out of a smoke-filled car, and brought another woman back with CPR a few days after that. As the cartoon caption says, maybe everything isn't hopeless bullshit. Maybe Martin from *High Noon* was wrong about the tin star meaning nothing. It matters. It had damn well better matter.

You remember as a new cop, a veteran officer drove you around the district and gave you the insider's tour, pointing out this corner where he got stabbed and that block where a father was gunned down in front of his two children. You've been on the job for a while now and have your own memories of the city. As you drive, you pass through an intersection where you once chased a murder suspect in your squad car—pure evil this man, you were duty bound not to let him get away—and you remember keenly how you and your partner nearly died in that same intersection when the semitruck didn't hear your siren and whisked right in front of you, so close, so very close. Inches away. No, less than that. Millimeters. No, it had to be closer. What's smaller than a millimeter? But then you caught up to the killer's car and stopped him cold. To have looked death square in the face and come out the other side with your quarry in handcuffs—that feeling is better than any drug.

You round the corner and see a teenager slouching against the wall of a liquor store. He reminds you of the teen you first arrested for a felony when he was fourteen. Rotten parents, even worse life. You tried to look out for him; he wasn't your friend, but he was far from your enemy. He chose his own path and made it to seventeen before getting shot through the mouth in a dope house. You keep driving, past the duplex where a man, out of work and despondent, held a butcher knife to his neck and you think about how you talked to him and called him by name and convinced him to put the knife down just by listening and letting him know that he counted. You see the parcel warehouse up ahead, where an active shooter murdered three of his coworkers and shot two more before you went in with a contact team to stop him, cavernous space, low light, fire alarm blaring, floor slick with blood, and when you found him and shouted at him to put the gun down, he murmured something to you before turning the weapon on himself. These are memories you feel at some cellular level. Some of them you don't know quite what to do with. Some are threaded through with lasting regret. The dying woman you couldn't save. The missing child you never found. You'll make new memories today, but the old ones linger and echo. With each corner you turn, they're out there, waiting for you.

The sad and the sublime.

The ghosts and the devils.

Afterword

You get asked a lot of questions as a cop, whether you're on or off duty. I'm using this space to answer some of the most common questions I've fielded over my police career as well as a few that seemed a bit out of left field. If you are an inquisitive member of the public, perhaps your question will be answered below. If not, consider attending one of the educational programs that many departments offer, like Coffee with a Cop, where the police can give you their perspective and you can give them yours. You can also drink coffee together, which is the liquid lifeblood of any worthwhile endeavor.

Question: Why did you want to be a cop?

Answer: To help people. This is true of me and of most cops. In fact, every recruit dutifully recites this in the academy when asked by the instructional staff why they chose the police profession. But if you want to get a cheap guffaw from a veteran cop at the station, tell him you're looking forward to helping people today. It's not that you don't want to help people. It's just not something you say. It sounds too hokey. Try saying it to your lieutenant once when he's having a bad day. Have an exit strategy for when he chucks a stapler at your head.

Question: I got pulled over for the same moving violation by two different cops. One gave me a ticket, one didn't. What gives?

Answer: For starters, how about you drive better? But to field your question, police officers have broad discretion on whether to issue a citation. Some cops pull cars over solely as a pretext to look for felony suspects or guns, not because they are all afire about traffic enforcement. If there are no weapons or contraband and the driver has no warrants and a valid driver's license and didn't commit a particularly heinous violation, they lose all interest in you and you will be released without a ticket. Other officers are strictly letter of the law. Their philosophy is no breaks, no deals, everybody gets cited. When they were kids, they heard the story of Jack and the Beanstalk and wondered if it was okay for Jack to have committed burglary. In Milwaukee, such officers were called "ropes." They're the kind of person who will give someone a citation for putting a flyer on a car windshield, a law so obscure most cops don't even know it's illegal unless they are a savant or studying for a promotional exam.

Question: Do the police have quotas for arrests or tickets?

Answer: They don't. With the exception of places like Ferguson, which purportedly employed a civic system overwhelmingly reliant on the income generated from citations (in short, a system that required people to break the law), the police do not arrest or cite to fill quotas. There are folks who get cash for every arrest they make, but those people are called bounty hunters. In California, ticket quotas are actually illegal. Now that doesn't mean the shift supervisor won't tell you to get out there and write some movers because he's getting hammered by citizen complaints about speeding cars on the block. But there's no listed numerical goal.

Question: Say you're at work and are suspected of engaging in an unlawful enterprise. Can the police search your desk?

Answer: It sort of depends, which is the stock answer to many legal questions. It boils down to whether you have a reasonable expectation of privacy at your workspace. Employers can typically give the police consent to search an employee's desk, file cabinet, locker, and work computer if the company has regular access and control over those places. If a desk drawer is locked, that changes things. Your personal laptop is off-limits. So is your person, unless the officer can articulate specific probable cause that you are carrying evidence/weapons/contraband. But what if your pants are work pants, provided by and returnable to the company? I dunno. I don't have all the answers. Some days all I have is more questions.

Question: If I record a crime with my phone, can the police take my phone away from me?

Answer: We'd hope you'd share your phone video with us because you're a concerned citizen who wants to contribute to our shared mission of reducing crime and enhancing the quality of life in the city. But unless you are in some way party to the crime, we can't seize your phone without a warrant or consent. We can only ask for it politely. Law enforcement and citizens alike get confused about this issue. But the bottom line is this—in the vast majority of jurisdictions, if a cop takes your phone under these circumstances without your permission, that's called theft. Feel free to lodge a complaint.

Question: Should I have a gun in the house to protect myself and my family?

Answer: Ask yourself this: could you kill someone if your life or the life of a loved one depended on it? If you waffle on this answer, even for a moment, or if you mentally picture purposefully winging a perpetrator in the arm or leg or firing off a warning shot, the answer is no, you probably couldn't. And you need to reconsider that gun and invest in an excellent home security system or a guard dog instead. Because when it comes to home defense, guns aren't just for scaring people. And when you fire one at someone in proximity, odds are you will seriously injure or kill them. Hesitate, and all you will do is make an awful situation worse as the suspect shoots you first or takes your gun away and uses it on you and your family. So know yourself and how you tick. And plan accordingly.

Question: How have your coworkers received your writing?

Answer: They've been pretty kind. Some have approached me with my first book in hand and asked me to sign it. In fact, some of the crooks I've dealt with over the years have even displayed mild interest in my literary trajectory. Shortly after *400 Things Cops Know* came out, I had a *Wall Street Journal* photo shoot on the unit block of 6th Street in San Francisco, a place where I have arrested many people. This piqued the curiosity of one 6th Street crack dealer, who I'll call L-Mack.

"I've hit it big, L-Mack," I told him. He shrugged and then photobombed all of my subsequent pictures, much to the amusement of my wife, who wanted to put one of the shots on our family Christmas card.

Question: Why did you leave the Milwaukee Police Department?

Answer: I relished working for the MPD and Milwaukee is my kind of town. I never would have left. But then I met my wife-to-be. When she took a job in San Francisco, I tagged right along. It was atypical because there's not a lot of lateral movement among cops. You get to a department, you stay there. And the few guys you know who do leave for another agency often return a few months later with a newfound appreciation for the place they thought they detested. But even if you know you're a lifer at your department, it's fun to talk about other agencies, sometimes wistfully. "Berkeley PD has fatigue abatement," a coworker will insist. "You get two fifteen-minute naps built into your shift. I'm telling you."

Question: I often see two patrol cars pulled up next to each other, driver's side to driver's side, in a parking lot or at the side of the road. What are those officers talking about?

Answer: There's a 15 percent chance they are discussing that new wrinkle in case law as it applies to search and seizure, or how to most effectively combat the recent rash of hot prowl burglaries. There is a 25 percent chance they are talking about their kids' sports teams. There is a 60 percent chance they are extolling the virtues of the leggy new civilian clerk, for we are cops, not monks, or engaging in an in-depth discussion on why farts smell worse in the shower. I have done the research and these percentages are exact. Cops need to decompress a bit. We see a lot of horrific things. So when you clear an assignment and have an opportunity to talk to your fellow officer, it's your chance to laugh, to fume, to make uncensored and sweeping generalizations about everything from social ills to local politicians (which are not mutually exclusive). This banter is far from a PG rating. It's called cop talk and it's essential to the job, both to build camaraderie and to make sense of your day. And if a recording of that conversation leaks and goes viral or a citizen overhears it in a place where the cops had a reasonable expectation of privacy and feathers are ruffled, so be it. Want to hear something highbrow and civilized? Go find a duchess.

Question: Ever encountered a serial killer? I've seen these movies . . .

Answer: Hollywood would have you believe there is a serial killer around every corner, but the FBI's violent crime center conservatively estimates there are between one hundred and two hundred serial killers in the United States and Canada. Some meticulously plan their crimes while others kill in the heat of the moment. Some are socially competent and charismatic, far from the kind of person who would spook you until it was too late. Others are inept with poor hygiene. A handful take trophies (hair, clothing, jewelry). Most are lone white males.

It's easy to assume serial killers are mostly the products of the fevered imaginations of novelists and screenwriters looking for material. But Rolf Mueller ran into one on a July day in 1991 and arrested him after a roll-around fight in a small apartment, a subsequent search of which revealed the remains of eleven corpses, including a man's severed head in the refrigerator and a 57-gallon acid drum filled with human torsos. The suspect? A polite and unassuming third-shift employee of the local Milwaukee chocolate factory, fellow by the name of Jeffrey Dahmer.

Question: Do officers have to live in the city they police?

Answer: Milwaukee had a residency requirement when I was there, which caused a fair amount of grumbling among the rank and file who wanted homes far from the clamor and wished to dodge situations where you're in your front yard and someone comes up to you and says "Remember me" and you have to rack your brain to recall if you arrested this guy once for aggravated assault or you were just both in Toastmasters years back. San Francisco has no such requirement, which is nice, because the current median home price for a single-family residence is $800,000. I know an SF sergeant whose primary residence is in Arizona. He stays in a cut-rate hotel during the workweek and flies home on weekends.

Question: Do cops ever go on strike?

Answer: No. Bus drivers, sanitation workers, and nurses all strike from time to time. Not cops. Nonstrike clauses are written into every law enforcement labor agreement. The last time a major metropolitan police department walked off the job was 1981, in my town of Milwaukee, partly in response to the callous remarks of a city alderman after Officers John Machajewski and Charles Mehlberg were murdered in an alley while investigating a tavern robbery. It wasn't clear how many of the city's two thousand officers walked off the job, but by nightfall, all district station doors were locked to the public. The work stoppage lasted sixteen hours. If you were a criminal in Milwaukee during that time, you were probably pleased with this development and figured it opened up some opportunities to expand; once you know the cops aren't coming, anything goes. If you were everyone else, I'm guessing that was a pretty long sixteen hours.

Question: What are you looking for when you have some down time and are just driving around in your patrol car?

Answer: It's all about the hierarchy of crime. Violent offenses come first. Then property violations. Then drugs, then traffic tickets. When you're on the street, you're looking for the guy who just started doing something different from what he was doing a moment ago. You come around the corner and there's a man picking his fingernails or fiddling with his shoelaces or talking unnaturally loud. The things people do when they're nervous and trying to act too casual. Or you watch the fellow who's meandering on a street where everyone else is walking briskly toward a destination. Sure, maybe he's just waiting for his buddy, or has some time to kill before a job interview. Or maybe he's sizing up his next robbery victim. Give him a second look.

But sometimes you're just out there hunting for a tasty grilled chicken sandwich that's gonna hang off both sides of the plate. Because you can't fight crime all day. At some point, you need to stop and have a meal.

Question: What's the best cop show? Cop movie? Cop song?

Answer: For TV, the best is *The Wire*. No other program is even in the conversation. As far as movies, *The Departed* had its moments, but I'm going to go with *L.A. Confidential*. The best song about cops is "State Trooper" by Bruce Springsteen. While I'm on a roll, the best quote about the police from a nonpolice movie is from Marty in *The Cabin in the Woods*: "Statistical fact: Cops will never pull over a man with a huge bong in his car. Why? They fear this man. They know he sees further than they and he will bind them with ancient logics." But, and this is likely your most pressing question, how about the best world-weary movie cop answering machine message? It comes courtesy of Bruce Willis as burned-out Pittsburgh detective Tom Hardy in the film *Striking Distance* whose machine wearily intones: "This is Hardy here. Go."

Question: What are some of the differences between Hollywood and reality?

Answer: Movie cops love their tough-guy lines. The hero officer will shoot a serial killer in a bar and then say something like "First round's on me." Or punch out a gunman in a supermarket and then proclaim "Cleanup on Aisle Four." I strive to be the most professional officer I can be. As such, I have resisted the temptation to call a criminal "hairball" or "dog breath" as Belker used to on *Hill Street Blues*. My resolve weakens annually.

Real cops aren't supposed to say those things for all the obvious reasons. When they do, it doesn't go well. Rolf Mueller told me of a Milwaukee officer who, many years ago, responded to a seasonal robbery in progress and came face to face with the robber, who still had gun in hand.

"Merry Christmas, motherfucker," the cop said before shooting the suspect. A citizen witness heard this and complained, and the cop was suspended.

Now, the officer shouldn't have said what he said, although he was in a high-stress situation and might not even have been fully aware of the words coming out of his mouth. But a formal citizen complaint? Here you had a cop who put himself in harm's way, foiled an armed robbery, and stopped the suspect cold, preventing him from hurting anyone. The witness's first thought was to take issue with the officer's salty language instead of sending him a holiday ham. That doesn't seem quite right.

Here's another difference—movie cops rarely handcuff anyone. They just haul the suspect away toward the squad car, even the dangerous felons who have a propensity for fleeing police. Maybe the movie cops are thinking, how could this man possibly escape when I have a semi-firm grip on one loose side of his jacket?

Also, the whispered pffftt that gun silencers make on the screen is pure Hollywood. Silencers on handguns don't silence them at all. They're still loud, they're just not make-your-ears-bleed loud. But what some silencers can do is erase a bullet's striation marks as it passes through the gun barrel, making it nearly impossible to link the bullet to the weapon that fired it.

Finally, although many police films and shows are laughably unrealistic, I am told that firefighter movies and TV programs that show the glory boys with lots of free time to exercise and cook elaborate meals and engage in romantic hijinks without seemingly doing any meaningful work—I am told by department insiders that these films are strikingly accurate.

Question: Would you want your children to be cops?

Answer: I'm not sure. I'd be glad if they were interested in a service-related field. I'd lament how the job would coarsen them. Honestly, I'd probably push them toward firefighting. When she was five, my daughter gave me a flower and told me to give it to the bad guys. I asked her why and she said so they wouldn't be bad anymore.

What I'd really like to do is to freeze my children in time so they'd always think this is how the world works.

Further Reading

Apprehensions and Convictions by Mark Johnson. Quill Driver Books, 2016.

Ghettoside: A True Story of Murder in America by Jill Leovy. Spiegel & Grau, 2015.

I Love a Cop by Ellen Kirschman. The Guilford Press, 2018.

The Onion Field by Joseph Wambaugh. Delta, 2007.

Fist Stick Knife Gun: A Personal History of Violence by Geoffrey Canada. Beacon Press, 2010.

Don't Shoot by David M. Kennedy. Bloomsbury USA, 2012.

Cop in the Hood: My Year Policing Baltimore's Eastern District by Peter Moskos. Princeton University Press, 2009.

Blue Blood by Edward Conlon. Riverhead Books, 2005.

A Good Month for Murder by Del Quentin Wilbur. Henry Holt & Co., 2016.

Verbal Judo: The Gentle Art of Persuasion by George Thompson. William Morrow Paperbacks, 2013.

Homicide by David Simon. Holt Paperbacks, 2006.

Shots Fired: The Misunderstandings, Misconceptions, and Myths About Police Shootings by Joseph K. Loughlin and Kate Clark Flora. Skyhorse Publishing, 2017.

Emotional Survival for Law Enforcement by Kevin Gilmartin. E-S Press, 2002.

The Gift of Fear by Gavin de Becker. Dell, 1999.

Tactics for Criminal Patrol by Charles Remsberg. Calibre Press, 1995.

Acknowledgments

This book has been a collaboration, through and through. Thanks to SFPD Lt. Sean Perdomo for his legal acumen, Sgt. Bassey Obot for his knowledge of tactical operations, academy instructor Ben Dorcy for his medical expertise, Inspector Ronan Shouldice for his mastery of evidence and forensics, the good unnamed Sgt. for his command of explosives, Sgt. Nico Discenza for his thoughts on homicide investigations, Sgt. Tim O'Connor for his contributions on flash bangs, and Sgt. Davin "Jedi Master" Cole for his rundown of the K-9 unit.

Many thanks to Richard and Kent Sorsky, Jaguar Bennett, and everyone at Quill Driver Books. It has been a pleasure.

A long overdue thank you to Sally Van Noord, my high school English teacher, who offered me patient writerly guidance, despite my first effort in her class being "Dark Toaster," a short story about a self-aware kitchen appliance.

Thanks to Rebecca Leimbach, who took the photo of my sergeant's star that is on the cover of this book.

To Andy, Brent, Angela, and Mark, all of whom took a look at the first draft. Your feedback made this book better. I appreciate that and I appreciate you.

To Mr. Greg Braun, father of my academy classmate Greg Braun Jr. Although I'm ashamed to say it took me over a decade to reach out to him after his son's suicide, he received me with grace and told me about his efforts to help people like Greg Jr., including a Milwaukee coffee shop called Dry Hootch that provides a gathering space for veterans. A portion of the author's profits from this book will go toward its important work. Learn more at www.dryhootch.org.

To Greg Braun Jr. who served his city and his country.

To all veterans and cops who are hurting. Help is out there for you. Your department or unit will have a dedicated counseling wing or can refer you to one. Please use it. Or call the National Suicide Prevention Lifeline at 800-273-8255. It's free and confidential.

To the dispatchers, the cop's lifeline. The best ones project a steady, knowing calm, can help manage complex and ever-changing scenes, and are as tuned in to an officer's voice as a parent is to a child's, monitoring it for signs of distress and proactively sending help without being asked. We couldn't do this job without you.

And finally, to all police spouses and partners, who make sacrifices on a regular basis. It's not just the low-simmering dread of getting the phone call that something happened at work. It's the day-to-day grind. Lots of weekends alone with the kids. Many a canceled date night because the 12th Street Boyz just shot up the block and your wife has to run the scene. Plenty of moving quietly around the house at noon so as not to wake your husband, who is asleep after pulling the graveyard shift. Thank you, better halves, one and all.

And speaking of police spouses and better halves, thank you to my wife Jennifer, my best editor and my best friend.

Index

Also by Adam Plantinga

"The new Bible for crime writers" —*The Wall Street Journal*

"Truly excellent—a mix of hard-boiled autobiography and streetwise poetry." —Lee Child

400 THINGS COPS KNOW

CRIME SCENE DO NOT C

Street-Smart Lessons
from a Veteran Patrolman
Adam Plantinga
"The new Bible for crime writers"—*The Wall Street Journal*

$14.95
Paperback

"A mix of hard-boiled autobiography and streetwise poetry."
—Lee Child

"Wise and witty, fascinating and fun ... a *lot* of fun!"
—Joseph Wambaugh

"Gritty, funny, and truthful ... a surprise on nearly every page."
—Edward Conlon

**WINNER OF THE
2015 SILVER FALCHION AWARD
BEST CRIME REFERENCE**

400 Things Cops Know

Street-Smart Lessons from a Veteran Patrolman

by Adam Plantinga

400 Things Cops Know shows police work from the viewpoint of the regular cop on the beat—a profession that can range from rewarding to bizarre to terrifying in one eight-hour shift.

Written by a veteran police sergeant, *400 Things Cops Know* takes you into a cop's life of danger, frustration, occasional triumph, and plenty of grindingly hard routine work.

In a laconic, no-nonsense, dryly humorous style, San Francisco police sergeant Adam Plantinga tells what he's learned from 13 years as a patrolman, from the everyday—like how to drive in a car chase without recklessly endangering the public—to the exotic—like what to do if you find a severed limb in the street.

Part memoir, part practical advice and above all, a series of unvarnished truths about everyday life as a cop, *400 Things Cops Know* puts the reader into the middle of the police experience. Sometimes heartbreaking, sometimes hilarious, this is an eye-opening revelation of life on the beat.

"Essential for crime writers and anyone interested in the reality of police work." —George Pelecanos

Available from bookstores, online bookstores, and QuillDriverBooks.com, or by calling toll-free 1-800-345-4447.

An explosive memoir by a one-of-a-kind cop

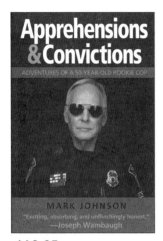

$18.95
Hardcover

"Hair-raising,
hilarious and
heartfelt."
—Winston Groom,
author of *Forrest Gump*

"Exciting,
absorbing, and
unflinchingly
honest."
—Joseph Wambaugh

"Comic, convincing,
and colorful."
—Don Noble,
Alabama Public Radio

Apprehensions & Convictions

Adventures of a 50-Year-Old Rookie Cop

by Mark Johnson

At age 50, Mark Johnson wanted a career change. What he got as a new life of danger, violence, and stark moral choices. *Apprehensions & Convictions* is Johnson's explosive memoir of how he became the oldest rookie in the Mobile, Alabama, Police Department. In a crisp first-person narrative that is by turns action-packed and contemplative, Johnson writes frankly of the experiences, challenges, disillusionments and dangers that transformed him from a social worker to a cop.

Defying the skepticism of his wife, the derision of the younger cops who called him "Pawpaw," and his own self-doubts, Johnson rose to become a detective and a highly decorated officer.

In salty, slangy language that crackles with the energy of the streets, *Apprehensions & Convictions* presents vivid portraits of addicts, dealers, prostitutes, pimps, thieves, murderers, crime victims, and ordinary citizens.

A fascinating story that sweeps from the Johnson's rookie days to a climactic confrontation with an escaped cop killer, *Apprehensions & Convictions* is a compelling memoir of a remarkable life.

"Gritty, thoughtful, and harrowing. Johnson is the real deal and so is this book." —Adam Plantinga

Mystery and police interest from Quill Driver Books

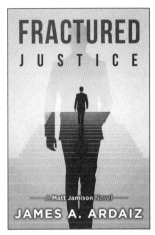

$16.95
Paperback

Fractured Justice

by James A. Ardaiz

A young prosecutor takes on an elusive serial killer and a flawed justice system in *Fractured Justice*. Assistant DA Matt Jamison is called to a meticulously staged crime scene on a canal bank in rural Central California—the latest in a series of murders that have killed three young women in one month. As a fourth victim is abducted and investigators race against time, Jamison must cope with a sophisticated and evasive killer, an arrogant defense attorney, and a fragile witness. Featuring an intricate plot, a chillingly sophisticated villain, a dogged and determined protagonist and a clear-eyed assessment of how the justice system operates, *Fractured Justice* is a gripping, fast-paced and coldly realistic thriller.

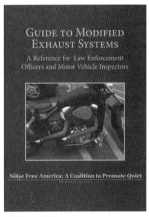

$14.95
Paperback

Guide to Modified Exhaust Systems
A Reference for Law Enforcement Officers and Motor Vehicle Inspectors
by Noise Free America

Ear-splitting motorcycle noise is a public health hazard and a destroyer of property value. **Guide to Modified Exhaust Systems** is a visual spotters' guide to help police officers, vehicle inspectors, and concerned citizens easily identify illegally modified exhaust systems. Illustrated throughout with color photographs of illegal exhausts, this slim, pocket-size paperback provides unequivocal photographic evidence for a citation that will stand up in court.

Available from bookstores, online bookstores, and QuillDriverBooks.com, or by calling toll-free 1-800-345-4447.

ABOUT THE AUTHOR

Adam Plantinga holds a BA in English with a second major in Criminology/Law Studies from Marquette University, where he graduated Phi Beta Kappa and magna cum laude in 1995. He has been a police officer for seventeen years and is currently a sergeant with the San Francisco Police Department. Plantinga's first book, *400 Things Cops Know*, received rave reviews from star crime writers such as Lee Child, Edward Conlon, and Joseph Wambaugh and was hailed as "the new bible for crime writers" in the *Wall Street Journal*. Plantinga lives in the Bay Area with his wife and daughters.